OVERLAND BY THE YELLOWHEAD

OVERLAND
BY
THE
YELLOWHEAD

J. G. MACGREGOR

WESTERN PRODUCER BOOK SERVICE
SASKATOON
1974

Copyright © 1974 by J. G. MacGregor

Western Producer Book Service
Saskatoon, Saskatchewan

Printed and Bound in Canada
By Modern Press

1

ISBN 0-919306-44-6

DEDICATED TO
Mrs. M. L. Peterson whose continuing
zeal has done so much to preserve
the history of Tête Jaune's pass.

BOOKS BY J. G. MACGREGOR

Blankets and Beads (1949)

The Land of Twelve Foot Davis (1952)

Behold the Shining Mountains (1954)

North-west of Sixteen (1959)

Pack Saddles to Tête Jaune Cache (1962, reissued 1973)

Edmonton Trader: The Story of John A. McDougall (1963)

Peter Fidler: Canada's Forgotten Surveyor (1966)

Edmonton: A History (1967)

Vilni Zemli (1969)

The Klondike Rush through Edmonton (1970)

A History of Alberta (1972)

Overland by the Yellowhead (1974)

ACKNOWLEDGMENTS

I am indebted to many individuals for their generous help in supplying information about the Yellowhead Pass. Of them all, Mrs. M. L. Peterson of the Jasper-Yellowhead Historical Society deserves the most credit not only for the large amount of material which she placed at my disposal, but because she was always keenly interested and extremely helpful. In her gracious way she went to untold trouble to help my project along.

To Ian D. Coates, vice-president of that society, I am very much in debt. Because he read several chapters and suggested corrections in them, he materially reduced the number of errors that the work will turn out to have. In discussing several points and by lending me material which I did not know existed, he was most helpful and generous.

Albert Siemens, a graduate student in history at the University of Alberta, also read and criticized some chapters and he too made material available.

To my friend Ted Abram, who allowed me to quote from a wealth of material he has written and on several occasions took time to talk to me and to write, I am heavily in debt. Dr. Walter Morrish, who enjoys talking of the days he spent there, did much to give me a correct conception of Tête Jaune Cache. Many others: Tommy Ross, Charlie Whitten, Alex Wylie, of Jasper; Stan Carr, of Tête Jaune Cache, Ross McKee, of Edmonton, and Reg Easton of the Yellowhead Highway Association all helped immensely. It is unfortunate that one book can only contain a few of the stories they had to tell. Mrs. Alex Law, granddaughter of the Mrs. Henderson who rode eastward through the pass in 1880, was also most kind.

Many librarians have, as usual, borne my importunities and supplied information. Once more, W. E. Ireland of the Provincial Archives of British Columbia repeated his former kindnesses and moreover, gave me permission to quote from the *British Columbia Historical Quarterly*. Eric Holmgren of the Alberta Provincial Library made the facilities under his charge available, and the staff of Edmonton Centennial Library helped with microfilms and in many ways. Miss Marshall of the Edmonton Regional Canadian National Railways Library was very kind in digging out material for me.

Mrs. Mary Balf, Curator of the Kamloops Museum Association, helped me with several useful suggestions and sent me a copy of the Trapp journal as well as putting me in touch with Dr. Ethlyn Trapp, of West Vancouver, who graciously allowed me to quote from her father's notes.

Mrs. B. R. Arends by being so kind as to let me quote from her memoirs enabled me to catch some of the spirit of the little town of Jasper during its formative days.

The Hudson's Bay Record Society kindly extended me the courtesy of quoting from its masterful publications.

For the many interesting pictures they made available to me I am greatly indebted to the Jasper-Yellowhead Historical Society, the Provincial Archives of British Columbia, the Public Archives of Canada, and the Glenbow-Alberta Institute.

Finally, I am very grateful to Geoffery Lester who made such a splendid job of preparing the maps which illustrate the text.

PREFACE

Of the dozen main corridors through Canada's majestic Rocky Mountains the Yellowhead Pass is the most interesting. Starting at Roche Miette, the eastern guardian of the Jasper valley, and ending where Mount Robson, its western bastion and the highest mountain in the Canadian Rockies, overlooks the Fraser River, the pass is unrivaled in beauty and charm. Neither the lowest pass through the Rockies nor the one with the longest white man's history, this, the most practical route from the prairies to the Pacific, is also the most historically fascinating.

Ascending the Athabasca River through Jasper National Park leads to two historic passes: the Athabasca Pass, used by the earliest fur traders, and the Yellowhead Pass, through which many forms of transport carry prairie products to the Pacific coast. As the Athabasca River descends from its source in the famous Columbia Icefields it picks up the waters of two important tributaries each flowing in from the west and each forming the approach to a pass over the summit of the Rocky Mountains. The upper tributary which enters the Athabasca some ten miles upstream from Jasper town is the Whirlpool, by which the fur traders ascended to the Athabasca Pass. The lower tributary which joins the Athabasca River at Jasper is the Miette, which leads to the Yellowhead Pass.

In 1810 Nipissing and Iroquois Indians told David Thompson, Canada's greatest surveyor, of the Athabasca Pass which led to the Columbia River and ultimately to Oregon. From then on back and forth through the Jasper valley and across the Athabasca Pass that fur traders' transport route carried men, material, and messages between the Pacific coast and Lake Winnipeg or Montreal. For decades it was a vital link in what one may call the first, and for a long time the only, trans-Canada highway.

During its earlier decades when the voyageurs and fur trade brigades passed and repassed along it the prairies to the east and the mountains to the west were virtually uninhabited wildernesses. On the prairie side of the pass a few busy fur trade posts, mere dots in the vastness of grass or forest, mainly Portage la Prairie, Fort Ellice, Fort Carlton, Fort Pitt, and Fort Edmonton, were the only points of civilization between present-day Winnipeg and the Rocky Mountains. In the maze of mountains white men had tiny posts at Fort George on the Fraser River, with Fort Fraser, Fort McLeod, and Fort St. James on remote lakes far to the north and west, as well as Fort Alexandria farther down the Fraser, and Fort Kamloops on the Thompson River.

Eventually the Athabasca Pass lapsed into disuse and travelers began crossing the mountains by the Yellowhead Pass which took its name from an Iroquois, Tête Jaune, or Yellow Head. About 1823 he made his first known crossing of that pass and left his furs at his famous cache. For many years after that, fur trade employees heading west for Fort George used his route sporadically.

Although it did provide a way of getting to Fort George, its importance as a route to the Kamloops area was not realized until the days of the Cariboo Gold Rush of about 1860. Then, during 1862 the Overlanders, the first Canadian contingent to head for the Cariboo mines, struggled through Tête Jaune's pass, and turning left at Tête Jaune Cache, headed for Kamloops. The Overlanders had found a new route from the prairies to central British Columbia. From then on by way of the Yellowhead Pass and the North Thompson River travelers began to use that new route. During the 1870's it had every hope that the CPR would follow the Overlanders' route, but for national if not for engineering reasons, that hope died. After a lapse of decades and just before the start of World War I, railway men, elbowing each other out of the way, first pushed two transcontinental railways through it and then with the wisdom of hindsight, immediately tore one up.

Some forty years later, at the end of World War II, the people in Jasper began thinking of other transcontinental means of transportation and hoped that the Trans-Canada Highway would pass through their valley. But as they had been back in 1883, when the CPR crossed the mountains by the Kicking Horse Pass, they were disappointed, because Canada's first Trans-Canada Highway was also built through the Kicking Horse Pass instead of the Yellowhead. By that time, however, the prairies to the east of the pass and the mountainous region to the west could both boast of large populations and prosperous cities which were ready to rally to the cause of the Jasper folk and their Yellowhead Highway. The struggle to obtain a paved highway through this logical pass took another twenty years. With prairie folk from Portage la Prairie to Edmonton putting their shoulders to the wheel and mountain dwellers from such diverse cities as Kamloops, Prince George, and Prince Rupert, backing them up, the Yellowhead Interprovincial Highway, an alternate Trans-Canada Highway, was finally opened in 1970 — nearly a century and a half after Tête Jaune had pioneered it.

Once more the old Yellowhead Route had been re-established — this time for all time. Once more, but now in high-speed cars, men can travel the historic route across the prairies and through the mountains which the Overlanders of '62 took from Winnipeg to Kamloops and Prince George. The historic old trails, the Carlton and Jasper trails, had been converted into a high-speed highway which from Portage la Prairie west passes through parklands sublimely beautiful and mountain scenery celebrated for its grandeur.

While from end to end the Yellowhead Interprovincial Highway abounds in scenic wonders, no portion of it has such a concentration of haunting beauty and historic interest as that section in the Jasper valley which winds across meadow and mountain from Roche Miette to Tête Jaune's old cache. For that reason, to the regretted exclusion of so much of interest along the other hundreds of miles of that highway, I have chosen to concentrate on it.

But one must not forget Tête Jaune the Iroquois who started it all. For a century and a half after his trip, while writers ascribed his feat to such white men as Jasper Hawse and François Decoigne, definite knowledge of the true Tête Jaune remained hidden in the limbo of old fur trade records. By a curious but happy turn of events, Jasper Hawse, a worthy but mediocre old trader who helped his superior, Decoigne, build the second white man's house in the magnificent valley, had his name bestowed on the area. William Henry, who had built the first house, is remembered by a mere railway siding called Henry House.

It was the voyageurs, however, passing and repassing by the Athabasca Pass, who stamped their character on the valley. Listen to the names they left behind; Roche Noire and Roche Bistre, the Maligne Range and the Bosche Range, Jacques Creek and Range and Lake, not to mention mischievous old Roche Bonhomme standing hand in hand with his gay servant girl Grisette.

Following the voyageurs into or out of the icy streams a long line of travelers trod the Athabasca Pass: corpulent Father De Smet; curious Paul Kane, the artist; canny George Simpson of the Hudson's Bay Company, and David Douglas, the botanist, whose memorial is the Douglas fir of the Jasper valley. Later on as the Athabasca Pass fell into disuse, other adventurers made their way through the Yellowhead Pass: Dr. Cheadle in 1863 prodding the cadger Felix O'Byrne; Mrs. Schubert, heavy with child, shepherding her brood to the Cariboo in 1862, and the equally courageous Mrs. Henderson, solacing her children in 1880 on her way east to a homestead at Edmonton.

The whole region — the wide blue valley at Jasper, the narrow, dark defile of the Caledonia valley, the lakes of the upper Fraser, and the salmon spawning grounds at Tête Jaune Cache — is filled with the spirits of men and women, Indian and white, who in their day on this majestic stage played valiant parts and passed down the stream of time.

And of a summer morning when sunshine streams into the great redolent basin at Jasper and mists rise to hover for a while far up the green valleys of Pyramid Mountain or the Colin Range and finally lift fitfully to reveal the sturdy profile of buffoonish old Bonhomme, the whole valley comes alive with memories of the staunch voyageurs. But, of a fall evening when the fading light blackens the carpet of pines blanketing untold miles of mountain slopes and leaves only the lanterns of yellow aspens glowing, and when half a mile away in a series of coughs, followed by a rumbling roar and finally a flute-like bird call, the bull elk cry out yearningly to all the cows in the valley — then Bonhomme, winking at his Grisette, laughs quietly over the joke the voyageurs played on their *Anglais bourgeois* about Miette smoking his pipe on his mountain.

It is of these men and a hundred others, of their doings, and of the spell they cast over the trail that Tête Jaune trod that I have written in this tribute to a few of the pioneers who opened up a corner of Canada, the fascinating Yellowhead Pass.

J.G.M.

CONTENTS

MAPS

ILLUSTRATIONS
(following page 130)

1

DAVID THOMPSON FINDS ATHABASCA PASS
1810

Both the Yellowhead Pass and Tête Jaune the Iroquois, after whom it was named, have been overlong in receiving the recognition they deserve. Only recently this low elevation pass, the easiest corridor from the prairies to British Columbia, this pass which the CPR surveyors wooed so ardently in the 1870's and then deserted so suddenly, has come into its own. Now with its two railway grades, its paved Yellowhead Highway and its large-diameter Trans-Mountain Oil Line, it has come to fruition as a major transportation route over the summit of the Continental Divide.

Less fortunate was Pierre Hatsinaton, the Iroquois with the itchy feet and the taint of white blood which lent a light tinge to his hair and earned him the nickname of Tête Jaune, the Yellow Head. Scarcely ten years after he had served the white fur traders by leading the way over his pass and building what they called Tête Jaune's Cache, he lay in some unknown mountain valley, scalped and dismembered. This immigrant to the West, this Iroquois, who, with an arrogance not even exceeded by the white men, intruded on the natives' lands, fell prey to the Beaver Indians whom he antagonized. His crowning indignity, however, was heaped upon him by white hands. After the passage of decades the white race which he had befriended so far forgot him as to ascribe his nickname Tête Jaune to men of their own race, Jasper Hawse and François Decoigne.

Behind the Beavers' hatred is the story of the Iroquois influx into the valleys of the Smoky, the upper Peace, and the upper Fraser rivers, areas all sparsely settled even by Indian standards. Before that influx, a few Shuswap lived in the Jasper and Mount Robson areas, while the Beaver Indians dominated the Alberta foothills between the Athabasca and Peace rivers. Then, almost simultaneously, came the white men and Indian immigrants from eastern Canada. Because the white men came carrying trade goods, the natives welcomed them. Because the immigrant Indians, particularly the Iroquois, came as interlopers, killing their game and trapping on their ancestral lands, every Beaver hated them.

In 1793, filled with the white man's curiosity and urged on by his commerce, Alexander Mackenzie made his famous trip up the Peace River and across to the Fraser River at Prince George, and went on to become the first white explorer to cross the wide part of the continent to the Pacific Ocean. In his wake came others of the North West fur trading company, and by the fall of 1805 Simon Fraser was busy building a trading post at Hudson's Hope. Approaching the mountains from another direction, by ascending the Saskatchewan River, the traders built Forts Augustus and Edmonton in 1795 and Rocky Mountain House in 1799; and in 1801 Duncan McGillivray and David Thompson put out the white man's first feelers towards a pass from the Saskatchewan to the Columbia.

In the meantime other interesting groups of explorers made their way into the Rocky Mountains, venturesome Indians from the East; Chippewa (also referred to as Ojibwa, Ottawa, Nipissing, and Bungee), Iroquois, and Algonquin. Originally, the XY and the North West fur trading companies had brought several men of these tribes to the West, in some cases as voyageurs and in other cases as employees hired to trap for the companies. Many of them had found the country and the life to their liking and after their period of indenture was over, had remained in the West. Then, since their way of life in the East was feeling the pressure of the white man's presence, several scores of these tribesmen decided to load up their canoes and to migrate to western Canada on their own. In many cases they brought their wives and children.

David Thompson, speaking of the period around 1798, mentioned that about 250 Indian immigrants from the East came up the Saskatchewan River to the vicinity of Fort Augustus and sought advice about where to go to live and trap. The Algonquin and Nipissing took the advice given and headed north and west. Most of the Iroquois, however, expressing scorn of the Plains Indians, went south and invaded Blackfoot lands. Before long the Blackfoot became annoyed at their arrogance and on one occasion alone killed twenty-five Iroquois. After that, according to Thompson, the remainder chose their hunting grounds in the forests along the east flank of the Rocky Mountains.

Before long those immigrants became relatively numerous in the hitherto sparsely populated Jasper-Hudson's Hope mountains, and perhaps being more restless than the natives, had soon explored every pass, stream, or valley in the north Rocky Mountains. Whenever the fur traders decided to push into hitherto unknown parts of the huge mountainous areas of what they called New Caledonia, they employed those versatile and venturesome Indians as voyageurs and guides. During the first decade of the nineteenth century the North West Company employed them along the Peace and Fraser rivers, and later on used them on the Columbia. After 1819, when at the mouth of the Smoky River the Hudson's Bay Company established St. Mary's House, its most westerly post on the Peace River, it began hiring the Iroquois, including Tête Jaune.

For centuries, of course, the natives of the Rocky Mountain areas had used the Yellowhead, Athabasca, and Albreda pathways over the summits separating the Athabasca, Fraser, Thompson, and Columbia rivers from each other. With the arrival of explorers, traders, and immigrant Indians, those passes came increasingly into the white man's ken.

In 1806, Simon Fraser worked his way up the Peace River, crossed over to the Fraser at Prince George, and a year later built Fort George there. During 1808 he set out and explored the river to its mouth near modern Vancouver. To the new Fort George post any natives living upstream for some 315 river miles to the summit of Yellowhead Pass could now take their furs. East of that pass, some 250 miles, lay the rival companies' posts of Fort Augustus and Fort Edmonton, accessible from the Jasper area by descending the Athabasca River and then crossing over the height of land between it and the Saskatchewan. During 1799 or 1800, in an attempt to garner the furs from the foothills, the two companies set up crude outposts; Pembina House (H.B. Co.) and Boggy Hall (N.W. Co.), both some six miles south and east of modern Lodgepole, together with Nelson House (H.B. Co.) and Whitemud House (N.W. Co.), both near the mouth of Wabamun Creek south of Duffield.

By 1806 the Indian immigrants, the Iroquois and the Nipissing, were familiar with the upper Athabasca and the Jasper area and on the island in Brulé Lake had built a crude windowless shelter which the white men who came later called "Hunter's Shack." About that time they also set out to do some exploring and started using the Athabasca Pass. According to David Thompson they were using it as early as 1808.

Very few years elapsed after the Nipissing's discovery of the Athabasca Pass before white men put the Indians' knowledge to their use. The first of these was David Thompson, who, after allowing the Piegan Indians to prevent him from using Howse Pass as he had done previously, had to fall back upon the Nipissing's knowledge and set out to cross the Athabasca Pass. Perhaps it was fortunate that in October, 1810, he did so, because by being forced to detour he became the first white fur trader to tread the one pass which for decades formed part of the first trans-Canada highway and to look up the other which today carries the Yellowhead Highway.

On September 15, Thompson had set out from Fort Augustus to follow his usual route by way of Rocky Mountain House and Howse Pass to the Columbia, and if all had gone well he could have expected to be in the milder climate on the upper Columbia about a month later. But things did not go well, and by October 12 his canoe brigade, with which he seems to have been out of touch for two or three weeks, had been turned back and he was stranded in a camp on the cliffs near the mouth of the Brazeau River, hiding from the Piegan. By that date, his right-hand man, William Henry, appeared at Rocky Mountain House and reported David Thompson's whereabouts to his cousin, Alexander Henry. Next day the cousin went down the river to find out what was going on and found Thompson "on top of a hill 300 feet above the water, where tall pines stood so thickly that I could not see his tent until I came within 10 yards of it. He was starving . . ."

Burdened beyond his capacity and suffering the consequence, Thompson had reached a low point in his daring life. In humility and hardship during the next two months he was to pay a bitter price for his weakness with the Piegan. Alexander Henry and he discussed a new plan he had formed "to open a new road from North branch by Buffalo Dung lake to Athabasca river, and thence across the mountains to the Columbia—a route by which a party of Ncpisangues* [Nipissing] and freemen passed a few years ago . . ." Henry promised to gather the scattered brigade of canoes together and send them down to Thompson.

At Boggy Hall Thompson regrouped his forces, and on October 29 set out for the Jasper valley. Thomas, an Iroquois, led the party along the scarcely visible trace of a route which some Assiniboine Indians occasionally took to reach that destina-

*Editor's note: The original and often quaint spellings of names and words have been retained in the quotations. In order not to interrupt the flow of the language, "sic" is not used to indicate obvious errors.

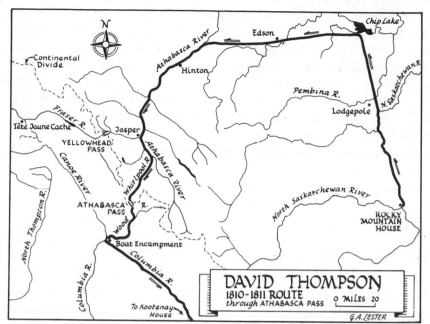

tion. The party consisted of Thompson, William Henry, twenty-four men, twenty-four pack horses, and nearly the same number of dogs. The explorer detailed four men to hunt to feed the contingent and assigned two to chop a path through the windfall; Thomas was the guide, and the remainder had their hands full packing and unpacking the horses and hazing them through the snowy forest. During the first part of their trip the weather was much colder than was normal for that time of year.

The men were typical voyageurs of French Canadian stock; some possibly all white and some of varying proportions of native blood. In different degrees all of them had the many vices and weaknesses as well as the many amazing virtues of voyageurs in a combination which, as David Thompson was to find, made them hard to lead. Undoubtedly his failure to cope with the Piegan had lowered their morale and it soon became apparent that Thompson was to have trouble with them. As far as they have been recorded, the names of twenty of them were: Messrs. Battoche, Bourré, Canada, Joseph Coté, B. D'Eau, B. Delcour, Desrosier, Du Nord, L'Amoureux, La Course, La Fortune, B. Le Tendre, Luscier, Mousseau, Pierre Pareil, Pichette, Baptiste Pruneau, René Vallade, Vaudette, and Villiard.

Owing to having to chop their way through fallen timber, their progress was slow. ". . . We went eight miles in six and a half hours, and put up, without any supper.'' On October 30 they chopped and fought their way another six miles. They traveled beside the Pembina River until November 7, then at a point where some teepee poles had been left standing, they swung off to the northwest.

For the next few weeks they struggled forward, passing close to Chip Lake, and from then on following essentially the route taken by Highway No. 16. On November 26, near modern Medicine Lodge, they left the stream which even that early had been named after A. N. McLeod, a partner of the North West Company. It is probable that he was the first white man to see that stream.

Somewhere west of Obed, on November 29, Thompson's party struck the Athabasca River. On December 3, Thomas led them to the small, dirty, windowless Hunter's Cabin on an island toward the upper end of Brulé Lake. Whoever had built it must have done so during the wintertime as a shelter from storms and must have been traveling on foot, because near it there was no pasture for horses. Because of the lack of pasture, Thompson's party had to move back downstream a few miles, either to Solomon Creek or to the site of Brulé town where they found ''a small fountain of water among pines and aspens, with plenty of grass for the horses.'' They remained there for twenty-five days.

Their trip from Boggy Hall had taken more than a month, and because of the absence of any trail, the amount of deadfall they had to chop through, and an unusually snowy November, it had been a most discouraging affair. Their hardships, some of which they could lay to Thompson's trepidation, had reduced their morale to a low ebb, and Thompson began having trouble with his men.

His observations indicate that their camp was near the north end of Brulé Lake, and there Thomas, the Iroquois, told him that it was too late in the season to take horses much farther. Consequently, Thompson set the men to making snowshoes and sleds for the next stage of the trip and to building ''. . . Log Huts to secure the Goods, and Provisions, and shelter ourselves from the cold and bad weather . . .''

By that time many of the men were utterly disaffected and on the verge of mutiny, and on December 14 Thompson, perhaps making the best of a bad situation, sent seven of them back with a horse each to take letters to Alexander Henry asking him to send pemmican and supplies. Between that date and the end of the month the temperature hovered around thirty below. When the men reached Henry they learned he was also out of provisions, so that, undoubtedly to their great relief, they did not return to Thompson at once.

Meanwhile, at Brulé Lake the explorer continued his preparations, and on December 29, leaving about ten of the horses with William Henry, who apparently was to remain in the Jasper valley for the winter, set out to make the final dash across the summit of the Rocky Mountains. "I gave the men their loads for the sleds . . . each sled that has 2 Dogs—B. D'Eau, Coté, Luscier and L'Amoureux have 120 lbs. and necessaries for the journey, and Vallade, Battoche, Pareil and Du Nord each 1 Dog and sled, have 70 lbs. per sled. 4 horses loaded with meat, having 208 lbs of Pemican, 35 lbs of Grease and 60 lbs of flour also accompany us to ease the dogs under the care of Villiard and Vaudette. Thomas the Iroquois for guide and Baptiste for hunter."

Since, generally speaking, the Athabasca River was frozen over they traveled along the ice or on the banks as suited them. On the first day—Thompson noting the sand which drifted out of Brulé and Jasper lakes—they made very little progress. On December 31, because the dogs could not cope with the heavy loads, he had to build a cache and proceed with reduced loads. All the while his men were most unco-operative. On January 2, with the temperature at twenty-three below, "the men had beaten two of them [dogs] to be useless; a Canadian never seems to be better pleased than, [when] swearing at, and flogging his Dogs. It is quite his amusement, careless of consequences." As a result, Thompson had to rearrange the loads again, and for a day or so they advanced slowly. On January 5, at a point near the latitude of the town of Jasper and after crossing a brook twenty yards wide "where the hunters formerly made a hut for the winter," he continued up the Athabasca. "Having secured the goods and provisions we could not take with us, by 11 AM set off with eight Sleds, to each two dogs, with goods and Provisions to cross the Mountains, and three Horses to assist us as far as the depth of the Snow will permit. We are now entering the defiles of the Rocky Mountains by the Athabasca River . . ."

Here he learned from his men that there was "a strong belief that the haunt of the Mammoth is about this defile." On questioning the men and making them admit that none of them had actually seen such a creature, he pointed out that if indeed it did live in this vicinity, they should at least be able to see some of its tracks.

On January 6, he recorded: "We came to the last grass for the Horses in Marshes and along small Ponds, where a herd of Bisons had lately been feeding; and here we left the Horses poor and tired . . ." This would have been on La Prairie de La Vache.

On January 7, when the temperature was four below, they turned up the Whirlpool River and next day, after marching ten miles, Thompson felt what he concluded was the mild weather from the Pacific Ocean. On January 9 they found themselves climbing steadily and as a result they had to take half loads and then go back for the other half. The next day they passed another hard ascent over deep snow to the height of land and, moreover, had to carry wood with them for the evening fires. That night, camped somewhere near the summit and in sight of a glacier a third of a mile away, their wood soon burned out and they passed the rest of the long night without fire. Nevertheless, to Thompson the appearance of the height of land between the Atlantic and the Pacific oceans was "a most exhilarating sight." He wrote: "Many reflections came on my mind; a new world was in a manner before me, and my object was to be at the Pacific Ocean before the month of August, how were we to find Provisions and how many Men would remain with me, for they were dispirited, amidst various thoughts I fell asleep on my bed of Snow."

Early the next morning they hastened down a descent so steep that even the dogs had a bad time as the sleds swung past them; in a day or so they came to the junction of two brooks. That evening Thomas came in to report that he had killed two moose. The men brought in the meat, ate some, and dried the remainder, while Thompson wrote messages on boards which by means of several of the mutinous men, most of whom he was not to see again, he sent back to William Henry so that he could copy the messages and forward them east. At the same time, he sent other men "to collect and bring forward the Goods left on the Way; which they brought except five pounds of Ball, which being in a leather bag was carried away by a Wolverine."

Rather naturally the wolverine did not waste much effort on the bag of musket balls. After being discarded, it lay at the summit of the pass for over a hundred years, until in 1921 one of the party of the Interprovincial Boundary Commissioners found a pile of 114 corroded musket balls. Some of these now repose in various Canadian museums.

On January 14, continuing down the slope, Thompson found the wet snow to be from three to three and a half feet deep, so that the dogs could no longer haul all the loads. At that juncture the party abandoned everything not absolutely necessary, including David Thompson's tent. The men's courage was steadily sinking. ". . . my Men had become so disheartened, sitting down every half mile, and perfectly lost at all they saw around them so utterly different from the east side of the Mountains, four of them deserted to return back; and I was not sorry to be rid of them, as for more than a month past they had been very useless, in short they became an incumbrance on me, and the other men were equally so to be rid of them . . ."

By January 18 Thompson had reached a point on the Wood River a mile from the Columbia, and for the next few days traveled desultorily down the larger stream. Finding such progress impractical, he ordered a return to the mouth of Canoe River. There, on January 26, "Du Nord, Bapt. Le Tendre and Bapt. D'Eau deserted. Luscier returned ill and Pareil and Coté I sent with letters to Mr. Wm. Henry and to bring more goods. Vallade and L'Amoureux stay here with me. I wrote letters on boards to Mr. Wm. Henry and to the partners."

Thompson's courageous or perhaps desperate persistence in pushing through the Athabasca Pass earned him the honor of being the first all-white man to travel the route which during succeeding decades was to be an important part of the first trans-Canada highway.

While Thompson was earning that distinction, his associate, William Henry, was also establishing a record, and in 1810-11 became the first all-white man to winter in the Jasper valley. Henry was the son of Alexander Henry the Elder and a cousin of Alexander Henry the Younger, who had helped David Thompson while he was at Rocky Mountain House on the Saskatchewan River. William Henry appears to have joined the North West Company as a clerk in 1801 and by 1810 was stationed at Cumberland House. When during that summer David Thompson started west from there, Henry was second in command of his expedition. As such, on December 29, 1810, Thompson had left him with instructions to winter in the Jasper valley, and in doing so to form a sort of base camp upon which, if necessary, Thompson and his men could fall back.

As noted, Thompson hurried forward over the pass and William Henry was left free to study the location and to build a base camp at whatever appeared to him to be the most strategic point. On January 12, 1811, and January 26, Thompson sent messages back to him, requesting him to send some goods and provisions. The two men whom Thompson dispatched on January 26, Pareil and Coté, crossed the summit, called on William Henry, and were back with goods at Thompson's camp on the Columbia by February 17.

Later that month he set his men to the difficult task of making boards by splitting cedar to build a clinker-built canoe without nails. Birch trees grew in the vicinity, but because of the mild climate, according to Thompson, the bark was too thin to be serviceable. So his men "split out thin boards of Cedar wood of about six inches in breadth and builded a Canoe of twenty five feet by fifty inches in breadth, of the same form of a common canoe, using cedar boards instead of Birch Rind, which proved to be equally light and much stronger than Birch Rind, the greatest difficulty we had was sewing the boards to each round the timbers. As we had no nails we had to make use of the fine Roots of the Pine which we split . . . ."

About the middle of April, 1811, Thompson and his small crew started up one of the most difficult stretches of the Columbia. By the beginning of May he had ascended the river to the vicinity of the mouth of the Blaeberry River, which was the stream he had descended in 1807 when he had reached the Columbia the first time. On May 4 he met two Nipissing Indians in a canoe and next day met the Grand Nipissing and three Iroquois, all of whom had previously crossed the mountains from Rocky Mountain House and who on this occasion were heading for the valley of the Canoe River, where they proposed to hunt and trap. The Grand Nipissing told him that for the previous three years he had trapped on this section of the Columbia and on the Canoe River. Thompson naturally discussed the geography of the area with those venturesome trappers and from their information formed a general idea of the relationship of the Canoe, Fraser, and Athabasca rivers. At the same time, he prevailed upon some of them to take another message over the summit to William Henry.

After that he went on up the Columbia, crossed over to the Kootenay River, and after much wandering about in the present-day states of Idaho and Washington finally descended to the Columbia's lower reaches, and on July 15, 1811, landed at Fort Astoria, which the Pacific Fur Company was building at its mouth. If in the minds of his employers, the North West Company, Thompson had been supposed to reach the mouth of the Columbia before the Americans did, his expedition was a failure. Being turned back by the Piegan in the fall of 1810 and taking so long to descend the Columbia had both combined to bring about his frustration.

In any event, on September 18, 1811, he was back at his former shelter at Boat Encampment. At that point he had hoped to find some supplies or at least some message from his North West Company associates on the east of the summit, but was disappointed. He wondered if William Henry might be trying to send him supplies by a new route down the Canoe River. Leaving a message fastened to a tree at Boat Encampment, he started up that river. After ascending some forty-eight miles, he was overtaken by two men in a canoe at some point which must have been within ten miles of modern Valemount. Those men told him that the day after he had started up the Canoe River several men whom William Henry had sent over the Athabasca Pass had reached Boat Encampment with pack horses. Amongst the men were voyageurs who had been with Thompson some months earlier; Canada, L'Amoureux, Mousseau, and Vaudette. In a few hours Thompson descended the forty-eight miles of the Canoe River which had taken him nearly four days to ascend, and upon his arrival at its mouth dispatched a canoe loaded with goods and nine men to Kettle Falls.

On September 29, 1811, Thompson started north to cross the Athabasca Pass, and in six days reached William Henry's camp in the Jasper area. Loading up what supplies he and a few men and horses could convey, he recrossed the pass and by October 13 was back at Boat Encampment. From there he sent the horses back to the good pasture in the Jasper valley.

Again on this trip Thompson was to hear of the huge mysterious animals, as he noted in his *Narrative:*

"On the sixth of October we camped in the passes of the Mountains, the Hunters there pointed out to me a low Mountain apparently close to us, and said that on the top of that eminence, there was a Lake of several miles around which was deep moss, with much coarse grass in places, and rushes; that these animals fed there, they were sure from the great quantity of moss torn up, with grass and rushes, the hunters all agreed this animal was not carnivorous, but fed on moss, and vegetables. Yet they all agree that not one of them had ever seen the animal; I told them that I thought curiosity alone ought to have prompted them to get a sight of one of them; they replied, that they were curious enough to see them, but at a distance, the search for him, might bring them so near that they could not get away . . ."

Shortly afterwards David Thompson set off for the company's trading posts in what are now the states of Washington and Idaho, and remained in that general area until on April 22, 1812, he started up the Columbia from Kettle Falls. With him were six canoes laden with a significant shipment of furs,

122 packs, sent from the Columbia area over the Athabasca Pass. On May 5, he reached Boat Encampment, and next day, leaving most of the men to dry the furs and to wait for better traveling conditions, he set out with three hunters to make his last trip over the pass.

At various times in crossing Athabasca Pass, Thompson's men had expressed fear of avalanches and Thompson had made light of their worries. On this his last trip across, he discovered that at "the height of land, where we camped in January last year and where my Men expressed their fears of an avalanche coming on them, and which then appeared to me not likely to happen from the direction I supposed they would take, we found an avalanche had taken place, and the spot on which we then camped was covered with an avalanche, which had here spent its force, in heaps of snow in wild forms round which we walked."

Shortly after crossing the path of the avalanche he sent men forward to get horses, and in due course they returned and met him near the Athabasca River. The same day Thompson arrived "at the House of Mr. William Henry, who had everything in good order." From this one can assume that Henry was still living in the Jasper valley.

There has been much speculation about the exact site of "William Henry's camp" and whether or not it was the same as "William Henry's House." When Thompson left most of the horses with Henry at the end of Brulé Lake, there is no doubt that the junior man was to remain in the Jasper valley for the winter and was to size up the situation there and to find a logical location for a base camp. During the winter Henry must have studied the valley and talked to any natives, Iroquois or Nipissing, who were familiar with it. Having done so, he would have decided to establish his base a short distance below the mouth of the Miette River. Amongst other factors which would have influenced him would be the fact that an outpost there would be at the highest point to which in most seasons it was practicable to bring canoes up the river.

At that point on the east bank of the Athabasca below the mouth of the Miette River he would have set up his winter camp, and there, in the course of some months, he would have erected his first house. When on October 4, 1811, Thompson came back for supplies, he set up his instruments at what he called "William Henry's campment," and calculated the latitude as 52° 53' 24" (the same latitude as Jasper Park Lodge). The next day he took another reading, and although the writing in his journal is a bit shaky, it appears to be 52° 54' 5" (the latitude of a point between lakes Edith and Annette). On May 12, 1812, when he returned to "William Henry's House" he determined the latitude as 52° 55' 16" (just north of Edith Lake).

Long before October, 1811, Henry would have started to build his house so that it seems safe to assume that what in the late fall of 1811 Thompson called the "campment" was the same spot which in May, 1812, he called the "House." Thompson's readings would indicate that the house was a mile or so north of where the modern Historic Sites and Monuments Board's cairn is—somewhere on the bank of the river but in sight of Lac Beauvert.

On May 13 Thompson set out for Fort William by canoe, and a week later was at the mouth of the Lesser Slave Lake River. On June 6, after descending the Beaver River from Lac La Biche, he reached Ile-à-la-Crosse.

During 1811-12 Thompson had crossed the Athabasca Pass twice in each direction and every trip had been most difficult. In spite of difficulty, the pass formed a link in a route by means of which the North West Company traders could bypass the Piegan, and as a result, Thompson recommended it to his employers. When they considered it at their meeting at Fort William in July, 1811, they voted against it, saying: "After a full discussion it was determined that the Route newly proposed, and which Mr. Thompson last winter attempted to pass thro', would be attended by more expence and difficulty than the old one and that therefore the Trade should continue to be carried on by the Route of the Saskatchiwane River."

In spite of the North West Company's decision, Thompson's new route continued to be used as year after year the threats of the Piegan made it advisable to do so regardless of the fact that transport over it was costly. Ultimately it became the regular route to the Columbia, and in time the traders cut a pack trail through the heavy woods and the deadfall. For decades after it formed part of the first trans-Canada highway across the mountains. While it remained in use as a trade route, most of the great figures of the fur trade, as well as a number of scientists and missionaries, traversed it. But to David Thompson, whom Elliot Coues called "the greatest geographer of his day in British America" goes the credit for traveling it first and for mapping it. (*New Light on the Early History of the Greater Northwest.*)

2

THE FIRST TRANS-CANADA HIGHWAY

ALTHOUGH the council of the North West Company had decreed that the trail which Thompson had pioneered up the Whirlpool River was not to be used in future, events conspired to keep it in use. For the next few years the Jasper valley and that route were the exclusive domain of the North West Company.

While in general the North West Company employees were better post keepers than record keepers, fortunately several of them did leave memoirs which got into print—Alexander Henry the Younger, D. W. Harmon, Simon Fraser, and Ross Cox, to mention a few whose writings throw some light on the area under consideration. From them it is possible to get a fairly good idea of what went on in the Jasper valley and west of there in the days before 1821 when the Hudson's Bay Company with its extensive record-keeping facilities took over the rival company.

When David Thompson left for the East for the last time, the North West Company was well established in the area which it called New Caledonia and which was roughly equivalent to present-day British Columbia. Servicing its posts on the Columbia River and its tributaries had involved the company in the route by way of Rocky Mountain House on the Saskatchewan River and the Howse Pass, and later on had caused David Thompson to find his way over the Athabasca Pass. Some of the partners of the company had wondered about the possibility of servicing posts in what is now the state of Washington by descending the Fraser from Fort George and then cutting across to the vicinity of Kamloops. They must have wondered also about effecting a connection from Jasper through what is now known as the Yellowhead Pass to the Fraser on the one hand or to the Canoe and Thompson rivers on the other. Although by 1812 the Iroquois and the Nipissing were fairly familiar with the two routes, the company did not take any active steps to use them.

For the time being, the North West Company's brigades continued to follow in Thompson's steps over the Athabasca Pass. The first record of the passage of one of those brigades was left by Gabriel Franchère, who accompanied a large contingent eastward over the pass in 1814 and whose *Narrative* has come down in published form.

Franchère had been an important member of the staff which John Jacob Astor had sent to the mouth of the Columbia and which was in the process of establishing Fort Astoria when in July, 1811, David Thompson had finally made his way down that river to tidewater. Shortly afterward the War of 1812 between the United States and Canada had broken out, and one of its results was the transfer of Astoria in the fall of 1813 to Canadian hands in the guise of the North West Company, which immediately renamed the post Fort George. Franchère, still loyal to John Jacob Astor, had refused to accept service with the new proprietors and was allowed to accompany the North West Company's 1814 brigade to eastern Canada.

Split up into small groups, the large party left Fort George on April 4, 1814, and worked its way up the Columbia. At Boat Encampment, Franchère and over a score of companions set out over the portage. On May 13 they "entered the mountain valleys where there were not less than four or five feet of snow. We had to ford the river ten to a dozen times in the course of the day, sometimes in water up to our necks. These frequent crossings were necessitated by precipitous rocks, almost impossible to get around without plunging into the woods for a great distance. The river is very swift and dashes over a stony bed. One of our men fell, thereby losing a sack of salt pork that we had carefully preserved as a last resource . . . ."

After what seemed to Franchère an interminable climb up the steep western approach to the summit, the party came to the top of the slope and expected to be on the very top of everything, only to find that in reality they were in a mere trough between still higher mountains. In his astonishment at the stupendous scale of the mountains he expressed himself in a rather confusing statement:

"This mountain is situated between two other much higher mountains, compared to which it is only a hill—that is to say, it is no more than a valley . . . ."

They had little time to gaze around in amazement for they had to press on through the deep snow to the eastern slope, where they were "forced to follow exactly in the tracks of those ahead of us and to plunge to our knees into the holes that they had made. It was as though we had put on and taken off, at each step, a large pair of boots.''

They worked their way down the Whirlpool River, crossed the Athabasca upstream from the junction of the two large rivers and continued until they camped at what their guide called Cow or Buffalo Prairie. "During the day," Franchère noted, "we had seen the carcasses of several buffalo." By that time the voyageurs and guides had become so familiar with the difficult route that they had bestowed names on some of the camping spots, and called this one "Campement Prairie de la Vaches," a nàme still in use.

Traveling on the east side of the Athabasca, undoubtedly to avoid the Miette River which is difficult to cross near its mouth, they evidently started to scramble up old Fort Point, but their guide called them back and they passed around behind it. Then they "came upon an old trading post that the North West Company had once built but had abandoned some four or five years previously. The site of this post is as charming as can be. Suffice it to say that it is built on one of the banks of the beautiful Athabasca River and is surrounded by smiling and lush prairies and superb groves."

Franchère may have been referring to what Thompson called a hunter's hut, but he probably meant William Henry's House which had been built during the late months of 1811 and may have occupied the same site as the hut. Not being a North West Company employee, his knowledge of that company's affairs was a bit sketchy. By the time of Franchère's visit in 1814 William Henry was stationed at a post on the Willamette River in Oregon, and his house was not occupied.

Franchère left on horseback and traveled on the east side of the river; others of his party availed themselves of a bark canoe. Near the mouth of Jacques Creek he caught up with some other men of the brigade and when the canoe arrived he traded places with one of the men and floated downstream until they "doubled a promontory that is called Miette Rock. We sounded the river at the foot of this rock and found it fordable. Messrs. Clarke and Stuart, who were on horseback and who had not followed the usual route through the interior, descended the length of the promontory and passed at the fording, in this way avoiding the long and fatiguing route caused by the slopes which we had constantly to mount and descend." In this quotation is the first mention of Roche Miette and of the difficult trail over Disaster Point. Like travelers who came along during the next century, that brigade tested the current where the river rushed around the foot of the point; if it was possible to cross it, they did, but if the water was at a high stage, they had to climb over the trail.

That night Franchère camped in the vicinity of modern Pocahontas, and next day went along the sandy east shore of Brulé Lake on horseback. The party forded the shallow water, came to Rocky Mountain House at the north end of the lake, and found François Decoigne in charge.

At that time Rocky Mountain House would be so new that the chips would still be lying around. After William Henry left the Jasper valley in the fall of 1812, the North West Company apparently sent someone else to take care of its interests there and to build what they may have hoped would become a permanent outpost at the north end of Brulé Lake. According to the company's minutes, that post was called Rocky Mountain Portage House, and during 1813 its staff consisted of one interpreter, one horse keeper, two hunters and two engagés, one of whom was a young Indian.

The minutes do not mention Decoigne, who, though still young, had previously established Fort De L'Isle on the Saskatchewan River in eastern Alberta. Neither do they mention Jasper Hawse, whose christian name came to be bestowed on his house and indeed on the whole area. In 1806, according to the company's records, he was listed as an interpreter. In 1813 the company probably intended that Jasper Hawse, still an interpreter, was to go in and build the outpost on Brulé Lake. If that was the case, it is strange that Decoigne was living there in the spring of 1814 when Franchère came along. Undoubtedly he had been there all winter, and if so, it is likely that the post had been built under his direction the year before.

In any event, that Rocky Mountain House, which soon came to be called Jasper's House, was not intended to be anything more than an insignificant outpost. Few Indians lived in the surrounding area, so that its trade was expected to be small. The Jasper region had been opened up so recently that the company was still not certain of what the future held, and moreover, was undecided about the permanence of the route through the Athabasca Pass.

The picture may have come into focus a little more clearly by the time the company began to consider its program subsequent to 1814, because the minutes outlining the plan for that year declare—"This Establishment to be knocked up except a Couple of Careful men to be left at the Portage with Horses and provisions to facilitate the Communication with the Columbia."

The same minutes mention Decoigne but only because he was in trouble and had been ordered to go to Fort William. They say: "Mr. Decoigne broke in upon a Depot taking therefrom two Pieces—and being in other respects reported to be extravagant has been ordered out and goes to Montreal—nothing otherwise against his Character." Chastisement, however, sat heavily on Decoigne's make-up and by October 3, 1814, he had taken employment with the Hudson's Bay Company and within a year was operating that company's Lesser Slave Lake House.

On May 19, 1814, when Gabriel Franchère and some scores of brigade members reached Rocky Mountain House, all within a few days, the number Decoigne had to feed took him by surprise. At the time, his post hunters were well to the north looking for game along the headwaters of the Smoky River and he could supply very little food to the travelers. As a result, Franchère's immediate group had to kill and eat a horse and a dog. On May 24, with four crude, recently made canoes fastened together in pairs, Franchère and his men set out to descend the Athabasca River as far as the "Hunter's Lodge." Decoigne, on his way to face the music of the annual meeting at Fort William, accompanied them.

When the party got some fifteen miles downstream from modern Obed, they met with bad luck in the rapids, which for many decades bore the name of Rapids du Mort. As Franchère said: "But about two o'clock in the afternoon, after doubling a point, we swept into a considerable rapid where by the ineptness of those who paddled the [two bound] canoes in which Messrs. Pillet, Wallace, McGillis, and I were seated, one struck a point of rock and was broken and the other capsized; and we all found ourselves in the water. Two of our employees, Olivier Roy Lapensée and André Belanger, were drowned; and only by the greatest effort were we able to save Pillet and Wallace, along with a man named J. Hurteau. The first had already gone down in the rapids and was carried into another. He had lost all his strength and was able to do no more than to put up his hands and arms from time to time."

Franchère found Lapensée's body, buried it, and erected a cross, but no one could find Belanger's body.

Since they were short of food, the party had to allow hunters to take time out to shoot an occasional moose, so that they were seven days before they came to the Hunter's Lodge. It was apparently at or near what is now the town of Fort Assiniboine, and because it was already assuming some importance in the still tentative route of communication, Franchère found four birchbark canoes there. His party loaded two of them, and on May 31 continued down the Athabasca. On the night of June 1 they camped at another strategic point on the system of waterways, the mouth of the Pembina River. Of it Franchère said:

". . . ascending the Pembina for two days and afterward crossing a tongue of land about seventy-five miles wide, one comes to Fort Augustus on the Park, or Saskatchewan River. Messrs. McDonald and McKenzie had taken this route and had left us a half-sack of pemmican at the mouth of the Pembina."

The next day they passed the mouth of Lesser Slave Lake River, another important point, and a day later left the Athabasca and started to ascend the Lac La Biche River. Going on to Lac La Biche they found Antoine Desjarlais, who had left the North West Company's employ in 1805 and now made his living by trapping and fishing. Of him, Franchère related an interesting bit of information: ". . . This man, with his family, lived by hunting and appeared quite content with his lot. No one disputed his possession of Lake La Biche, of which, it might be said, he was the master. He begged me to read to him two letters he had had for two years and of which he did not know the contents. They were from one of his sisters, and were dated from Vercheres . . ."

Under François Decoigne's guidance, the party descended the Beaver River and by way of Moose Lake cut across to Fort Vermilion on the Saskatchewan River, not far upstream from what is now the Alberta-Saskatchewan boundary. Undoubtedly because of his previous residence in that general area, Decoigne felt that this was the best route to take when heading for Fort Vermilion. For several years after Franchère's visit, many North West Company voyageurs on their way to Jasper and the Columbia River used that same route by way of the Beaver River and Lac La Biche. At the same time, however, the Northwesters, when heading west, occasionally used the

Saskatchewan River to Fort Augustus (Edmonton) and then por-
taged across to the Pembina, or went even farther to Fort
Assiniboine. As yet no one had decreed that one particular route
should be used when going west to Jasper.

Three years elapsed after Franchère's crossing of the
Athabasca Pass before anyone left another written record. This
was Ross Cox, who many years later wrote a good account
of his experiences in a book called *Adventures on the Columbia
River*. On May 28, 1817, on his way east in charge of a brigade
of eighty-six people, he set out from Boat Encampment. The
mountains impressed Cox and his associates, and even though
some of the voyageurs had crossed the Athabasca Pass on previous occasions, they nevertheless were amazed at their immen-
sity. At the summit, Cox wrote, one of them exclaimed: "I'll
take my oath my dear friends, that God Almighty never made
such a place."

Enough time had elapsed since David Thompson had first
pushed his way over the pass and many voyageurs had struggled
over it that various spots had become labeled with names
everyone knew. After trudging their way up the Wood River
for about twelve miles from Boat Encampment, Cox's party
came to some ten miles of "battures" (braided gravel flats).
Then after struggling through a point of woods, they came out
upon a few more miles of battures. After trudging over these,
they reached the mouth of Pacific Creek, and in ascending it
climbed some 2,700 feet in about five miles of the Big Hill or
Grande Côte to the top of the pass. Then they had to descend
about 1,700 feet before reaching the main stream of the
Athabasca. Some ten miles down the Whirlpool River from the
summit they came to Camp Fusil.

When Cox reached Camp Fusil no Jasper House employees
were there to meet his party, although he found five horses
grazing and discovered their gear hanging on nearby trees. Har-
nessing and loading them took only a few minutes and Cox
hurried down the Whirlpool River. He crossed to the east side
of the Athabasca and eventually arrived at "an uninhabited
house, heartily tired. This place is called the 'Old Fort,' and
was built several years before as a hunting lodge for trappers;
but owing to the scarcity of provisions was subsequently abandoned . . ."

On June 4, Cox and his men loaded the horses and went
about three miles down the east side of the Athabasca, when

their "progress was arrested by a bold mountain torrent, which fell into the Athabasca. It was too deep to ford, and we were again obliged to have recourse to our old expedient of rafts in order to cross it." It was the Maligne River, which was never easy to cross. At the turn of the century when many packers were traveling back and forth through the Jasper valley, those who took the trail along the east side of the Athabasca experienced similar difficulties with that river. On most occasions when they found the Maligne too dangerous to cross, they circumvented it by driving their horses into the Athabasca and swinging round where the waters spread out after they passed the island at its mouth.

After having crossed the Maligne, some of Cox's party decided to raft downstream, as navigation of the main river from that point to Rocky Mountain House was free from obstructions. Cox, however, stayed with the pack horses and "continued on through a handsome country with a tolerable pathway until sunset, when we encamped on the border of a small rivulet which runs into the Athabasca." That would be one of the creeks toward the north end of the Colin Range and across the river from the mouth of Snaring River. Five hours after starting next morning at 3 a.m., they reached an unoccupied "hunting-lodge belonging to the Company." It was most likely in the vicinity of Talbot Lake. There they found that their hunters had left the carcass of a buffalo· for them. It was thin, but "to such half famished devils it was an unexpected luxury."

After relaxing for a while the group pressed on, had some problems crossing Rocky River, and came to "Le Rocher de Miette, over which we had to pass."

Cox described some of the difficulties one of the earliest pack trains experienced in crossing Disaster Point thus: "We commenced our task a little after eleven; and at half-past two arrived at its base on the northern side, where we remained an hour to refresh our horses. The road over this rock is tolerably good, but extremely steep. The horses surmounted it with great labour; and the knees of the majority of our party were put to a severe test in the ascent. From the summit we had an extensive view of the country . . ."

After getting over that spur of Roche Miette, Cox went on and camped at the upper end of Brulé Lake, perhaps where Franchère had camped three years earlier. At 8 a.m. on June 6, after they had traveled for some time on the east side of the lake, the men at Rocky Mountain House sent a canoe over for them. "This building was a miserable concern of rough logs, with only three apartments, but scrupulously clean inside. An old clerk, Mr. Jasper Hawes, was in charge, and had under his command two Canadians, two Iroquois, and three hunters . . ."

Presumably Jasper Hawse had been in charge since Decoigne had left three years earlier and by that time the voyageurs were already speaking of the place as Jasper's House. Apparently the company's resolution of 1814 to maintain that outpost as a convenience for the brigades was still in force.

Cox also noted that La Rivière à la Boucane (Smoky River) was not far away, and said that it got its name "in consequence of some of the hunters who first visited this place having alleged that they saw a volcano near its source, which emitted great quantities of smoke. On making inquiry from our people, I could not learn that they had ever seen an actual eruption; but they assert that in the autumnal months the ground is quite hot, and that smoke issues from it in various places; during which period, they add, a strong sulphite smell pervades the atmosphere." Since the upper reaches of the Smoky are so bountifully blessed with rich coal deposits, the smoke must have come from fires in some of the seams of coal.

Cox also said that some of the Cree who had worked their way west up the Athabasca "have a curious tradition with respect to animals which they state formerly frequented the mountains. They allege that these animals were of frightful magnitude, being from two to three hundred feet in length, and high in proportion; that they formerly lived in the plains, a great distance to the eastward; from which they were gradually driven by the Indians to the Rocky Mountains; that they destroyed all smaller animals, and if their agility was equal to their size, would have also destroyed all the natives, . . ."

Just as David Thompson had heard of huge animals from his voyageurs, so Cox heard another version. Perhaps the mountains overawed those prairie or woodland natives and therefore lent credence to a belief in mysterious creatures.

On June 7, 1817, with two good bark canoes and six men in each, Cox "took leave of the melancholy hermitage of Mr. Jasper Hawes" and set out down the Athabasca. Following the usual route, the party descended the Athabasca to the mouth of the Lac La Biche River, ascended it, and headed for Ile-à-la-Crosse and Cumberland House.

By the time Cox went east the North West Company was facing financial problems, and within four years was to amalgamate with the Hudson's Bay Company. He was the last traveler associated with the North West Company to leave a written record of affairs in the Jasper valley and along the rivers approaching it from the east. From all the journals left by travelers up to that time, the situation with respect to the trade routes and posts just prior to the time that the North West Company passed out of existence emerges fairly clearly and can be briefly summarized.

Coming in by way of the Peace and Parsnip rivers, Simon Fraser had established Fort George in 1807 and the next year descended the Fraser River to tidewater. Then within a year or so the North West Company built other posts in the area north and west of modern Prince George and called the region New Caledonia.

Approaching the mountains by way of Rocky Mountain House on the Saskatchewan River in 1807, David Thompson had crossed them through Howse Pass and subsequently his company had gone on to establish posts in the Columbia watershed. In 1809, Joseph Howse of the Hudson's Bay Company had also crossed that pass, which by one of fate's ironies came to bear his name instead of Thompson's. Then, because of his friction with the Piegan, David Thompson had been forced to find another pass over to the Columbia and in doing so had crossed Athabasca Pass in 1811. By 1817, when Cox crossed that pass, the North West Company had come to use it in preference to Howse Pass. By 1817, however, the Hudson's Bay Company had neither penetrated New Caledonia nor interfered in the North West Company's affairs in the Jasper valley.

The pass up the Miette River to the headwaters of the Fraser, and which by means of that river could have provided communication with Fort George, was not used, or at least was not used enough to warrant some reference to it in the scanty North West Company records available. It was certainly known and used by the Iroquois and the Nipissing. At that period the New Caledonia district was one entity supplied by way of the Peace River, while the Columbia district was another quite separate entity which maintained contact with Eastern Canada by way of the Athabasca Pass and River but got the bulk of its supplies by sea.

During the years prior to 1817, Fort George, like Jasper House, was an insignificant outpost which was apparently occupied sporadically. When David Thompson was in the vicinity of Athabasca Pass he had tried to obtain information from the Iroquois and Nipissing about possible routes through what is now known as the Yellowhead Pass leading to the Thompson River on the one hand and the Fraser on the other. Several years elapsed before anyone made any practical use of this knowledge.

By 1817 the problem of maintaining overland contact with the Columbia district was still in the experimental stage, and the North West Company had not been able to give much thought to which was the best route to get from Lake Winnipeg to the upper Athabasca River and the Jasper valley. The company had a post on Lesser Slave Lake and at least temporary outposts at the mouth of Lesser Slave Lake River on the Athabasca and at Lac La Biche. Somewhere in the vicinity of modern Fort Assiniboine there was a company-sponsored hunter's lodge and the staff knew and used a trail heading southeast to Edmonton. Travelers from the east bound for Jasper House or the Columbia went by way of Lac La Biche and the Athabasca River. Up to this time the Hudson's Bay Company had not succeeded in going far up the Athabasca or Peace rivers, and was not concerned with what the Scots of the North West Company called New Caledonia.

A few buildings had been erected in the Jasper valley by 1817. William Henry's House at the head of practical navigation on the Athabasca was unoccupied, except when passing brigades took shelter in it. Jasper's House, presumably built in 1813 jointly by Decoigne and Jasper Hawse, was occupied by the latter. One other definite building was a hunter's lodge which the North West Company had caused to be built. Undoubtedly a few company employees remained in the Jasper valley when their time of service expired and a few freemen were finding the area a congenial place to live and were associating with a handful of Iroquois who also had taken a fancy to the area. One or two of them may even have built shacks in preference to teepees.

Except for short stretches, the brigades setting out to cross the Athabasca Pass generally traveled on the right or east side of the Athabasca River. Sometimes in doing so they passed over Disaster Point, and at other times, depending upon the stage of the river, forded the stream. They crossed the Maligne River, which, although difficult, was preferable to crossing the Miette. The various camping spots along the Whirlpool and Wood rivers were already named. Up to this point the Hudson's Bay Company had not invaded the area.

Both that situation as well as the fortunes of the overexpanded North West Company, which was locked in bitter rivalry with the Hudson's Bay Company, were on the point of changing.

3

TÊTE JAUNE LEADS THE WAY
OVER YELLOWHEAD PASS

THE Hudson's Bay Company started one of the earlier acts of the bitter rivalry with the North West Company when in 1819 it erected St. Mary's House on the Peace River. Not only was it the most westerly of that company's posts, but it was built at the mouth of the Smoky River, the stream which rises on the slopes of Mount Robson, north of Yellowhead Pass. At last the Hudson's Bay Company began sending tentacles toward the Fraser River.

In February that year, John Clarke, who was to establish the post, wrote his superior explaining that he was planning an expedition which was leaving "with a band of Iroquois . . . to cross the mountains to New Caledonia," to see if its natives could be induced to trade with the company. José Gaubin, whom he chose for the trip, set out that same month and returned to St. Mary's House three months later.

In December, 1819, Ignace Giasson took charge of a push up the Smoky. According to written instructions dated December 18, from Colin Robertson, Giasson was to be accompanied by John Harper, Charlo Phillip, and an Iroquois guide named Pierre Hatsinaton and was to ascend the river to the "Grand Forks of the Smoky River" where he was to meet some other Iroquois and to wait there till the spring of 1820.

In April, Giasson was to take John Harper and three Iroquois employees — Pierre Thestironsara, Pierre Hathawiton, and Jacques Anevagueron — and cross the mountains to make friends with the Indians who lived on the Fraser River upstream from present-day Prince George. In the copy of the letter sent to Giasson, Robertson, struggling to get the English letters and syllables to fit the Iroquois name, called the guide both Hatsinaton and Hathawiton, but in the copy he kept in his records he listed him as "Tête Jaune a free Iroquois."

On March 29, 1820, from Sheep River, Rocky Mountains (the vicinity of today's Grande Cache) Giasson sent a letter to Colin Robertson at St. Mary's House giving information on how he had spent the winter and referring to his guide, Pierre. On October 29, 1820, Giasson was back at St. Mary's House and planned to "return for some Furs they were obliged to leave in cache [at Grande Cache]."

When Giasson's party entered New Caledonia it took the North West Company by surprise. On June 10, 1820, James McDougall wrote in the Fort St. James journal that the Indians "have a Report of there being at the Forks of Fraser's River one of the H.B. Co's clerks and 3 men. . . ."

At last the Hudson's Bay Company had begun to invade New Caledonia and in the process had used the services of one or two of its French employees, and had hired the Iroquois, Tête Jaune. During the season 1820-21 George Simpson superseded Colin Robertson in charge of that company's operations in the area and made his headquarters at Fort Wedderburn (Chipewyan). On February 24, 1821, Simpson wrote to Duncan Finlayson, who was at St. Mary's House at the mouth of the Smoky River, advising him that he was sending a Mr. Brown to succeed Giasson in trading in the area up the Smoky and that Brown was to take "Eustace and Tête Jaune" with him. About that time, in the process of exploiting the Smoky River, the Hudson's Bay Company built an outpost somewhere in the vicinity of Grande Cache.

When George Simpson was writing his letter, the battle between the two companies was practically over. In 1821 the fight, which had floored the North West Company and brought the Hudson's Bay Company to its knees, resulted in their amalgamation. As a result of it the two organizations were combined to form a much stronger Hudson's Bay Company. Early in 1822 George Simpson was appointed Governor of the Northern Department, and in an effort to see what measures would have to be taken to co-ordinate the activities of the various traders and trading posts, one of his early acts was to make a tour of the Peace River country and the Lesser Slave Lake and Edmonton areas.

A period of uncertainty followed while Simpson applied his businessman's brain to grasping the logistics both of trading in the area and providing transportation for the Columbia and New Caledonia regions. After a few false steps, which he soon corrected and which included a plan to close out Edmonton House, a plan he did not carry out, he had the problem solved by 1824.

The main steps in the process, as far as they affect the Jasper area, all indicate a trial-and-error procedure which took some time to sort out. Under Simpson's guidance the Council of the Northern Department, which met in July each year, issued various decrees, which are recorded in its minutes. In 1822 the Council appointed William Connolly to take charge of the area, which included the upper Athabasca River, and directed that he do so from Lesser Slave Lake. He was instructed to close the outpost at Grande Cache and to put a good caliber trader in the person of J. F. La Rocque in charge of Jasper's House, which the Council referred to as Rocky Mountain House and which had continued to be occupied.

During the following winter George Simpson wrote to William McIntosh at Lesser Slave Lake, saying: "With Mr. Connolly I have had much conversation in regard to the tract of Country explored last summer by Mr. Annance; it lays between the head waters of the Smoky and those of Canoe and Fraser's Rivers, and by his account abounds with Beaver . . . and according to Mr. Connolly's report, it appears that a post established there from Lesser Slave Lake, will not only answer all the purposes of Jasper's House, for the Columbians, being only four days march from the Rocky Mountain Portage, but likewise be the most convenient resort for those [Iroquois and Freemen] Hunters, without incurring any additional expense . . ." What he was proposing was to build an outpost in the vicinity of today's Tête Jaune Cache. Tête Jaune himself, or Pierre Hatsinaton to use his Iroquois name, the man who had piloted Ignace Giasson into that area, was still around, hunting and trapping in the triangle between the Smoky River Post, Jasper, and Fort George, and from time to time accepting employment from the Hudson's Bay Company. During those years he must certainly have passed back and forth through the pass that now bears his name, Yellowhead, and on one occasion had made a cache at a spot known to all the freemen in the area as Tête Jaune's Cache.

Questions of posts and transportation were never very far from Simpson's thoughts. As early as July 31, 1822, when writing to the London office, he had considered building a post "at the Pambina Portage or Hunter's Lodge upon the Athabasca River." On May 8, 1823, he wrote: "I have given much attention to the affairs on McLeod's branch and Jasper's House (say Smoky River) and it is my opinion that they should both be established from Lesser Slave Lake . . . I have conversed with several Indians in regard to the State of the Pambina and

Athabasca Rivers, and they seem to think that there is abundance of Water at all Seasons for Boats; the Pambina Portage is about 50 Miles across, and Horses loaded with 2 pieces each can perform the trip in four days in the Autumn & six Days in Spring.''

The Council meeting held at York Factory (on Hudson Bay) on July 5, 1823, issued several other decrees. One appointed an interpreter and three men to Fort George on the Fraser. Since the time when the North West Company had stationed Hugh Faries there, it had been occupied intermittently. Another was that "the present Post of Lesser Slave Lake if practicable be abandoned & that a Post at McLeods Branch be substituted in place thereof.''

Still another decree was that Jasper's House be abandoned and that a new one be built on the Smoky River, presumably near Grande Cache, and that William Connolly take charge of it. The names of the few men, mostly Métis or Iroquois, who were to be associated with Connolly at Grande Cache are not recorded, but it is almost certain that Tête Jaune, the guide, was one man the company kept at its fingertips. The Council at York Factory ordered that J. F. La Rocque take charge of a new post which was to be built at the mouth of McLeod's River. The order to abandon Jasper House was not carried out, and the idea of building at the mouth of the McLeod was changed in favor of building Fort Assiniboine near the mouth of the Freeman River.

One is able to get a good idea of the situation along the upper Athabasca River in 1823 from the detailed journal John Work kept of his trip from York Factory to the mouth of the Columbia. At the time, Work, who was later to rise to prominence, was merely a clerk who accompanied the large Columbia-bound brigade under P. S. Ogden, which had ascended the Beaver River to Lac La Biche and then descended the Lac La Biche River to the Athabasca.

On the night of September 22, Work and the brigade beached their canoes at the mouth of the Pembina River. By traveling up the Athabasca for a day and a half they "arrived at a new House which Mr. McDonald the gentleman who is superintending the building calls Fort Assiniboyne, it is situated on the North side of the River. This is the House which was to have been built at McLeods Branch, the distance of which is four days work up the River, so that we were surprised at understanding that the buildings were here.''

Finally, on October 3, they reached Jasper's House at eight in the morning. Next day, using twenty-two pack horses, Work traveled overland, while Ogden, the senior officer, picked up some extra supplies and ascended the river with a few canoes. Part of the reason for taking the canoes was to move them farther up the river for the use of the rest of the brigade which would soon come east over the mountains. Work and his horses evidently followed up the right (east) bank of the Athabasca, and on the second day came to Roche Miette where, Work reported: "We crossed the river to the West side & then recrossed it again, which saved the necessity of ascending a very steep rock which is dangerous. This cannot be done except when the river is very low as it is at present . . ."

Like many other travelers, his party avoided the trail over Disaster Point by crossing the Athabasca twice. At 9 a.m. on October 6, Work "arrived at the little house (where a small house was formerly kept) about 9 o'clock where the canoes had arrived a short time before us. The canoes are to be left here as the river is very difficult to Navigate further up . . ." That was William Henry's old house, which, although unoccupied, had a band of freemen camping nearby.

On October 13, after having been able to take seventeen loaded horses all the way, the brigade reached Boat Encampment, where for twenty days Messrs. Ross and Kennedy and fourteen men had been waiting for them to arrive so that they could use the horses to cross over to Jasper House.

By the time the Council of the Northern Department met at York Factory on July 1, 1824, George Simpson had obtained a better grasp of the transportation problem, and the situation in the Jasper area was beginning to come into focus. Under his guidance the Council decreed that for the ensuing winter John Clarke was to take charge of the Smoky River-Jasper area and to make Lesser Slave Lake his headquarters. J. F. La Rocque was to be stationed at the post on the Smoky River, while William McIntosh and George Deschambeault were appointed to the new Fort Assiniboine Post. Apparently Jasper House was to be left with merely enough men to look after the horses there. The Council also ordered that provisions to fuel the next Columbia and New Caledonia brigades be accumulated at Ile-à-la-Crosse to the extent of 220 bags of pemmican of eighty pounds each. The Columbia brigade was expected to ascend the Beaver River and cross over to the Athabasca, while the

New Caledonia brigade was to go by way of the Methy Portage, Chipewyan, and the Peace River.

When the Council meeting at York Factory was over, George Simpson spent a few busy weeks supervising the company's affairs in the tremendous territory under his jurisdiction. At that juncture, Simpson, conceited and crafty but immensely capable, was the type of calculating businessman the company needed. To him fell the task of co-ordinating the forceful and often unco-operative men who as partners of the North West Company or chief factors of the Hudson's Bay Company had for long opposed each other bitterly. Now that the competition had ended, he was faced with a surplus of staff and with some uncertainty over the still unresolved problem of which were the best lines of communication to the Columbia and the New Caledonia districts. To get first-hand information on all those facets of his new empire, he decided to travel to the districts to see for himself.

After the Council meeting several of the chief factors spent a few weeks at York Factory before starting out to lead their brigades west towards their districts. Late in July, John Rowand, who was to rise to fame at Edmonton House, left with his heavily laden brigade. Finally, on August 15, George Simpson left, "accompanied by Chief Trader McMillan in a North Canoe with a complement of Eight Men besides my own Servant and an Indian Guide." Since his object was to travel as rapidly as possible, he needed an express canoe and had a specially picked crew of voyageurs. Driving his crew at a fierce pace for eighteen or more hours a day, he reached Ile-à-la-Crosse and took the Northwesters' route up the meandering and practically dry Beaver River to Lac La Biche. On September 16 his canoe caught up with J. F. La Rocque's, whose crew was toiling up that stream on their way to establish a post somewhere in the Yellowhead Pass.

At Lac La Biche Simpson met a couple of its earliest settlers, Jacques Cardinal and Antoine Desjarlais, both freemen. Hurrying on down the Lac La Biche River, he reached the Athabasca River and ascended it to Fort Assiniboine, where he arrived on October 2.

There, while he was still fretting about the inadequacy of the Northwesters' route up the Beaver River, he found the answer which was to provide the means of abandoning that route. It was in a note from John Rowand, who had come across from

Edmonton to meet him but who, after waiting four days, had found it necessary to hurry back to the Saskatchewan River post without seeing him. Simpson commented on Rowand's speed in his journal: ". . . the circumstances of Mr. Rowands having got to this place from Edmonton after accompanying his loaded Brigade from York thereby performing the Voyage in . . . Days shews how much shorter the route is by the Saskatchewaine than by the Beaver River and accounts for some arrangements I am about to suggest and have taken steps for carrying into effect without further delay which I have no doubt the Honorable Committee & Council will approve . . ."

After discoursing on the weaknesses of the Beaver River route, he continued: ". . . For this purpose I would recommend that the route by the Beaver River be abandoned altogether and by forming one Brigade of Seven Boats to start from York at the usual time say about the 20th July Forty Five Men instead of Seventy Nine will do the transport business of those Districts . . . With Cardinal the Freeman I made an agreement that he should in the course of this ensuing Winter and Spring get a Horse track or road cut from Fort Assiniboine to Edmonton House Saskatchewaine which I shall have occasion to speak upon hereafter . . ." In taking that step, Simpson caused the first pack trail in Alberta to be cut out. Undoubtedly Indians, in crossing from the vicinity of Fort Assiniboine to Fort Edmonton, had occasionally traveled the same general route and certainly once in a while the Northwesters had also used it when they set out from Fort Augustus to the spot near the mouth of the Freeman River, which they and Simpson sometimes called the Hunter's Lodge. With respect to the definite trail, however, Simpson's claim to fame is that he had it brushed out in spots so as to make it a pack trail and ordered that thenceforth it was to form a permanent and recognizable link in the route across the continent.

Simpson's journal states that his party left Fort Assiniboine at daybreak on October 3, 1824, to proceed toward the Columbia district. They "met a few Indians who gave us some fresh meat and without falling in with any adventure worthy of remark we got to the Rocky Mountain House commonly called Jaspers House, where Mich^l Clyne was in charge of the Even^g of the 10th.

"The Athabasca River is one of the finest streams I have seen in the Country . . . the banks finely Wooded and as we approach the Mountain high and prominent and the face in many places exhibiting strata of Iron & Coal . . .''

True to his businessman's outlook, George Simpson wasted little time emoting over scenery. Mountains he had known since his infancy on Loch Broom on the wild west coast of Scotland and later near Dingwall on the east coast, but as he ascended the defile of the Athabasca, past Hinton and Entrance, the stupendous naked wall of the outer range of the Rockies towering in the west must have stirred his Highlander's soul. And yet even with the blue of Brulé Lake stretching afar from Jasper House and with Roche Miette and many of its companions dominating its southern end, Simpson had space in his journal merely to say: "The situation of Jaspers House is beautifully Wild & romantic, on the borders of the Athabasca River which here spreads itself out into a small Lake surrounded by Lofty Mountains.''

With the next stroke of his pen, he got back to business: "This is merely a temporary Summer post for the convenience of the Columbians in crossing; the Winter Establishment was last Year on the borders of the Smoky River about 80 to 100 Miles to the Northward, but it was this Season determined that it should be removed to Moose or Cranberry Lake situated more in the heart of the Mountain near the height of Land and where we suppose Frasers River takes its source; the object of this change is to draw the Freemen further into the Mountain than they have been in the habit of going, where they are expected to make good Hunts as it has been rarely Wrought and thereby the lower parts of Smoky River and the Country they used to occupy towards Lesser Slave Lake will be allowed to recruit . . .'' Although that part of his plan was to fall through, Simpson was determined to build a post in the vicinity of Tête Jaune Cache.

At Jasper House what Simpson wrote in his journal provides the first glimpse ever penned of a prominent band of Métis which for decades was a dominant influence all along the mountains from the Peace River south to the Columbia and Fraser rivers and whose descendants still roam in the yet unspoiled wilderness of this area. He wrote: "Jacco Findlay and a band of followers (Freemen) were here watching the Shewhoppes in order that they might trade their Furs before they got to the Establishment and thereby make a profit on the hunts of these poor Indians, but I gave them notice that that practise must be discontinued as we should not allow Freemen interfere with and impose on the Natives & I addressed a circular Letter to Messrs Clarke McIntosh Rowand and Laroque begging they would narrowly watch the conduct of Findlays band . . ."

Undoubtedly those Finlays were descended in the male line from one or both of the early independent traders, James and his son James junior, who found their way into the West about 1759, and may well have had an admixture of paternity from the John Finlay who gave his name to the Finlay River and who may have been a relative of the other two. Jaco or Jacques Finlay, probably a brother of James junior, spent some time associated with David Thompson, and in 1806 crossed Howse Pass at his request. Since all the traders from Sir George Simpson and Sir Alexander Mackenzie down to the humblest engagé found the practice of celibacy incompatible with the freedom and rigors of a remote post, the Finlays, like everyone else, multiplied rapidly in the mountain air.

On the morning of October 12, 1824, while some of his party worked their way up the Athabasca with horses, Simpson "followed in the Canoes to William Henrys old House as far as the River is Navigable about 50 Miles higher up where they were laid carefully past in order to be ready for use next Spring and on the Morning of the 14th we started in a body with a cavalcade of Twenty-one Horses.

"Our route is about due West through defiles in the Mountains; the track for Cranberry Lake [Yellowhead Lake] takes a Northerly direction by Cow Dung River [Miette] which falls into the Main Stream at Henrys House."

While Simpson was busy making a note of today's Yellowhead Pass and was on firm ground when seeking information about topography, he allowed himself to be deceived in the field of natural history. At La Prairie de la Vache he saw tracks of buffalo and deer, and somewhere nearby his hunter killed two sheep and two goats. At this point his voyageurs, perhaps with the smirking connivance of his white associates, pulled the wool over his eyes. Simpson was so insufferably efficient and conceited that the yarn the men told him may well have been the joke of the camp. In any event, after remarking in his journal that goats frequented the highest pinnacles, he added: "Hunting them is a duty of some danger as no sooner do they discover an Enemy than they roll down showers of Stones when it is high time to give up the chace and look for safety under the cover of some projecting rock . . . The Sheep are not so shy, keep together in bands and do not frequent such inaccessible places; on the least alarm however they clamber up the Mountains and are equally expert in rolling down Stones on their pursuers . . .''

Following in the usual track, Simpson's party camped at the Grand Traverse. At the tarn at the summit he marveled that out of it water flowed to the Pacific on the one hand and to the Atlantic Ocean on the other. ''. . . I thought it should be honored by a distinguishing title and it was forthwith named the 'Committee's Punch Bowl'.''

On October 19, when he reached Boat Encampment, he wrote: ''. . . having disposed of the celebrated Athabasca Portage which altho not exceeding from Jaspers House 120 miles and from Henry's House 80 to 90 occupied us six Days in crossing.'' One can almost picture the self-satisfied smirk which accompanied those words.

At Boat Encampment he fell in with a band of Iroquois hunters on their way to trade with Mr. La Rocque, who was following along behind. For some years, Simpson noted, they had hunted ''. . . in the neighbourhood of Canoe River Cranberry & Moose Lake New Caledonia and the North branch of Thompson's River . . .'' They also told him that the Canoe River was ''navigable by half sized or Bateaux Canoes to its Sources in the Mountain from whence two small portages can be made to Cranberry Lake which is the head Water of Frazer's River and by that route Fort George, New Caledonia is not exceeding Ten Days march from hence . . .''

That information set the wheels of his brain meshing again over the ever-pressing problem of transportation, and he wrote: ''. . . My plan would therefore be to forward the New Caledonia outfit in two Boats & thirteen men in company with the Saskatchewann Brigade; from Edmonton cross over to Fort Assiniboine in three or Four Days then proceed in two Boats to Henry's House in the mountain in Ten Days; thence by Horses to Buffalo Dung Lake [Yellowhead Lake] (1 pipe across) in Two Days; thence by Land or Water to the head of Frazer's River in Three Days and thence by a fine bold stream to the different Posts. The returns to be taken out in like manner.'' For the first time a fur trader was giving more than passing thought to using the Yellowhead Pass as a freight route to Fort George. Vital to this plan, however, was the fact that J. F. La Rocque was intended to go up that pass and build a post in the vicinity of Yellowhead or Moose lakes.

From Boat Encampment Simpson went down the Columbia to the present Portland area, where he spent the winter, and then early in April, 1825, returned to Boat Encampment on his way homeward. Since J. F. La Rocque had not sent the horses over for them, Simpson and his men had to carry about sixty pounds each over the rigors of the mountain pass. As he was struggling along he, ". . . discovered that the Blackguard Iroquois had on our departure broached the Keg of which all partook except a few of my own Crew and about half a Doz. of them were so drunk that they could not come on . . . one of the people informed me that Isaac the Iroquois Chief (the leader of the Mutinous Dogs who were discharged from the Snake Expedition and one of those I had sentenced to transportation for Life from the Columbia for his uniform bad conduct) was the person who had broached the Keg in the Morn^g and had that moment in a fit of drunken rage sent his Provisions down the Stream to lighten his burthen; this information irritated me exceedingly and particularly so on account of the low state of our Provisions as we must either give the fellow a share of our own little stock or leave him to perish in the Mountain and seeing the dangerous consequences of allowing an offence of this kind pass unnoticed I was on the impulse of the moment induced to descend to the disagreeable duty of chastising him on the spot with the first Stick that came to hand, he will feel it for a few Days and recollect it while in the Indian Country and it will have a good effect on the whole of our Columbians who are by no means in a good state of discipline; and further to mark my displeasure of the conduct of our people this Day I knocked a Hatchet into the head of our Rum Keg and dashed the contents into the River which I have no doubt drew lamentations from some of them."

On April 24, when climbing the west side of the pass, Simpson had a strenuous time, as recorded in his journal: "In the foot of the Hill for about a couple of Miles the Snow was about 18 Inches deep but as we advanced it deepened to 6 feet; the labour of Walking without Snow Shoes was dreadful during the heat of the day sinking every Step 18 Inches to 2 feet we however by great exertion got to the top of the Hill at 5 P.M. having Walked 12 hours with these Indian Shoes on rough Shingle & in deep Snow; every Man in the Camp lame & exhausted."

Similarly, on April 26, going down the east slope, Simpson exclaimed: "Never did exhausted travellers turn out less disposed to renew a toilsome Journey than we did at 3 o'clock this Morn,ᵍ every man on the party requiring the aid of a Walking Stick our feet being much blistered and Lacerated by the rough Travel on the Battures and in the Bed of the River; we however improved as we got Warm upon it and continued a Steady pace until 10 O'clock having by that time forded the River 27 times when the joyful shout was given by one of the people that the Horses were in sight . . ."

The next day at 3 a.m. they mounted the horses which had been brought to them and "got to the Mountain House at 6 O'clock Chief Trader Laroque in charge."

The last time Simpson had seen La Rocque had been when he had overtaken him east of Lac La Biche the previous fall, and at that time it had been intended that the trader would winter somewhere in the vicinity of Moose Lake in the Yellowhead Pass. Now at the shack which La Rocque had built on Cottonwood Creek during the past few months and which Simpson called Mountain House, he listened to and reported La Rocque's explanation. "When Mʳ Laroque left York last Fall it was determined that he should Winter at Cranberry Lake in the heart of the Mountain but his craft was set fast by Ice in the Athabasca River which rendered it impossible for him to get beyond this place; he however took a Winter excursion in that direction and finds that no Establishment can be maintained further in the interior of the Mountain than where now situated large Animals being scarce and the Lakes producing no Fish which together with the improved footing on which I have placed Thompsons River District completely changes my views in regard to this Post (Rocky Mountain House) . . ."

In other words, even though La Rocque had built a shack or two, nevertheless Simpson decided that such a post was unnecessary. ". . . I think it will be to the Coʸˢ interest that this post be withdrawn altogether as the Furs will assuredly find their way either to Fort Assiniboine or Kamloops . . ." So once more, although he meant to leave one or two men there, Simpson was determined to discontinue fur trading in the Jasper valley. That fall La Rocque was transferred to eastern Canada. The shacks he had put up came in handy for travelers and thenceforth were referred to as La Rocque's House.

At noon on April 28, Simpson hurried on by canoe and

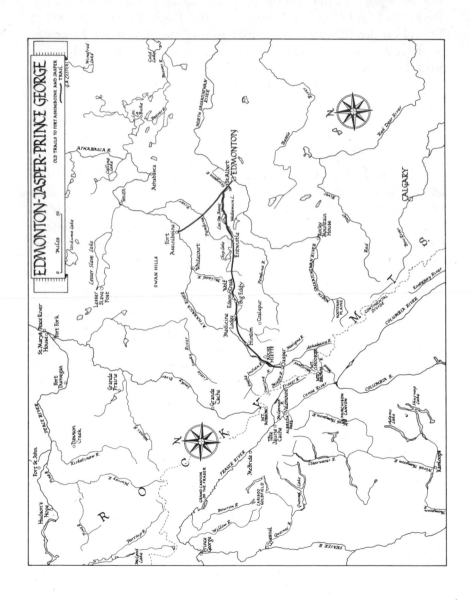

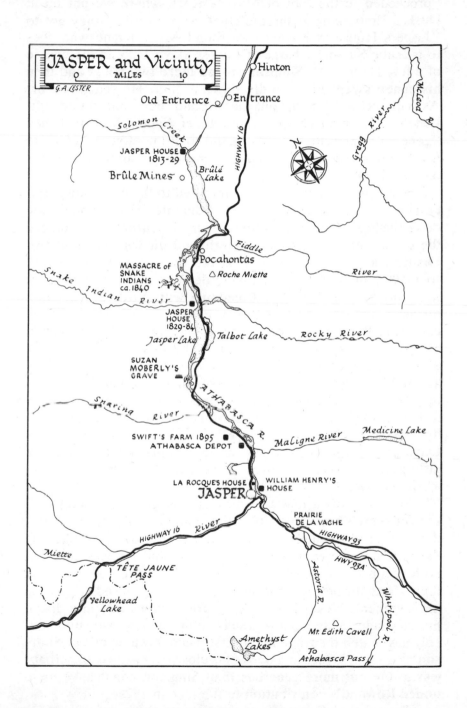

"proceeded to the foot of Mayots Rock where we put up at Dusk." Embarking at three o'clock next morning, they got to "Jaspers House at 8 where we found Mich¹ Klyne who goes to take the Summer charge of Lesser Slave Lake in the course of a few Days . . ." Simpson stayed there two hours and then his canoe swept him rapidly downstream. He reached Fort Assiniboine at 9 a.m. on the second day and found Mr. Deschambeault in charge, while Chief Factor McIntosh had "gone with his returns across Land to Edmonton agreeable to my directions last fall." At 3 p.m. Simpson set out for Edmonton on horseback.

Simpson was now wholly committed to the new transportation route from Fort Assiniboine to Edmonton House and thence down the Saskatchewan, as revealed in his journal: ". . . indeed the change of routes I have determined on will on these two Districts alone yield a saving to the Company of at least 12 to £1500 p annum if the Company determine on continuing the transport business of New Caledonia with York Factory and further I am satisfied that this discovery of Mine (as I alone can claim the merit thereof it never having been even dreamt of by any other) will enable us to do the Peace River business at a reduction of one third on the usual expences of that place as the Peace River outfits & returns can be taken by Horses in 5 Days between Dunvegan & Lesser Slave Lake, by Boats in 4 or 5 Days between Lesser Slave Lake and Fort Assiniboine, by Horses between the latter place and Edmonton in 3 or 4 Days and by Boats between that and York Factory and the difference of Expence between Boat and Canoe transport is at a fair estimate 33-1/3ᵈ p Cent."

Simpson was a new broom, busy sweeping the humps off the company's transportation system and equally busy clearing the way for his own promotion, and the latter involved pleasing the Committee members in faraway London. He was adroit at both occupations. There can be no doubt that he decreed that thenceforth the new route should be the one to be used in crossing the continent. Nevertheless, his journal shows him in a disappointing light. Although eventually John Rowand, who undoubtedly advocated the route in the first place, became one of Simpson's best employees and one of his close friends, a man perhaps less astute but more generous than Simpson might have mentioned Rowand's contribution to the idea in 1825.

Regardless of that, from the time of Simpson's decision,

the route for crossing the mountains and hence the continent — that is, up the Saskatchewan to Edmonton, across to Fort Assiniboine and thence up the Athabasca River to its headwaters at the pass — became the only trans-Canada highway and for decades continued in that role.

In 1825 Alexander Ross, a company employee returning from service in the Columbia district, accompanied Simpson on his journey eastward. In later life he wrote a book giving details of the trip which Simpson did not bother to tell. At the summit of the Big Hill, he said, the snow was eight feet deep. When the party camped near there, Ross says of the men:

"Instead of setting them to clear away the snow and pitch the tents as usual, they were ordered to lay a tier of long green wood on the surface of the snow; upon which, after being covered over with wet faggots and brushwood, a blazing fire was kindled and we prepared for rest. Travellers in severe weather, in these parts, generally sleep with their feet towards the fire; it was so with us, as no regular encampment was made. Each rolling himself up in his blanket, lay down on the surface of the snow, round the cheering fire; every one stuck his shoes and socks on a forked stick to dry, in order to be ready for an early start. This being done, sleep soon sealed up our eyes.

"We were not, however, long permitted to enjoy a bed of snow in peace; for hardly had we slept, when one poor fellow, who had placed his feet in rather doubtful proximity to the fire, was awakened by feeling it approach too near his toes. Thus warned, he started up, exclaiming, 'Le feu! le feu!' In a moment we were roused; but only to witness a scene of confusion, mingled with jests and shouts of laughter. It appeared that the fire had sunk down a considerable way, owing to the melting of the snow under it, and thus formed a miniature crater, over which feet and blankets, as well as shoes and socks, had experienced a too warm temperature. On jumping up, some, not aware of their position, slid down, with an easy descent, into the fiery gulph; but, fortunately, the melted snow which they carried down with them, and the activity of their comrades, who hastily dragged them up, prevented anything more serious than a fright."

From the Grand Traverse Ross estimated the distance to what he called Rocky Mountain House fairly accurately at ten miles. He mentioned that there his old friend La Rocque was in charge of "a neat little group of wood huts." After going down the river in a canoe, Alexander Ross came to ". . . another establishment, named 'Jasper's House,' still smaller; and of less importance than the first, so called in honour of the first adventurer who established it; but now in charge of a man by the name of Klyne, a jolly old fellow, with a large family. Attached to this petty post are only a few indolent freemen . . .''

In the spring of 1825 when Simpson and Ross left Jasper's House it was in charge of Michel Klyne, who had been moving around in the Athabasca district since 1804. Since Simpson had decided that this house was not worth maintaining as a fur trade post, Klyne was to move to Lesser Slave Lake, but presumably one or two employees of a lesser status were to stay there to look after the horses.

Simpson returned to York Factory in ample time to preside at the Council meeting there on July 2, 1825, and he was full of ideas involving the Columbia, New Caledonia, and the new route by way of Fort Assiniboine. When the minutes of that meeting came out, those ideas were embodied in various decrees. One of them ordered that the following spring C. F. Connolly in New Caledonia was to send the year's returns out to Fort Vancouver. Since, however, owing to the absence of large game in the New Caledonia area it was always chronically short of leather goods, they had to be shipped in from the East. Connolly was also ordered ''to employ ensuing spring two men with Indians to transport about Thirty Packs, containing dressed Leather, Pack Cords &c. &c. from the Rocky Mountains where the same are to be deposited by the Saskatchewan District for New Caledonia Outfit 1826.''

Hitherto those items had been supplied from the Peace River, but now George Simpson had decided that they were to be forwarded by way of Fort Assiniboine and that men were to ascend the Fraser and pick them up from the post in the Jasper valley. At last the fur traders were taking steps to use what they soon came to refer to as the Leather Pass.

Pursuant to the Council's decision, James McMillan was appointed to take charge of Fort Assiniboine and he was instructed to survey the route from Jasper House to the head of the Fraser River that autumn. On October 5, 1825, he left Fort Assiniboine on horseback to examine it. Tête Jaune, who presumably had accompanied McMillan, carried his report dated October 24 from ''Rocky Mountain'' to Connolly, who was in charge of the New Caledonia district.

Somewhat later, on November 25, in a letter addressed to

Dr. McLoughlin, who at the time was at Fort Alexandria lower down the Fraser, Connolly felt optimistic about the future supply of leather, and said: "The route which is here after to be followed is well calculated to provide this District with steady and ample supplies of leather, tho' it appears from McMillans report who this fall surveyed the intended route, that the transportation of it will be attended with some difficulty."

By the time the Council met at York Factory in 1826, transport matters were getting straightened out. Once more the minutes dealt with a supply of leather for New Caledonia, with the recommendation: "That a Requisition of 500 Dressed Moose and Red Deer Skins, 30 Parchment do., 2,000 fms. Pack Cords, 30 lb. Sinews, and 70 lbs. Babiche be provided and forwarded by the Saskatchewan District to Tête Jaune Câche on or before the close of September proxo." In them is the first written mention of Tête Jaune Cache.

That fall J. E. Harriott, who as the years went by was destined to play a large part along the Saskatchewan and Athabasca rivers and in the New Caledonia area, was put in charge of Fort Assiniboine. About the same time, the first official party to take supplies up the Miette River set out. Aemilius Simpson, who was not going with them, reported in his journal: "October 9, (Encampment nearly opposite Henry's Old Post, that being on the south side of the river and the encampment on the north side.) This day has been occupied in making arrangements for our Journey across the Portage, & the seperation of the Brigades for the Columbia & New Caledonia, the latter pursue a route, that has hitherto been passed by few, report says it is a good one which soon leads them to the Head Waters of Frasers River. October 10 . . . The Luggage and Horses having been sent across the River [Athabasca] to Henery's plain, we wished our friends Messrs. MacGillivray & MacDougal & the rest of the Brigade for New Caledonia, a farewell & commenced our Journey across the Portage . . ." Aemilius Simpson, who was going out to Fort Vancouver as the company's hydrographer, evidently stayed at La Rocque's House on Cottonwood Creek while the Columbia Brigade which he was to accompany was busy crossing the Athabasca to William Henry's old house.

Incidentally, Aemilius Simpson left some definite information about the location of the first Jasper House. Some years ago Shand-Harvey of old Entrance, a source of much reliable information on the history of the area, told the writer that the natives had indicated its site as being at the north end of Brulé Lake where the railway crosses Solomon Creek. Simpson's 1826 notes show the old post as being in latitude 53° 18′ 40″ on the west side of the lake. He arrived at it by entering the lower end of the lake and crossing it "S.W. 1½ miles."

4

THE LEATHER PASS

DURING 1825, the year before Aemilius Simpson made his way to Fort Vancouver, Thomas Drummond became the first botanist to visit the Jasper area. He was not a company employee but had been attached to Sir John Franklin's second expedition and instead of going into the Arctic regions, had chosen to investigate the flora of the Jasper area. Making Jasper House his headquarters, he spent an interesting year.

He left Edmonton towards the end of September with the Columbia brigade. From Fort Assiniboine some of the party traveled up the Athabasca River by boat, but he and several others spent eleven days following its windings to Jasper House on horseback. At the time, the old post had no official incumbent, as Drummond explained: "The Hudson's Bay Company have built a hut here for the accommodation of the person who takes charge of their horses, which are used for crossing the Portage of the Columbia; but the boats, after discharging part of their cargo at the head of the lake, proceed about 50 miles farther up the river, where the Portage commences, to the Upper House." The Upper House which Drummond visited was the one La Rocque had built. Since the Jasper valley was considered of little importance, neither of the posts had a white man in charge of them, so that when the brigade set out for Boat Encampment on October 18 he was left at the house as the only white man in the whole valley.

Anxious to spend the winter at the post on the Smoky River, he hired a native hunter to guide him along the crude trail which led up the Snake Indian River and which ultimately went on to Fort St. John. As a rule, the party traveled about fifteen miles and then camped for a couple of days while the men scoured the valley for game, but not far up the river they met with an unexpected delay, which Drummond described: ". . . the hunter whom I had engaged was accompanied by his brother-in-law, an Iroquois Indian, whose wife was in labour. According to the custom of these tribes, the woman quitted the tent in which she had lodged, until she should be delivered, and owing to the extreme severity of the weather, the ground being covered with snow, and the mercury indicating 38 degrees below zero, both the mother and her infant perished. The despondency which this event excited in the minds of the survivors, was so deep, that ten or fifteen days elapsed before they could be induced to quit the spot.''

After they had ascended the valley about forty miles, the snow became so deep that the party gave up the idea of going on to the Smoky River and swung off to the east until they reached the ''Baptiste River so named after my hunter'' (Berland River). During the winter, which was so severe that most of the pack horses starved, Drummond spent three or four months along it. In April he returned to Jasper House and when on May 6 the brigade from the Columbia came along, he was camped in solitude living on the whitefish he caught in Talbot Lake.

That summer Drummond wandered around ''with the old Canadian who had charge of the Company's horses''—undoubtedly Jacques Cardinal. He spent some time at Rock Lake and then went farther north to the Smoky River where he remained until the end of September. While there, his hunter killed buffalo and made pemmican. Later in the fall, Drummond crossed the Athabasca Pass to Boat Encampment and then, after returning to Jasper House, continued east until he reached Edmonton House in December, 1826.

Judging from the long list of plants and mosses which he compiled, that year-long sojourn of Jasper's first botanist was highly gratifying. On one occasion, however, he must have wondered if he had chosen the best vocation, for he had ''a narrow escape from the jaws of a grizly bear; for, while passing through a small open glade, intent upon discovering the moss of which I was in search, I was surprised by hearing a sudden rush and then a harsh growl, just behind me; and on looking round, I beheld a large bear approaching towards me, and two young ones making off in a contrary direction as fast as possible. My astonishment was great, for I had not calculated upon seeing these animals so early in the season, and this was the first I had met with. She halted within two or three yards of me, growling and rearing herself on her hind feet, then suddenly wheeled about, and went off in the direction the young ones had taken, probably to ascertain whether they were safe. During this momentary absence, I drew from my gun the small shot with which I had been firing at ducks during the morning, and which, I was well aware, would avail me nothing against so large and powerful a creature, and replaced it with ball. The bear, meanwhile, had advanced and retreated two or three times, apparently more furious than ever; halting at each interval within a shorter and shorter distance of me, always raising herself on her hind legs, and growling a horrible defiance, and at length approaching to within the length of my gun from me. Now was my time to fire; but judge of my alarm and mortification, when I found that my gun would not go off! The morning had been wet, and the damp had communicated to the powder. My only resource was to plant myself firm and stationary, in the hope of disabling the bear by a blow on her head with the butt end of my gun, when she should throw herself on me to seize me. She had gone and returned ten or a dozen times, her rage apparently increasing with her additional confidence, and I momentarily expected to find myself in her gripe, when the dogs belonging to the brigade made their appearance, but on beholding the bear they fled with all possible speed. The horsemen were just behind, but such was the surprise and alarm of the whole party, that though there were several hunters and at least half-a-dozen guns among them, the bear made her escape unhurt, passing one of the horsemen (whose gun, like mine, missed fire,) and apparently intimidated by the number of the party."

The next spring, in the Jasper valley, another botanist, the great David Douglas, noted some of the firs which came to bear his name. Accompanying Edward Ermatinger, he crossed the pass from Boat Encampment. A few comments in both those men's journals help to throw additional light on the affairs in the vicinity of Jasper. On May 3 they met "J. Cardinelle at Campment d'Orignal with 9 horses." That interesting individual who over the years became almost synonymous with the Jasper valley was undoubtedly the same man to whom George Simpson had referred three years earlier and Drummond had mentioned in 1826.

In fur trade annals Cardinal is an old name, which, even at the time of Ermatinger's visit to Jasper, went back many decades. Generation after generation his progenitors had worked farther and farther west from Quebec, and in almost any record of fur trade activity some men of the staunch Cardinal breed are mentioned as playing a valiant role. When in due course the trade extended up the Saskatchewan River, the Cardinals came with it. In 1809, when Alexander Henry, cousin of the William Henry who built the first house in Jasper, was at Fort Vermilion on the Saskatchewan River in eastern Alberta, he mentioned a Cardinal combination of a father and son on whom he placed great reliance. At the time the father was living in one of the North West Company's huts with his native wife and five children.

Spreading out from there and acquiring more than a passing acquaintance with all the rivers, byways, and lakes of northern Alberta, some of the Cardinals made trips to Cold Lake, Lac La Biche, and Lesser Slave Lake. When George Simpson was at Lac La Biche he found Cardinal living there but familiar with all of northern Alberta and hired him to cut his pack trail from Fort Assiniboine to Edmonton. By the time of Ermatinger's trip, Jacques Cardinal apparently had shifted his headquarters to the Jasper valley, where in due course Camp de Cardinall, Jacques Creek and Pass, and a range of mountains were all named after him. Jacques left his horses at La Rocque's House, and at 4:30 a.m., May 4, accompanied Ermatinger in one of two canoes which carried them down to Jasper's House that evening. Next morning Ermatinger continued downstream, and during the second day caught up with George McDougal, who was held up by ice. McDougal had left Stuart Lake in New Caledonia on March 18, using the new route, and touched at Fort George on the 24th, Tête Jaune Cache on April 1, and reached Jasper's House on April 18.

David Douglas who crossed the pass with Ermatinger threw additional light on some of the hardships experienced. On his way up the west side in the course of one particular six-mile stretch he explained that "we made as many traverses or fordings of the river, which was two and a half to three feet deep, clear, and with a powerful current. Though the breadth did not exceed twenty-five to fifty yards, the length of time passed in the water was considerable, for the feet cannot with safety be lifted from the bottom, as if once the water gets under the soles of the feet, which should be glided along to prevent this, over goes the whole person. In very powerful currents, it is necessary to pass in a body, and the one supporting the other, in an oblique direction."

At the summit, not content with merely crossing the pass, he climbed the mountain on his left as he faced east. Of that experience he wrote: "Being well rested by one o'clock, I set out with the view of ascending what seemed to be the highest peak on the North. Its height does not appear to be less than 16,000 or 17,000 feet above the level of the sea . . . The view from the summit is of too awful a cast to afford pleasure. Nothing can be seen, in every direction, far as the eye can reach, except mountains, towering above each other, rugged beyond all description . . . This peak, the highest yet known in the Northern Continent of America, I felt a sincere pleasure in naming 'Mount Brown,' in honour of R. Brown, Esq., the illustrious Botanist, a man no less distinguished by the amiable qualities of his mind than by his scientific attainments. A little to the southward is one nearly of the same height, rising into a sharper point; this I named 'Mount Hooker,' in honour of my early patron, the Professor of Botany in the University of Glasgow. This mountain, however, I was not able to climb . . ." For decades, because of his exploit, Mounts Hooker and Brown were cited as being two of the highest mountains in Canada.

Douglas also mentioned his meeting with Jacques Cardinal, who treated him to an excellent supper of mutton and then "regretted he had no spirits to offer me. Pointing to the stream, he jocularly said, 'there's my barrel and it is always running.' The kind fellow also afforded me a part of his hut."

During the fall of 1827 Ermatinger accompanied the brigade back through the Athabasca Pass. Since his journal entry for October 2, the day he went upstream from Jasper House, gives a good idea of what the brigades were like, it is worth quoting:

"The 4 canoes were sent off about 8 o'clock this morning to proceed to the Portage, the 2 large ones, laden with each 15 packs Leather and 3 Cassettes or cases and manned by 6 men—and the 2 old ones each 12 packs 1 Cassette and manned by 5 men. Provisions 1 bag Pemican pr canoe. At noon our horses being collected and the baggage tied etc. our van marched and the whole party were off from Jasper's by 1 p.m. All the gentlemen and families go by land to lighten the canoes. Our pieces for this amount 66 packs Leather and parchment, 18 bags pemican with our private baggage and the number of horses we are to employ on the Portage amount to 54. We encamped at 5 p.m. below the point of mietts Rock, which is high and difficult to pass. The mares are to follow us light to the Portage."

On October 5 both the Columbia and the New Caledonia brigades set off from La Rocque's House, and again Ermatinger's journal fills in some details:

"Having separated and prepared the Baggage the Columbia people set off about 10 a.m. with 15 horses—3 employed as saddle horses for Messrs. Todd, Ermatinger, Mr. McLeod's wife and 2 children, the other 12 laden with the following Baggage . . . Mr. McDougal has 40 horses to transport his packs, etc. Memo. of Art. given to Mr. McD. for his voyage — 8 bags Pemican, 2 canisters tea 3 lb., ½ keg biscuit, 1 moose, 1 canister sugar, 8 lb., 4 flagons spirits, ½ cheese.'' The McDougall to whom he refers was George, who was in charge of Fort Alexandria and who, of course, accompanied the New Caledonia brigade.

There is also Edward Ermatinger's journal for his trip east over the pass on which he left Boat Encampment on May 1, 1828. Once more Cardinal met the travelers with horses—that time at the Grand Batture, west of Camp d'Orignal, and in due course they reached Jasper House where they found Michel Klyne in charge. He descended the river with them as far as Fort Assiniboine, where J. E. Harriott decided to accompany them across the portage to Edmonton House.

For a year or so Michel Klyne's movements are hard to follow. When in the spring of 1825 George Simpson passed Jasper House, he decided to send Michel to take charge of the post at Lesser Slave Lake for the summer. Klyne, who spent most of his life in the fur trade, was the type of worthy but not outstanding man who as occasion dictated could be sent around to fill in here and there. As such, he apparently had come back to Jasper House by the time Ermatinger happened along. From then on till 1834, he remained in charge of the post.

Although George Simpson does not mention him, Klyne was probably at Jasper House when he paused there in the spring of 1829. On that occasion, the Governor was making a swing around another vast part of his far-flung domain. In July, 1828, he traveled up the Peace River to see the New Caledonia area for himself, and then descended the Fraser River. He went on to Fort Vancouver, and on his way back to the Red River Settlement in May, 1829, passed through Jasper.

During the fall of 1828, Simpson called at Fort St. James on Stuart Lake to see Chief Factor William Connolly. About the time he was there, or perhaps soon after he left, Connolly received news about Tête Jaune. John Tod, writing from McLeod Lake, advised him that the venturesome Iroquois was reported dead. The Beaver Indians' enmity had finally overtaken him and somewhere in New Caledonia they killed Tête Jaune, his brother Baptiste, and their wives and children. Tête Jaune, who had served the white man well, the man who had led the way through the Yellowhead Pass, had come to the end of his travels, all unaware that because of his cache his name would pass down the ages.

Whether or not Simpson heard of Tête Jaune's death, he nevertheless familiarized himself with everything that went on in the area. Moreover, he familiarized the natives—nay, even startled them—with a display of the importance of his august personage such as they had never dreamed possible. Archibald McDonald, who accompanied him, has left a wonderful description of Simpson's pageantry as he entered Fort St. James. "The day, as yet, being fine, the flag was put up; the piper in full Highland costume; and every arrangement was made to arrive at Fort St. James in the most imposing manner we could, for the sake of the Indians. Accordingly, when within about a thousand yards of the establishment, descending a gentle hill, a gun was fired, the bugle sounded, and soon after, the piper commenced the celebrated march of the clans—'Si coma leum cogadh na shea,' (Peace: or War, if you will it otherwise) . . The guide, with the British ensign, led the van, followed by the band; then the Governor, on horseback, supported behind by Doctor Hamlyn and myself on our chargers, two deep; twenty men, with their burdens next formed the line; then one loaded horse, and lastly Mr. McGillivray [with his wife and light infantry] closed the rear. During a brisk discharge of small arms and wall pieces from the Fort, Mr. Douglas . . . met us a short distance in advance, and in this order we made our *entrée* into the Capital of Western Caledonia."

Because he thought that a piper would add an impressive touch to his entourage, Simpson had asked the company to engage one and send him to Canada. Accordingly, in March, 1827, from the Highlands of Scotland, the company acquired "a young Man of the name of Colin Fraser fully qualified for a Piper," and sent to Canada a man who was destined to spend some fifteen years in charge of Jasper House.

When Simpson started his tour of New Caledonia in 1828, Colin took his place in the Governor's canoe. A few days later, Simpson, who had a habit of bearing down on men less hardy than himself, wrote: "We are getting on Steadily considering the state of the Water & the Weakness of some of our Men . . . the Piper cannot find sufficient Wind to fill his Bag . . ." In a letter written from Dunvegan, he said: "Colin breaks in by degrees I rub him against the grain as frequently as worth, he is a piper and nothing but a piper."

In any event, Colin completed his tour with the Governor and on it, in 1829, got his first view of the Jasper valley before he returned to York Factory for a period. In the fall of 1835 he was promoted to the rank of Post Master and appointed to take charge of Jasper House as the successor to Michel Klyne.

Some years before Colin Fraser arrived Klyne must have become fed up with what Ross Cox called a "miserable concern of rough logs" and in 1829, with approval from higher up, not only built a new Jasper House but built it several miles farther up the valley. The new post was at the lower end of Jasper Lake, not far from the mouth of Snake Indian River, and it is the one which, with occasional rebuilding, persisted until the era of railway surveys.

Undoubtedly Klyne's main task was to keep an eye on the company's two or three hundred horses, which were so necessary in the transport system. As early as 1824 Simpson had augmented the herd by ordering John Rowand, of Edmonton, to provide "20 good young cut Horses and a few breeding mares and entire Horses for the mountain transport." Some of them were to be left at Fort Assiniboine and the balance were sent on to be cared for by the regular horse-keepers at Jasper.

Starting about 1826, brigades bound for New Caledonia set out from the unoccupied La Rocque's House on the west side of the Athabasca River. It is likely that a pack trail had been developed from Jasper House along the west side of the river about the same time that another was worked out through the Yellowhead Pass and down the Fraser.

Fort George was the western terminus for the so-called leather brigade, which during the years from 1826 to 1828 made the trip over the Yellowhead Pass from the Jasper valley. The minutes of the Council in 1827, for instance, ordered that a specified amount of leather goods was to be provided and shipped from Edmonton House to Tête Jaune Cache by the close of October, 1829, and that Chief Factor Connolly was to have it picked up there. The other supplies for New Caledonia, of course, were to come from Fort Vancouver.

Taking the leather over the Yellowhead Pass and on to Fort George so late in the season must have been a risky venture. In the fall of 1828 J. E. Harriott and P. W. Dease were expected to bring it across from Jasper but they had some difficulty not detailed in the records, which resulted in hardship in New Caledonia the next season. As a result, the minutes of Council for 1829 ordered that leather and grease "which have usually been furnished by the Saskatchn. District be from henceforward provided at Dunvegan together with a sufficient quantity of Grease to make up the ladings of two Canoes to 50 Pieces in all, deliverable when called for after the month of August in every Year." Moreover, Connolly, writing to Simpson on March 4, 1830, to confirm the fact that the Council's orders would be carried out, said: "The necessary steps will be taken to send for our supplies of Leather &c. to Dinvegan and altho the voyage thither is longer than that to Tête Jaunes Cache I trust that it will never be attended with such vexatious circumstances as have of late occurred in fetching those supplies from the latter place."

Thenceforth, for at least the next two years, leather for New Caledonia was to be sent by way of the Peace River.

For two or three years commencing in 1828, bad luck dogged J. E. Harriott. About a year later, when he had been made Chief Trader at Stuart Lake in the New Caledonia district, it struck through his half-breed wife, Margaret Pruden. On January 20, Waccan, one of the natives employed by the company, brought a message to Chief Factor Connolly to the effect that "Harriots wife whom he had left at Alexandria was raging mad: I had to allow him to go for her with two Man to assist him . . ."

During the winter of 1829-30 Harriott was once more stationed in the New Caledonia district and towards spring his wife presented him with a daughter, who was also named Margaret. When a few weeks later he set out for York Factory, taking his wife and child along, Mrs. Harriott's illness apparently struck again. While his movements are hard to follow, it appears that the party was on its way east over the Athabasca Pass. In any event, along the way his wife simply disappeared from the brigade, having wandered off accidentally or deliberately. Although the party stopped and searched, no one could find any trace of her. Whether she fell off a cliff or got lost and froze to death, no one ever knew. With a great deal of difficulty the party managed to keep her infant alive and finally the baby girl was left at Edmonton House in Chief Factor John Rowand's care.

In September, 1835, A. C. Anderson arrived at Fort George

from the Columbia district and was assigned to go through Tête Jaune's pass to Jasper House to meet a party of new recruits from Canada, with whose aid he was to take a consignment of leather back to Fort George. When he reached Jasper House he found that owing to adverse weather the party from the east was late. When it did arrive, Colin Fraser, who had been posted to Jasper House, came with it and Anderson set out for Fort George. According to John McLean,"when they reached the heights of Frazer's River, they found the ice beginning to form along its shores. They persevered, however; sometimes forcing their way through the ice, sometimes carrying the canoes and property overland where the passage was blocked up by the ice. But all their efforts proved unavailing, for they were at length completely frozen in."

By that time they were in serious straits because the supplies that remained could be stretched over only four days of scanty fare, and no matter whether they tried to return to Jasper House or to continue to Fort George, they faced a grueling trip of fifteen days. Anderson decided that they should return to Jasper, and when the men stumbled in there they were fed, although the post itself, as was not unusual, was on very short rations. Faced with that dilemma, Anderson led them back to Edmonton House, and as McLean says: "They succeeded in reaching it, though in a most deplorable condition, half starved and half frozen, none of the party being provided with winter clothing; but they were most hospitably received by the kind-hearted bourgeois Mr. Rowand; and, after remaining a few days to recruit their strength in this land overflowing with fat and pemmican, and receiving their supplies, they set off on their return, and reached their destination without accident."

By the time they passed Jasper House again, the early weeks of December were wearing away. Back at Fort George everyone was worrying about them, and McLean set out with five men and dog sleds laden with fish to try to help them. He had proceeded only a short distance up the Fraser when he met them all safe and sound but considerably chastened by the inhospitable manner in which the unprecedentedly early winter in the pass had treated them.

That was the fall during which Colin Fraser assumed charge of Jasper House. By that time the Hudson's Bay Company's affairs in the Jasper valley had settled down to a humdrum routine. The first Jasper House at the north end of Brulé Lake was tumbling into ruin, and although the brigades passing back and forth still used La Rocque's House on Cottonwood Creek on an overnight basis, it did not have a regular occupant. Undoubtedly some of the houses beside it were used by the growing half-breed and Iroquois population of the valley, and some of those people were employed from time to time by the company.

Occasionally, a relatively small number of Indians, who for generations had been genuine natives of the area, looked in on Jasper House. Some, who came in from the west, were the Shuswap who brought their furs across the Yellowhead Pass from the upper Fraser. Whereas a generation or so earlier they had at times lived in the Jasper valley and even sallied out to hunt in the Alberta foothills, the hostility of an increasing population pushing in from the east had made it too dangerous for them to do so. Now when they came to trade at Jasper House they hurried to and fro and spent as little time in the valley as possible.

At times, too, a few of the Carrier Indians from the area below McBride came in to trade and in small bands even lived in the Jasper valley. Judging from the information that Father De Smet has left, they were the same people whom the traders sometimes called the Snake Indians and at other times referred to as Snaring Indians. J. Shand-Harvey, an old forest ranger who entered the Jasper area in 1907, stated that the Iroquois told him that the Snaring Indians caught mountain sheep, bear, and buffalo by snaring them. In any event, early in Colin Fraser's sojourn in the valley, the Indians who came crowding in from the east practically wiped them out in a massacre which took place near Jasper House.

The Indians from the east consisted of a very few Cree and many Assiniboine or Stoney. During Fraser's time the Assiniboine were scattered about between Jasper and Edmonton House and in the vicinity of Fort Assiniboine, which was built to receive their trade. In his time too the traders called the stream which enters the Athabasca immediately below Jasper House the Assiniboine River. On modern maps it is labeled the Snake Indian River. It was on the flat at its mouth that about 1830 the Assiniboine massacred the Snake Indians and perhaps it is but ironic justice that its modern name perpetuates the memory of the victims.

The slaughter took place where the remnant of thirty-seven of the Snake Indian band was camped on the point of land immediately upstream from the mouth of the Snake Indian River. Not far away was a larger camp of their long-time enemies, the Assiniboine. On the fatal day on the pretext of making a permanent peace, the Assiniboine tricked the few able-bodied Snake men into coming to their camp. Once the Snake were seated around the fire, their enemies shot every one of them. Then they rushed over to the Snake camp and killed everyone except for ten who escaped and three young women aged about seventeen, whom they took captive and carried to their camp.

Once their passions cooled, they began to worry about what pressures the Hudson's Bay Company might exert against them and decided to move some two hundred miles down the Athabasca to Fort Assiniboine and they took the three girls with them. It is doubtful if the Stoney would have harmed their captives because it was Indian practice to adopt such young women and to treat them kindly once they gave up trying to escape. Eventually the girls would probably have been taken in marriage by some of the younger men.

For some years a Métis family named Bellerose had established itself at Fort Assiniboine—a family that for several decades was to make its mark in that area. When the senior Bellerose noted the arrival of the Assiniboine, he also learned that the three Snake girls were lying naked and bound in one of the teepees. That night he sneaked into the teepee, cut their bonds and turned them loose. All he could give them was a knife and his fire-bag containing a flint, a steel, and some punk.

In the darkness the young women fled up the river toward the mountains and within a few days had reached the mouth of the Berland River. There, unfortunately, they quarreled and separated. Two of them, taking the fire-bag, continued up the Athabasca. They were never heard of again—undoubtedly they perished.

The third girl, naked and armed only with a knife, worked her way up the Berland River for about thirty miles and decided to winter there. For a while she lived on berries and squirrels. With the sinews of their tails she made snares and succeeded in catching enough rabbits not only to feed herself, but to clothe herself with their skins. Porcupines and marmots fell victims to her club and she was able to dry their meat as well as to kindle a fire in the primitive way by revolving the point of one dry stick rapidly in a hole made in another. Her preparations for winter were so successful that she lived on that spot until the following summer.

During that mild but mosquito-ridden season she moved farther west to a little lake some twenty-five miles east of where the forestry road from Entrance to Grande Prairie crosses the Berland, and hence into the territory of the Iroquois. That fall, nearly a year after she had escaped from Fort Assiniboine, an Iroquois from the Grande Cache area came upon her tracks. They mystified him but he decided that they must have been made by a weetigo, that is, an Indian who had run amuck, eaten human flesh and been banished from everyone's society. He did not have time to investigate further but went on his way.

The next summer, after the girl had lived alone through two winters, the Iroquois and his friends worked their way down the Berland River. When he reached the vicinity of the tracks he had seen, he decided to search for the weetigo if it should still be alive and to his surprise he saw snares set, trees barked, and the same strange tracks, still fresh in the mud. Following them he came to a cave-like hole in a high bank, probably an abandoned bear's den. In front of it, however, was a stack of brushwood beside a still smoking fire. Hiding nearby, he waited. Presently a wild creature in a short skirt of rabbit skins came up bearing a load of rabbits. As she bent over to stir up the fire, the Iroquois realized that she was a woman, and knew at once that she must be one of the three women who had escaped from the Assiniboine.

As he jumped to catch her, she screamed and ran. While he soon caught her, she fought him so fiercely that he had the greatest difficulty subduing her. Finally he made her understand that he meant her no harm. Even then he had quite a struggle to take her back to his camp.

There the women were kind to her, and although for a while she acted like a wild creature, she finally fell in with their ways and lived with them for two years. After that she was taken in by the occupant of Jasper House and settled down to help his wife with domestic duties. She lived there for two years, and then when a family of Carrier Indians came in to trade, she went off with them.

While that tragedy at the mouth of the Snake Indian River must have taken place during Michel Klyne's regime, it was nevertheless fresh in everybody's mind when Colin Fraser began his long sojourn in the valley.

5

COLIN FRASER'S REGIME

FOR fifteen years, looking out at the valley from his post on the shore of Jasper Lake, Colin Fraser led a lazily idyllic life, for the prospect from Jasper House, a mere dot in the broad basin where two valleys intersected at right angles, was both charming and magnificent. Approaching the basin from the south, the eager Athabasca had slashed its way through a great mountain chain which in front of the post and five miles away towered five thousand feet above it. After flowing through the basin, the river had torn another gap in a parallel range which behind and three miles away rose four thousand feet above Colin Fraser's solitary retreat. In that range and just across the river, Roche Miette, the guardian of the gateway to the mountains, reared its great cubical block. Each of the two chains of mountains through which the river had cut a gap stood on maps as memorials to the French voyageurs; the downstream one separated into two sections, the Miette and Bosche ranges; the upstream one, De Smet's and Jacque's ranges. Later, after Colin Fraser's time, another slightly more distant range of mountains contiguous to Jacque's came to be marked on maps as Colin's Range.

The Snake Indian River, which emptied into the Athabasca a short distance behind the post, had shaped the broad valley that ran back for miles towards the northwest. Standing beside his home and looking in the opposite direction Colin could peer far up towards the misty blue recesses of the Rocky River valley. Up either of those vast pine-carpeted troughs, the view toward the distant peaks was superb. But for sheer grandeur the long vista sweeping south along the six-mile lake, lifting through the notch at its end, rising to meet the misty blue wall of the Palisades, and terminating at the towering snow-capped triangle of Pyramid Mountain surpassed all other views.

Whether in the brittle beauty of winter, the misty green softness of spring, or the heavy clouds of summer, the view in any direction was magnificent. But in the fall when the gold of the aspens fringing the lake, dotting the hillsides or dappling the mountains contrasted with the gray-blue of the lake, and when the deepening blues of receding ridges and the icy blues of the peaks ranged against the azure sky — in the fall, nothing could surpass it. Blue was the dominant color, blue merged with the green of nearer pines and the black of distant spruces, and splashed all over with gold. With little to do but blow his pipes, dream nostalgically of the glens of Sutherlandshire, and watch the play of shadow upon ridge or dune or peak, Colin Fraser, the patriarch of the Jasper valley, begetting all the while, watched fifteen summers flow through the valley.

For some time prior to taking charge of Jasper House, Colin Fraser had acted as an interpreter in the Saskatchewan district. During that interval, probably in 1831, he married Nancy Gandry, daughter of Joseph Gandry and Lesette Châtelain, a descendant of one of the earlier French traders, Louis Châtelain. When in the fall of 1835 Colin received the minor promotion to Post Master at Jasper House, he and Nancy and their two-year-old daughter Betsy, started their long residence in the magnificent valley.

For company they had a number of Métis of mainly French ancestry. Because their progenitors had come west in the fur trade and because the company employed them full time, part time, or only occasionally, their loyalties lay with it and everybody regarded them as part of the organization. Whether much or little of their livelihood came from the company's coffers, they nevertheless found the broad, scenic valley a good place to live and to pasture whatever horses they owned.

Prominent in Jasper's primitive but lively social circle were many whose descendants still enjoy the Alberta foothills country. When Colin Fraser went to Jasper, the aging J. B. Berland was still there and had already given his name to what everyone had called Baptiste's River but which came to be called the Berland. In Colin Fraser's time Eustache Decoigne, James Finlay, George Ward, André Chalifoux, and several Desjarlais lived in the valley. All of them had moved west, keeping pace with the extension of the fur trade. The Desjarlais would be close relatives to old Antoine Desjarlais whom Franchère had met at Lac La Biche. Leader of them all, however, was Jacques Cardinal.

Mingling with those Métis was another group of half-breeds mainly of Iroquois stock, led by Dominick Karayinter. After Colin Fraser arrived, one of the first men he met was that outstanding oldtimer, who by then had lived in the area over twenty years. In several battles of the War of 1812 he had fought with the British army, and when the campaign was over, seeking further adventures, he had arrived at Brulé Lake in 1814. For many a long year he had been the foremost man in the small Iroquois band. One of his associates was an equally stalwart Iroquois by the name of Louis Kwaragkwanté who had left the Montreal area about 1805 and had been in the vicinity of Jasper House since at least 1811.

Even though in small bands a variety of natives dealt at Jasper House, that outpost did an insignificant trade. Its main reason for existence was to act as a way station to help the brigades on their way over the Athabasca Pass, the hardest part of the whole trip across Canada. Fortunately the logistics of the fur trade made it necessary to cross the summit at the least difficult times in the year, the late fall and the early spring.

The west-bound brigade ascending the Athabasca, usually reached Jasper House about the end of October. When it did, the small staff there came into play by providing a supply of meat and having the transport horses ready for the travelers. Occasionally a brigade ascending the Columbia from Fort Vancouver was waiting to greet the west-bound crew at Boat Encampment and to make use of the horses in crossing to Jasper House. At that outpost, it in turn was provided with food, sleds and snowshoes, and every assistance needed to hurry it eastward. As the years of Colin Fraser's long regime slipped away, the importance of Jasper House diminished, but during those years he entertained a number of interesting people.

Two of them were the first missionaries of any faith to reach the Jasper valley, Fathers François Blanchet and Modeste Demers. Acting under the orders of Bishop Provencher of St. Boniface on Red River, they were en route to open a mission at Fort Vancouver in present-day Oregon. Along the way, at Fort Carlton, Fort Pitt, Edmonton House, and Jasper House they baptized many a voyageur's child and left a record of those baptisms.

At the end of September, 1838, they spent a week as guests of Colin Fraser, getting some of the weariness of the long trip from Edmonton out of their bones and recruiting their strength for the difficult trail over Athabasca Pass. They arrived in time to bury five-year-old Henriette Leblanc who had died September 24. During the time they spent at Jasper House they baptized thirty-two children ranging in age from eight months to eleven years, including three of Colin Fraser's daughters. They were

Betsy, who had been born on June 28, 1833, before the family moved to Jasper; Elizabeth, born December 17, 1835, and finally Marguerite, who was only nine months old.

As during the next ten years the Columbia brigades passed through, Colin Fraser, like all Hudson's Bay Company men everywhere, was keenly interested in what was going on in the company's Columbia district which the Americans were beginning to call Oregon. It was becoming obvious that the company would soon lose its hold there and have to withdraw.

In 1842 George Simpson made another trip to what he still called the Columbia district, and undoubtedly Colin Fraser, knowing he was going to do so, must have looked forward to a visit from his old friend and patron. Simpson, however, decided not to travel by the conventional route through Jasper but to pioneer another from Edmonton House through what is now Banff and the Kootenay River. On his way from the Red River Settlement to Edmonton House Simpson struck across the prairies with a cavalcade which brought the first carts all the way to Edmonton. He was one of the pioneers of the trail which after a lapse of more than a century became the modern paved Yellowhead Highway.

At Fort Vancouver Simpson began taking steps which would insure that when the day came that the Americans took over Oregon, his company's position would not be irretrievably weakened. One of those was to order that in 1843 a new post, to be called Fort Victoria, should be built on Vancouver Island. When that time came, this was the post which Simpson planned to make the company's headquarters on the coast.

In the meantime, although the company continued to operate Fort Vancouver, its business fell off, with the result that the size and the frequency of the brigades coming and going through Jasper were reduced considerably. And with that reduction Jasper House's importance, which had never been great, was cut further. In spite of that, Colin Fraser was still destined to play host to two interesting visitors, Father De Smet and Paul Kane.

In the spring of 1845 the priest, a Jesuit with headquarters at St. Louis on the Mississippi, who was famous in the western States and in southwestern British Columbia, ventured north as far as Edmonton House. On his way back to the Oregon country he went through the Jasper valley. He was such a genial character and observed so carefully that the letters he wrote to his fellow priests throw a great deal of light on conditions in western Canada.

Speaking of the Indians along the upper Athabasca River, he recorded that some years prior to his visit the Assiniboine had claimed the area but by 1845 had more or less left it. When they did, many wandering families of the Carrier tribe "compelled by hunger, have quitted their country, traversed the east of the mountains, and now range the valleys of this region in quest for food . . . In winter they fare well: for then the moose, elk and reindeer are plentiful. The reindeer feed on a kind of white moss, and the paunch is considered delicious when the food is half digested. By way of a dainty morsel, the Indians pluck out the eyes of fish with the end of the fingers and swallow them raw, likewise the tripes with their whole contents, without further ceremony than placing them an instant on the coals, from thence into the omnibus or general reservoir, without even undergoing the operation of the jaws."

Having dealt with the true natives in the area, his report turned its attention to the interlopers, the Iroquois, and Father De Smet rejoiced when he found that some of their older folk had once enjoyed priestly consolation in the East. He said: "On the banks of Lake Jasper we met an old Iroquois called Louis Kwaragkwanté, or Walking Sun, accompanied by his family, thirty-six in number. He has been forty years absent from his country, during which he has never seen a priest . . . The little Iroquois camp immediately set out to follow me to Fort Jasper. Most of them know their prayers in Iroquois. I remained fifteen days at the fort, instructing them in the duties of religion . . . The number of baptized amounted to forty-four; among whom was the lady of Mr. [Colin] Fraser, (superintendent of the fort) and four of his children and two servants."

Seven years had elapsed since Father Demers had baptized three of Colin Fraser's children and now four more were presented to Father De Smet. Even though for weeks at a time the rugged Scottish piper may have found life in the Jasper valley dull, nevertheless it allowed him plenty of time to devote to domestic affairs.

While Colin was undoubtedly genuinely glad to play host to the priest, the problem of feeding the bands of Indians which assembled was too much for him. Accordingly he suggested, Father De Smet wrote, that "we should leave the fort and accompany himself and family to the Lake of Islands [Jarvis

Lake?], where we could subsist partly on fish. As the distance was not great, we accepted this invitation, and set out to the number of fifty-four persons and twenty dogs. I count the latter, because we were as much obliged to provide for them as for ourselves. A little note of the game killed by our hunters during the twenty-six days of our abode at this place will perhaps afford you some interest; at least, it will make you acquainted with the animals of the country, and prove that the mountaineers of Athabasca are blessed with good appetites. Animals killed — twelve moose deer, two reindeer, thirty large mountain sheep or bighorn, two porcupines, 210 hares, one beaver, two muskrats, twenty-four bustards, 115 ducks, twenty-one pheasants, one snipe, one eagle, one owl; add to this from thirty to fifty fine white-fish every day and twenty trout, and then judge whether or not our people had reason to complain; yet we heard them constantly saying: 'How hard living is here. The country is miserably poor — we are obliged to fast.' "

Before Father De Smet left the valley his Iroquois friends made a very kindly gesture "to prove their attachment . . . Each one discharged his musket in the direction of the highest mountain, a large rock jutting out in the form of a sugar loaf, and with three loud hurrahs gave it my name."

The fact that today a mountain peak some four miles west of old Jasper House bears the corpulent priest's name is not conclusive proof that it is the mountain in whose direction the voyageurs wobbled their muzzle-loaders. If at the time De Smet was sure of which mountain they meant, his description of it as a sugar loaf (conical) mountain and one perpetually covered with snow certainly rules out Roche Miette and maybe Roche De Smet as well. I am inclined to agree with Ian D. Coates of Jasper, who says that De Smet's description "fits in with Pyramid and he would have been looking at the North face at the time which I think was early April. I notice that in Dr. Cheadle's Journal there is an illustration 'View from the Hill opposite Jasper House — The Upper Lake of the Athabasca River and Priest's Rock.' This quite definitely is Pyramid, even though it is not in its 'correct' position — the Indians would undoubtedly have called the mountain Priest's Rock and not by the name of De Smet. As I mentioned, Pyramid is still known by some of the local Indians as Priest's Rock."

After the ceremony of naming the mountain, Father De Smet started south and near the Miette River met a family of

Carrier Indians. The woman who had escaped the massacre at the mouth of Snake Indian River was with them. As Father De Smet recounted that story it differed in minor particulars only from that in the previous chapter.

As he expected, on his approach to the Athabasca Pass the worthy priest met the spring brigade from Fort Vancouver. F. Ermatinger was in charge of it and with him were two strangers whose mission was of more than passing interest; H. J. Warre and M. Vavasour. Though they came posing as hunters and tourists, they were lieutenants in the British army who had been sent out to see what had to be done in case the United States and Britain got into a war over the Oregon country. They were instructed to study the line of communication across western Canada and to see what could be done to protect it in the event that there was danger of the American philosophy of Manifest Destiny making a move to invade the Canadian West.

After leaving Warre and Vavasour, De Smet came to the worst part of the journey over the deep snow of the summit, and "had to try the snowshoes for the first time in my life." That was the challenge of which John Rowand at Edmonton had warned him, because he was of the opinion that "it was absolutely impossible for me to accomplish the journey, on account of my corpulency, and they wished to dissuade me from attempting it."

Finally, however, after plowing through snowdrifts and wading through torrents, De Smet came to Boat Encampment "and in about an hour we found ourselves snugly seated and stretched out around the kettles and roasts, laughing and joking about the summersets on the mountains and the accidents on the Portage. I need not tell you that they described me as the most clumsy and awkward traveler in the band."

While Father De Smet had been floundering in the snow of the Athabasca Pass, Britain and the United States were discussing the fate of Oregon. About a month later, on June 15, 1846, they signed the Treaty of Oregon. Under its terms the boundary between the United States and Canada was continued west along the 49th parallel of latitude and most of the territory which the Hudson's Bay Company had called its Columbia district and which it had served out of Fort Vancouver, passed into American hands. As soon after that as was practicable the company removed its headquarters on the Coast to Fort Victoria and within a few years, the necessity which had called the Columbia brigades into being, ceased. Thereafter for decades few travelers used the Athabasca Pass and most of the reason for the existence of Jasper House likewise ceased.

Before that happened, however, Colin Fraser met his next interesting visitor when in the fall of 1846 in the course of his duties he had gone east to Edmonton and found that Paul Kane was about to travel through Jasper. Now regarded as one of Canada's outstanding early artists, Kane had persuaded George Simpson to let him travel with the Oregon cavalcade. On that trip he painted innumerable pictures of Indian life in the Far West and later on wrote one of Canada's most fascinating travel books, *Wanderings of an Artist*.

The brigade which Kane and Colin Fraser accompanied to Jasper was carrying the "Russian packs of otter skins." For several years the west-bound brigade forwarded these items to fulfill the terms of an agreement whereby the Hudson's Bay Company undertook to supply the Russian America Fur Company "with 3,000 land otter skins taken from the east side of the mountains." At times many of the pelts had been trapped in Ontario or Quebec and year after year they were forwarded through Jasper.

When Kane reached Fort Assiniboine, he found that though honored by the name of a fort, it was "a mere post used for taking care of horses, a common man or horsekeeper being charge of it." As usual the men took to boats and after a difficult voyage of twenty-three days, during which they poled and pushed their craft up the shallow icy river, they reached Jasper House in a howling blizzard.

On November 2, in the Jasper valley, Kane said: ". . . it is scarcely possible to conceive the intense force with which the wind howled through a gap formed by the perpendicular rock called 'Miette's Rock,' 1500 feet high, on the one side, and a lofty mountain on the other. The former derives its appellation from a French voyageur, who climbed its summit and sat smoking his pipe with his legs hanging over the fearful abyss."

Once more, in the same manner as the local people had told David Thompson about mammoths, and as they had explained to George Simpson how mountain sheep roll stones on their pursuers, they pulled Paul Kane's leg. In the best tradition of tall tales, the tradition which has produced the ogopogo and sasquatch, they invented a mythical hunter, a certain Miette, who climbed Roche Miette — presumably the face of Roche

Miette — for fun. Paul Kane must have failed to observe the twitch of their laughter wrinkles when wide-eyed and innocent they tried this tale on him.

Not that every single one of the voyageurs couldn't have climbed the mountain or that, if a sheep had been standing there, any one of them wouldn't have scampered up and shot it, but to climb the cliff for fun — c'est drôle, monsieur.

If one inclines to the belief (which I hold) that no voyageur climbed Roche Miette for the fun of it, then one must cast about for another explanation of the name. The earliest written reference to it is in Franchère's journal in which he calls it "La Rocher a Miette." If it was named in honor of a voyageur, he must have been in the area before that year. While some of the North West Company records of the area have passed out of existence and those that remain are scanty, no one seems to be able to find any reference to a voyageur of that name. Moreover, there are no references to such a name in any of the available Hudson's Bay Company records. That does not prove that Miette never existed, but a search of directories of cities having a large French population, Montreal, Quebec, Winnipeg, and others, including Edmonton, reveals how rare the name is. Even variants in spelling, such as Myette, Mayotte, Maiotte, and so on, are rare.

Both Roche Miette, the great guardian of the gateway to the Jasper valley, and the Miette River some thirty miles removed from the mountain — the river which carved out the Yellowhead route — both have come by their names prosaically. In my opinion, both names are derived from their long-time pre-eminence as the haunt of mountain sheep — the "My-a-tick" of the Cree which, rolled about on the voyageurs' Gallic tongues, became Myatt or Miette, probably pronounced with a long "i."

None of this, however, should detract from the pleasure tourist guides since Kane's time get by telling of Miette smoking his pipe. Like the stories of Indian maidens (princesses, of course), hunting for lost or strayed lovers and falling over cliffs in fogs, but still calling for their loved ones, the story of the voyageur Miette is too good to allow it to be forgotten.

Jasper House, of which he made a sketch, Kane found to consist "of only three miserable log huts. The dwelling-house is composed of two rooms, of about fourteen or fifteen feet square each. One of them is used by all comers and goers: Indians, voyageurs, and traders, men, women, and children being huddled together indiscriminately; the other room being devoted to the exclusive occupation of Colin and his family, consisting of a Cree squaw, and nine interesting half-breed children.'' In spite of Kane's apparent disappointment, Jasper House served its purpose, and while Colin Fraser may not have been wholly satisfied with it, he did not bother to take steps to improve it. Perhaps he was too busy with his family, which had grown since Father De Smet's visit by the addition of two children.

At Jasper House Kane met and made a sketch of Capote Blanc, who he understood was a Shuswap and one of the survivors of the massacre at the mouth of Snake Indian River. The artist described him as ''a very simple, kind-hearted old man, with whom I became very friendly.'' Whether the native was a Shuswap, as Kane said, or was a Carrier, which Father De Smet's comments would suggest, is a moot question.

Kane left Jasper House on November 5, and after a typically difficult time crossed the pass and reached Boat Encampment ten days later. He described his experiences so graphically, they merit extensive quotation even at the risk of being repetitious. As he was working his way along he fell behind the others of his party and came to the Wood River, where it was seventy yards broad and flowing swiftly. Finding that the other men had crossed the stream, he took off his snowshoes and waded in. ''The water was up to my middle, running very rapidly, and filled with drift ice, some pieces of which struck me, and nearly forced me down the stream. I found on coming out of the water my capote and leggings frozen stiff. My difficulties, however, were only beginning, as I was soon obliged to cross again four times, when, my legs becoming completely benumbed, I dared not venture on the fifth, until I had restored the circulation by running up and down the beach. I had to cross twelve others in a similar manner, being seventeen in all, before I overtook the rest of the party at the encampment.''

After descending the Columbia to Fort Vancouver and remaining there for nearly a year, he set out for his home in Eastern Canada and reached Boat Encampment again in October, 1847. As soon as he started across the portage he had plenty of justification to feel sorry for himself and the horses. ''My horse stuck in a mud hole until he sank up to his head, and it was with the greatest difficulty that one of the men and myself extricated him alive. What with the horses sticking in the mud, the packs falling off, the shouting to the animals in

Cree, and swearing at them in French, there being no oaths in the Indian language, I never passed such a busy, tiresome, noisy, and disagreeable day in my life . . ."

That night the party reached Campement de Fusil and Kane wrote in his diary: "A distressing occurrence took place here some years previously. Whilst a party were ascending this mountain, a lady, who was crossing to meet her husband, was in the rear, and it was not noticed until the party had encamped that she was not come up. Men were instantly sent back to seek her. After some hours' search, they found her tracks in the snow, which they followed until they came to a perpendicular rock overhanging a roaring torrent; here all traces of her were lost, and her body was never found, notwithstanding every exertion was made to find it. Little doubt, however, could exist that she had lost her way, and had fallen over the precipice into the torrent, which would have quickly hurried her into chasms where the foot of a man could not reach." Kane, of course, was referring to the loss of J. E. Harriott's wife in 1830.

On November 6 he reached Jasper House, where the men were obliged to pause while they made birch snowshoes and sleds. On November 15, accompanied by an Indian and a half-breed and with three dogs to pull his sled, he set out down the Athabasca. The river was not completely frozen over and ice jams and other problems made their trip one of rarely paralleled difficulty and danger.

On November 18 one of the dogs ran away. "This was a serious loss, as besides his use in drawing the sledge, we did not know but that we might want to eat him, our provisions were getting so scarce, and we met with very few rabbits, the only thing to be found on the route at this season."

Day after day for another week, clambering over blocks and ridges of ice, or crashing through into the freezing water, wet through, nearly frozen and perpetually hungry, the three men pressed on. When they camped for the night of November 27 they expected to reach Fort Assiniboine the following day, so they ate the last of their meager provisions. Next day they "started early in the morning, about three o'clock; this was an hour earlier than we usually got away, but we had nothing to cook and no breakfast to eat. I began to feel that my hardships were telling seriously on me. The mal de racquet tortured me at every step; the soles of my feet were terribly cut and wounded from the ice, which formed inside of my stockings as much as an eighth of an inch thick every day, occasioned by the freezing of the perspiration. It breaks in small pieces, and is like so much sharp gravel in the shoes; and I was weak from the want of food; but the hope of reaching a place of safety kept me up, and I toiled on over the bourdigneaux, which were very numerous today, steadily but slowly. At last, overcome with fatigue and weakness we had to encamp still far from the fort. We had a long consultation over our camp fire, as to whether we should eat the dogs or not, but their thinness saved them — the two would not have furnished us with a sufficient meal; besides, they could draw the sledge still; and that was a great consideration to us in our weak state; and we knew that if we met with no accident, we must reach the fort next day; still, if the dogs had been young, and in anything like condition, they would most assuredly have gone into the pot.

"November 29th — We again started very early in the morning . . . Our way was not very bad, in comparison with what we had come over; still we had to move on slowly from weakness, and it was not until four o'clock P.M., that we arrived at Fort Assiniboine, having travelled 350 miles in fifteen days.

"No sooner had we arrived, than all hands set to work cooking; luckily for us, this post is plentifully supplied with white fish . . . the memory of that feast hung over me, even in my dreams, for many a day afterwards. One of the women devoted herself to the rather arduous task of satisfying my appetite, whilst my two men cooked on their own account, thinking that nobody else would do it quick enough; and no cook who cared for his reputation would have dished up fish in the raw state in which they devoured the first two or three. I, however, controlled myself, and gave the woman a little time to prepare mine . . .

"Soon, seated on a pile of buffalo skins before a good fire, I commenced the most luxurious repast of which it had ever been my fate to partake. I had no brandy, spirits, nor wine, neither had I tea, or coffee — nothing but water to drink. I had no Harvey's sauce, or catsup, or butter, or bread, or potatoes, or any other vegetable. I had nothing but fish; no variety, save that some were broiled on the hot coals and some were boiled. But I had been suffering for days from intense cold, and I now had rest; I had been starving, and I now had food; I had been weary and in pain, without rest or relief, and I now had both rest and ease . . . How many fish the men ate, I do not know; but having satiated themselves, they all lay down to sleep. In the middle of the night they woke me up, to ask me if I would not join them in another feast, but I did not; much to their astonishment, as the woman had told them that she was afraid I was sick, as I only ate four fish [averaging six pounds] out of the seven she had prepared for me. However, in the morning, about five o'clock, I commenced again, and made another hearty meal; and then how happy I was when I lay down and slept again, instead of clambering over the rugged bourdigneaux!''

When he had relaxed briefly at Fort Assiniboine, Kane went on to spend Christmas at Edmonton, and ultimately went home to finish the scores of paintings he had started and to publish his *Wanderings of an Artist*. Traveling as he had done, intent on painting and describing life in the West as he saw it, he has left Canadians forever in his debt.

After Paul Kane's trip through Jasper, the size of the brigades dwindled each year as the Hudson's Bay Company closed out its operations in Oregon, until by 1854, except for an occasional wayfarer, travel over the route ceased. In the meantime, the company built up Fort Victoria on Vancouver Island into a place of some importance. On March 11, 1850, by the time Colin Fraser had been blessed with another two or more children, the colony of Vancouver Island was officially created. Thenceforth the company's New Caledonia district became increasingly oriented to Fort Victoria, while Jasper House, never a promising plant, withered on the vine.

By 1850 Colin Fraser was fed up with Jasper and wrote to his old patron, George Simpson, asking to be moved to some other post, saying that he had been ''now fourteen years and going about every summer through a very rough country with a large family.'' Simpson granted his request and put him in charge of nearby Fort Assiniboine, where he remained till the fall of 1853.

When Colin shook the blowing sands of Jasper Lake off his moccasins, Joseph Edward Brazeau, a trader well known in the West, took his place. A member of a prominent Creole family, he was born in St. Louis, Missouri, where about 1830 he entered the fur trade probably as an employee of the American Fur Company. Well-educated and speaking English, French and Spanish fluently, he was also remarkably proficient in six quite different Indian languages. After many years' experience in the United States, he joined the Hudson's Bay Company and in 1850 took charge of Jasper House. At various times he served at Rocky Mountain House on the Saskatchewan and at Edmonton. He married Marguerite Brabant, sired eight children, and died at St. Albert in 1870.

Brazeau's first four-year stretch at Jasper House seems to have been quite uneventful. By his time the brigades had almost stopped using the Athabasca Pass and before he left he saw the last one set out over it, so that, except for the various natives of the valley and André Cardinal, he had little company. In the fall of 1855 Roderick McKenzie succeeded him, and he in turn was followed a year later by J. R. Watson. Neither of them seems to have distinguished himself.

For the season 1857-58 Jasper House was officially unoccupied, although André Cardinal, the reliable jack-of-all-trades, kept an eye on the company's interests. About that time he was directed to round up as many as possible of the 350 horses which were ranging in different pastures in the valley and to take them to Edmonton.

In the fall of 1858 Chief Factor Christie at Edmonton sent a virile young man to reopen Jasper House. This was Ontario-born Henry John Moberly, who at the age of nineteen went to Rocky Mountain House on the Saskatchewan to work for the company. During the next summer, in 1856, when for a few weeks he was in charge of a shipment of supplies to Dunvegan, it included a supply of leather destined to travel to New Caledonia by way of the Peace River. Apparently the company had decided that it was not practical to send leather through Tête Jaune's pass.

When in the fall of 1858 Moberly started a residence of four years at Jasper House, he set out from Edmonton with André Cardinal, six young Iroquois, and some forty horses. He decided to take his pack train by way of Lac Ste. Anne and to follow what he called Indian "pitching trails" to Brulé Lake. Although in his memoirs he claimed to have been the first white man ever to take a pack train over what later became the Jasper Trail, his claim is a bit shaky.

In order to get his claim into proper perspective, it is necessary to consider "pitching trails." The natives, and by that time the Iroquois belonged in that category, found it necessary to move about from place to place over quite a large area. With their horses they often traveled for several days from one destination to another. Between those points they usually followed the same route, which would mean that in general they would travel up one stream valley and cross over to another. Rarely indeed did they chop obstructing deadfall out of their way. Instead, they circumvented it and their horses made their way through the trees or around muskegs in any manner they pleased. They left so little trace of their passage that anyone unacquainted with the country would have had the utmost difficulty finding which way they had gone. Even after several parties had taken a particular route the soil would scarcely be disturbed enough to make the trail stand out clearly as does a chopped-out pack trail.

With respect to the trail to Jasper, many years were to pass before it came to be an easily defined trail along essentially the same route as modern Highway 16. While Moberly, as an old man, may have felt certain that he had pioneered it, there seems to be little doubt but what André Cardinal had preceded him by a few years. Furthermore, in the fall of 1857, Father Lacombe and his Métis guide, Michel Nipissing, traveled overland to Jasper with two pack horses and a saddle horse each.

But even before that, J. E. Brazeau must have used that short cut from Lac Ste. Anne to Jasper Lake. In doing so either he or his native helpers left at least two landmarks which were well-known in 1859 when Dr. James Hector followed his guides from Jasper House to Edmonton and referred to them as Brazeau's cache and Brazeau's "lob-sticks." Judging from Dr. Hector's itinerary for February 25, 1859, Brazeau's cache was somewhere north of modern Peers. At least the set of Brazeau's lobsticks noted in Hector's itinerary for March 1 appears to have been west of Chip Lake, and was created to mark the place where the west-bound trail left the stream named after them to cut across west to the vicinity of today's McLeod valley. It appears certain from the evidence in Hector's itinerary that the first white man to mark the trail was J. E. Brazeau.

In any event, when Moberly reached Jasper House he found that the "buildings, so long untenanted, badly needed repairing, the chinks between the logs re-mudding, the chimneys patching and the windows fitting with new parchment . . ." Apparently he decided to rebuild the small outpost and probably did so the next year, for he liked the milder climate of the Jasper valley and looked forward to spending some time in an area which, for a good hunter, held much fascination. He and the Iroquois soon developed a high mutual regard and with them he spent much of his time hunting in the nearby mountains and going as far afield as the Grande Cache area. At other times he merely engaged regular hunters who pitched off along the foothills to the north or south. All of them had their own bands of horses which, having been raised in the mountains, were nearly as sure-footed as sheep.

On one expedition when he accompanied them, they killed more than seventy moose, besides caribou, bighorn and goats. Telling of it, Moberly said: "Our outfit consisted of four hunters and four meat-haulers with their respective families, my horse-keeper and his family, myself, a cook and an interpreter — in all ten lodges — with some hundred and fifty horses. The lodges were of dressed mooseskin, eight or ten to a tent, and were extremely comfortable . . . We commenced our hunting along the foothills, and as hunting in the locality had been followed for years we had good roads, or 'pitching trails' as they were called, for the reason that whole camps travelled them and pitched at accustomed intervals where feed for the horses was plentiful. Sometimes we made only a few miles, sometimes a fairly long move, remaining two or three weeks at each camp, until the vicinity was hunted out and the meat dried and cached."

It was in connection with such hunting that decades later Vincent Wanyandi told J. Shand-Harvey about stampeding game animals over cliffs. Vincent had been born near Jasper House about 1850 when the old fort was a post devoted to provisioning the brigades and when the Hudson's Bay Company bought all the meat the Indians could bring in. In those days moose and buffalo frequented the ridge separating the Wildhay River from the Snake Indian River, and once in a while, in a concerted effort, the natives would spend several days driving all game ahead of them until they converged on the cliffs near the mouth of Mumm Creek. During the last night of the drive the hunters kept the animals in a continual state of fear by making various noises all night. Then at daybreak they all yelled, shot off their guns and rushed noisily forward until the stricken animals were forced over the precipice. Down below, the women and old folk would be waiting to slit the beasts' throats and cut up their carcasses.

For days the Indians feasted while they dried the meat over fires. Then with the horses heavily loaded they set off along the north shore of Rock Lake and up Mowitch Creek, and over the pass to Willow Creek and down the Snake Indian River to Jasper House, where they sold their produce.

While Moberly sometimes participated in the Iroquois' hunts, his attentions were not restricted to that group of the valley's inhabitants. He was a young man about twenty-two and nothing was more natural than he should soon be captivated by the charms of the comely, capable and loyal mountain girl Suzan Cardinal. During their temporary but satisfying union, Suzan presented him with two sons, Ewan and John, who for decades were to be two of the leading figures in the broad, sunny valley.

One outstanding man who called on Henry J. Moberly at his newly refurbished post, was Dr. James Hector, a member of the Palliser Expedition. While he was a geologist and, therefore, found the mountains a rich pasture for his professional appetite, he was also a forerunner of the new era which was even then starting to send its tentacles into Western Canada. Part of the Palliser Expedition's purpose was to report on the feasibility of building a wagon road all the way across Canada to the Coast. Even as Hector was making notes on strata, he was also sizing up the possibility of using the Jasper valley for that route. After attending the New Year's celebrations in Fort Edmonton, Hector and three men set out in January, 1859, by dog team for Jasper. When he reached Fort Assiniboine he found it consisted of a few ruined and unoccupied log huts.

A week or so later and half an hour after wading across the Athabasca River at the foot of Roche Miette, Hector stumbled into Moberly's post. His description of crossing the icy stream is worth quoting: "After searching about for a crossing place in the dark without success, we took the most shallow place we could find, where the river was very rapid, and without taking the harness off the dogs, unfastened them from the sleds, and pitching them into the water, pelted them with pieces of ice, so that they swam for the other side of the river. We then got off the edge of the ice ourselves, and found the water took us above the waist, and getting the sleds, loads and all, on our shoulders, waded through the rapid, which was about 100 yards wide, and so reached the left bank. The wind, which had changed at sunset to N.E., was bitterly cold, so that the plunge into the water felt rather warm at first, but on re-emerging we at once stiffened into a mass of ice, for, as I found half an hour afterwards, the thermometer stood at -15°. In this state we again tackled the dogs, that were all frozen in a lump with their harness, and after a run of two miles through the woods, we reached Jasper House at 10 p.m.''

Hector was pleased with Jasper House and said: ''. . . the little group of buildings which form the 'fort' have been constructed, in keeping with their picturesque situation, after the Swiss style, with overhanging roofs and trellised porticos.'' His pleasure, however, did not save the inhabitants from occasional hungry spells. He arrived at a time when the three Iroquois hunters were having a hard time bringing in enough sheep to keep everyone supplied. To hunt the bighorn they used a few highly trained dogs, which followed their prey up the mountains and when possible turned them before they could reach some of the more inaccessible crags.

H. J. Moberly, of course, enjoyed hunting and he too had a dog which he valued highly, especially when he relied upon it to tree lynx. Those large cats formed a significant part of his family's diet that winter when lean mutton and fat lynx meat supplemented each other. To prepare what everyone agreed was a savory meal, a lynx would be stuffed with minced mutton and roasted whole. So far that winter, Moberly explained to Hector, of the eighty-three lynx which had been shot and eaten, he and his dog had procured about half.

Before leaving the Jasper valley, Hector, Moberly, an Iroquois hunter named Tekarra, and a Canadian named Arcand, set out up the Athabasca but failed to get to the summit of the pass. By climbing a mountain opposite the mouth of the Whirlpool River, Hector thought he was able to get a view of the mysterious mountains Brown and Hooker. Somewhat farther up the Athabasca he named Mount Christie after the Chief Factor at Edmonton House, and named another nearby in honor of Moberly. Since that time another name has supplanted Moberly's, but the name Christie has remained. In the part of his journal which told of that trip, Hector said: "On the 11th we reached a point opposite to Miette's House, where there was once a trading post, at a point where the track branches up the Caledonian Valley (Miette Valley) to Fraser River . . .'' This would be the remains of La Rocque's House.

In February, when Hector was ready to set out for Edmonton, his guide Tekarra estimated that twelve days' travel along the trail which here and there was blazed would take them and their dogs to Edmonton. Bad weather and difficult traveling slowed their progress until their food supply came to an end, and they were forced to tramp along in a half-famished state. Then, fortunately, Tekarra killed a moose, and as Hector said: "We at once made a fire by the carcase, which lay among fallen timber where the snow was about four feet deep. Our appetite was tremendous, so that, although the flesh of the animal was so lean that at other times we would not have eaten it, we continued cooking, eating, and sleeping the remainder of that day, and the whole of the next, by which time there was little left of the moose but the coarser parts of the meat. Our three dogs also, who had eaten nothing but the bones of the grouse and our cast-off moccasins since leaving Jasper House, enjoyed themselves to the full; indeed both the dogs and masters conducted themselves more like wolves than was altogether seemly, excepting under such circumstances." That food supply saw them through to the Roman Catholic mission at Lac Ste. Anne.

By 1859, when Hector visited Jasper, the trail from Edmonton to that point was at least blazed in a crude sort of way. By that year too, and mainly during the previous decade, other changes had taken place in the area between the two posts. The mission which Father Thibault had started at Lac Ste. Anne in 1844 had been operating several years. To that mission in 1852 came the great Father Lacombe. And soon after Hector's visit Sister Superior Emery and Sisters Lamy and Alphonse of the Grey Nuns came to teach, nurse, and minister to the Indians and Métis, who looked upon Lac Ste. Anne as their spiritual headquarters.

From the mission the priests worked out a cart road which split off from the Fort Assiniboine Trail at a point a few miles north and west of modern St. Albert. It provided the first leg of what was later to be the pack trail to Jasper. Once the mission was established, the Iroquois, who had never forgotten the religious training their grandfathers had enjoyed near Montreal and who had rejoiced in Father Demers' and Father De Smet's ministrations, began to journey to Lac Ste. Anne for spiritual consolation. Their visits contributed to making the trail from Jasper to the mission somewhat more definite.

Meanwhile, Fort Assiniboine had fallen on evil days. Colin Fraser had been in charge of it from 1850 to the spring of 1853, but then, since the necessity for the Columbia brigades was passing, it lost its main reason for existence. Consequently, he had asked to be transferred to another post, and as a result, took charge of Lesser Slave Lake until the spring of 1862.

While those changes were taking place east of Jasper, interesting events were under way in New Caledonia to the west. Ever since Tête Jaune had made his first trip over the pass, the interior of British Columbia had remained a land of dense forests, roaring rivers, and gloomy valleys. Here and there, stuffed with salmon at times and starving at other times, a few natives eked out a precarious existence, supplementing what the woods and streams yielded by trading furs at far-spaced Hudson's Bay Company posts. Thus it had been for decades; thus for all anyone could guess it would always be.

Then in 1856, near the junction of the Thompson and the Fraser rivers and not too far from the fur trade post of Fort Kamloops, some prospectors found gold — a double handful of nuggets. The next year, in a mad hunt for the new resource, some of the company's employees mingled with Indians and American 49'ers who had worked north from California's gold rush. During 1858 over twenty thousand bearded miners poured through Fort Victoria and struggled up the Fraser, astounding fur traders and antagonizing the Indians. To cope with part of the problem which the prospectors posed, the colony of British Columbia was created on November 19, 1858. The eyes of the world turned to it and to the Fraser River gravels. The old district of New Caledonia, now the Colony of British Columbia, had a new resource, and fur trading found itself shouldered aside.

By the time Dr. Hector visited Moberly in January, 1859, and looked west up Tête Jaune's pass toward the headwaters of the Fraser, its lower reaches were lined with miners. A month or so later, when Hector was safely back at Edmonton House, the prospectors were panning as far up the Fraser as Quesnel. By that fall a few hardy adventurers were picking away at the gravels in the Cariboo, eighty straight-line miles west of Tête Jaune Cache — eighty rugged miles. Six months later, in the spring of 1860, the first of a generation of miners passed through Jasper. The party, consisting of Timolean Love, D. F. McLaurin, A. Perry, and Tom Clover, had bypassed the Cariboo, ascended the Fraser, and crossed the Yellowhead Pass on their way to Edmonton House and Fort Garry. Undoubtedly they looked in on Jasper House, which was temporarily unoccupied while Moberly was away at Edmonton.

About that time Moberly's itch to move along became too strong to resist. When he heard that his old patron, Sir George Simpson, had died, he left the company's service in the fall

of 1861. At the end of October, accompanied by a young
half-breed, he made his way to Tête Jaune Cache. There, living
with a couple of Shuswap, he found the woman survivor of
the Snake Indian massacre. From those friendly people he
obtained a canoe and a warning about the Grand Canyon of
the upper Fraser, which was some 110 airline miles downstream.
On the second evening after he embarked he came in sight of
the dangerous reach of water. He had no trouble getting through
the Grand Canyon, which, over the years, was destined to drown
a score or so of men. Not only did the hardy trader survive
the experience, but he was the first man to write about it afterwards.

While his memoirs deal simply and briefly with such incidents as running the canyon, or indeed with his adventures in
the Jasper valley, they say nothing about his wife Suzan. Unlike
Colin Fraser who remained faithful to one wife and took his
growing family along as he moved from post to post, Moberly
simply saddled his horse and rode away from Suzan and the
boys — whether with relief or regret one can never know.

6

OVERLANDERS OF 1862

DURING the summer of 1862, belaboring their oxen over the trail Moberly had used from Lac Ste. Anne mission to Jasper and capsizing their canoes in the rapids of the river by which he made his exit from this story, a contingent of hopeful miners from Ontario crept through the Yellowhead Pass. With the gleam of gold in their eyes and the smoke of a hundred campfires in their hair, the Overlanders of '62 headed for the Cariboo.

That spring from the growing cities of Ontario many adventurers started for the gold fields, and by June had assembled at Fort Garry, where they gained a few recruits. At that point they met Timolean Love, one of the party of miners which a year or so previously had crossed the Yellowhead Pass on its way to Fort Garry. Traveling by carts from there in two main parties totaling 175 men and one woman, the Overlanders trekked slowly across the prairies and reached Fort Edmonton about the end of July.

The woman, who turned out to be remarkably able and courageous, was Catherine, aged twenty-seven, Irish-born, and the wife of Augustus Schubert, a German immigrant living at Fort Garry. With them the couple took their daughter and two sons, all under seven years of age. For the children's sake, these adventurers took a milking cow along yoked with an ox. Like her husband, Catherine rode a horse, but it was rigged with a basket for each of the two smaller children. The elder boy rode with his father.

At Edmonton some sixty men gave up the idea of going to the Cariboo and decided to prospect along the headwaters of the Saskatchewan River. The remainder, now numbering about 115, abandoned most of their carts and headed west for Lac Ste. Anne. They traveled in two main parties led by Thomas McMicking and Stephen Redgrave, but within the larger divisions the Overlanders were not only split into smaller groups but were strung out into little batches of men battling muskeg here and there and extending nearly two hundred miles from front to rear. When the McMicking group, which was in the van, was in sight of the mountains near Hinton, Redgrave was leaving Edmonton, some two hundred miles behind and nearly a month later. In the foremost group, of course, were the most energetic men, those who could not stand wasting time, and to them fell the tasks of chopping deadfall out of the way and bridging the small, deep streams along the first part of the route over which they were still using carts. Those who straggled along behind benefited by the work done by those who preceded them.

Before leaving Edmonton on July 29 the McMicking party had wisely hired André Cardinal, who, though having been born in the Jasper valley and having resided there most of his life, had recently settled near Father Lacombe's new mission at St. Albert. His payment was to be fifty dollars in cash, an ox, a cart, and one hundredweight of groceries. He undertook to take them as far as Tête Jaune Cache, and the Overlanders found him friendly, trustworthy, capable, and resourceful. As it left Edmonton, the McMicking party, which included Mrs. Schubert, had about 140 assorted horses, mules, and oxen each transporting 140 to 250 pounds.

Of the departure of his party, Stephen Redgrave wrote: "At 11 a.m. started with a pack on my Back for Jasper House which is in the mountains. Another & myself had an ox packed with our provisions, the ox not being used to pack commenced kicking & playing up fearfully, first one strap & then another breaking, plates knives & forks fly^g in the air, flour spilling on the ground, ox running away frightened to death . . . however we tried again & kept the pack on, only sometimes the old brute would fling it off but we managed to get thro to the Mission."

The first night the McMicking party reached St. Albert. Two days more traveling over a rough, muddy road in a drizzling rain, brought them to Lac Ste. Anne. Before reaching there they had to build a couple of temporary bridges, and of one of those Sellar wrote: ". . . we came to a small river about 30 yds wide & very deep where we had to unpack our animals & build a bridge before we could get across. This took us some time, as the timber was all on the West bank of the river, & the water was so cold that no person would Volinteer to swim over & cut down the timber, after considerable jawing about who had done the most at places like this Wm Gage, A. Anderson, D. Oney, & myself proposed to go over, so we caught two Oxen, tied our clothes upon their horns, & drove them in & got them by the tails & swam after them across & then fell a large poplar tree across the river for the rest to cross upon.''

At Lac Ste. Anne the Overlanders met Father Lacombe, who the year before had started a new mission at St. Albert. By the time Sellar reached it, about twenty half-breeds and freemen, including André Cardinal, had settled near it. At Lac Ste. Anne the travelers found Colin Fraser, now the father of twelve children, who was in charge of the Hudson's Bay Company's post which he had opened a few months previously.

The mission there, with its signs of civilization, its church bell, its devoted nuns, and the milk, bread, butter, and potatoes they were given, made a deep impression on the travelers. Except for Dr. Symington, none of them could repay the kindnesses they received in anything more tangible than verbal thanks. The doctor, however, reciprocated Father Lacombe's kindness in a manner which, if not material, was greatly valued. Sometime previously the priest had been the recipient of a battered cabinet of medicines, but could not dispense them because he was unaware of their uses and properties. The physician looked them over and supplied the necessary names and information, so that thenceforth they were invaluable to the good Father.

At Lac Ste. Anne the Overlanders abandoned the last of their carts, for beyond there it was impossible to take them. From there onward everything had to be packed on reluctant horses and downright unwilling oxen. Pushing forward, they passed Lake Isle, and with many a tribulation crossed the Pembina. Several of the diarists commented on the coal seams exposed in its banks. Others noted the fact that at that river they saw signs of the first frost. It was now August 4, and the summer was wearing away.

The months had slipped by rapidly since most of them had left their Ontario home towns in the last week of April, filled with the assurance that sixty days would see them in the Cariboo. When the foremost party had reached Edmonton on July 23, some ninety days had gone by and they were still far from their destination. And now at the Pembina River they had seen their first frost and the Fraser was still over two hundred rugged miles away.

Somewhere in what is now the Niton area, Sellar had trouble with muskeg, and wrote: "At 6²⁰ struck into a fearful slough covered with dry spruce poles about 3 inches thick. It was the worst of any that we had meet on our journey, I have often

heard tell of the slough of dispond but after this I shall be able
to tell where it is. It is about 150 roods wide, the surface is
a kind of open mose [moss] while beneth the mose it appears
like floating tan bark & as I had to drive my horse through,
I was thankful that he was the best in the crowd . . .''

Then, a day or so later when crossing Wolf Creek, they
found the grave of a gold seeker who had been buried in 1860.
It was covered with birch bark and inscribed on a tamarack
tree was his name, James Mockerty. After following the McLeod
River for some days and crossing the height of land to the Athabasca and then turning up Prairie Creek, along much the same
route taken by Highway 16, the McMicking party camped somewhere in the Pocahontas area. Sellar went into a rhapsody when
describing the mountains, although his spelling couldn't match
his sentiments: "This sceanery around the camp was delightful,
though no person could help feeling more or less awe over them,
when they realized the fact that they were standing in a mear
chasm, while the rocks on either side towered thousands of feet
above & appeared as if they hung by a mear thread which at
any moment might break, & we be buried in oblivion.''

Across the river Jasper House looked unoccupied, even
though during 1861 and 1862 J. E. Brazeau was nominally in
charge. They discussed whether to cross over to it or whether
to keep on along the right bank of the river. Deciding on the
latter course, they had to cross the shoulder of Roche Miette,
and on top one of their horses dropped off the trail. ". . . all
got along well till we were up about 1400 feet, when the horse
that H. Blachford [had] missed a foot . . . canted end over
end about 400 feet down packs & all when he landed against
a tress . . .'' Luckily they were able to rescue the horse, although
not long afterward another party had two horses killed in a similar
manner.

Next day they swam the stock and made rafts to cross
to the west side of the Athabasca, and shortly before they came
in sight of the Miette River, André Cardinal pointed to a heap
of rotten logs all grown over with brush and said, if they understood and reported him correctly, "That is old Henry House.''
Since they were on the west side of the river, the logs would
be all that was left of La Rocque's House.

Like the Hudson's Bay Company's leather brigades of some
decades earlier, the McMicking party started up the Miette
River, following what traces of a trail were left. On the second

night, having crossed the almost imperceptible height of land which was the summit of Yellowhead Pass, they camped on what was known as Cow Dúng Lake (Yellowhead Lake). At last they were beside water flowing west, the Fraser River itself. By that time their provisions were running dangerously low. One group killed an ox, and as they had little salt, they cut the beef into thin strips and dried it over the fire. The Schuberts killed a horse; others shot squirrels and small birds to eke out their scanty provisions. Some of the men shot a porcupine and a skunk, which were declared good eating.

After passing Moose Lake they came to the dangerous shale hill where the pack trail over the treacherous rocks climbed to nine hundred feet above the river. They did not venture to drive loaded horses across it but unpacked them and carried the loads on their own shoulders. By the time they camped by the Fraser that night it was a considerable river. Next morning after André Cardinal awakened them by shouting "Hurrah for Tête Jaune Cache" and promising that they would reach there during the afternoon, they set off jubilantly. Two or three miles before they reached that spot, one of Sellar's horses "carrying our cooking utentials & all the dishes & china Plates got tired of life & ran over the bank into the Fraser & was drowned sinking with all his cargo, & was washed up onto a sand bar about a mile below with nothing upon him except his saddle & another riding saddle which was lashed on to his pack one."

In spite of that mishap they reached Tête Jaune Cache at 4 p.m. on August 27, nearly a month after leaving Edmonton and four months after leaving Ontario. By that time their stock of provisions was nearly exhausted, so that they were doubly glad to see a camp of Shuswap Indians upon the opposite bank of the Fraser. The natives had salmon and berries, both of which commodities they dried, making the fruit—huckleberries and service berries—into cakes. Upon seeing the new arrivals they came over with a supply of each, disposing of their wares by barter for ammunition, articles of clothing, needles, thread, or whatever else might take their fancy. To the weary travelers, who for several weeks had been on short rations, the Indians' freshly caught salmon, each weighing from twenty-five to thirty pounds, were delicious. The travelers had long passed the point of fastidiousness over food, and even if the fish were in poor shape after their long swim from the sea and battered and bruised in their passage through narrow canyons and over shallow, boulder-strewn bars, the Overlanders devoured them with gusto.

Meanwhile, the rest of the Overlanders were strung out for about a hundred miles behind the McMicking party; the last group reached the Cache on September 16. The Redgrave men, for instance, did not pass Cow Dung Lake until September 7, when, as it was getting dark, the guide and five of the party went on, crossed a stream and camped on what they thought was the far bank of the Fraser.

Daylight showed that they were on an island, and during the night the river had risen so high that they could not safely cross the other channel. The water was too broken for a raft and there seemed nothing for it but to wait until the flood subsided. Joe, the guide, however, using a stout pole, managed to make the crossing and to return, but advised the rest that they dare not cross. Then in one of the strangest episodes of the entire journey, a man named Burgess bribed the guide to carry him and his pack across on his back, and the pair went off, leaving the others to follow or remain. Alexander and Thompson stripped, tied their packs and clothing on their shoulders, and tried to make the crossing, but were nearly swept off their feet, and it was all they could do to get back to the island again. Thompson, an old man, fastened his pants, which held all his money, on the top of his knapsack but the pants got loose and floated downstream. The old fellow, almost distraught, ran after them. Fortunately they caught on a small twig, but he had to go into the icy water to retrieve them.

The men intended to try to cross the next morning, but Thompson, by getting heated from his race and then chilled by the cold water, became quite ill and raved during the night. Partly because of his condition, the men decided to wait till those behind should come along and help them. They had to wait four days, and meantime were almost out of provisions. Alexander's diary entries for the last two days of their stay on the island describe their plight:

"Wednesday, September 10th. Still no sign of the Company. We are all beginning to feel very weak. If they don't come up soon it will be very serious work for us. Took our last meal this morning, hardly, a tea cup full of thin soup made with a bit of beef about the size of your hand, a thin piece of cake about the same size. Leader is very bad. We lie about the fire and smoke nearly all day, passing the pipe from one to the other, and, strange to say, I find the talk among men nearly starving is what they would like if they were at home . . .

"Thursday, September 11th. Well, nothing to eat this morning; a whole day with nothing to eat. Phillip went out this morning and shot two small Red Squirrels, just enough to keep life in and he was skinning them, when, thank God, we heard the voices of our jolly fellows. They camped at once and a good deal of indignation was felt at the guide, who would hardly have been safe in these hands at that time. After a plentiful dinner, we proceeded and camped on the shores of Moose Lake—a widening of the Fraser River."

During the Overlanders' long trek from Ontario three points on their route had stood out as landmarks; Fort Garry, Fort Edmonton, and Tête Jaune Cache. They had now reached the third objective, and the next jump would take them to their goal, the Cariboo. Though every hour had to be husbanded and every minute filled with activity if they were to reach that goal before winter closed the way, nevertheless their stay in the pleasant valley refreshed man and beast.

For well over a hundred miles they had been confined in a narrow, winding slit of a valley where almost at their elbows great mountains rose steeply, and now, all of a sudden, they had debouched into the widest valley they had seen in all that distance. At Tête Jaune Cache and mainly south of the river the terrain opened up to become a broad expanse over ten miles long and five miles wide, carpeted with good pasture. In that open area even the river relaxed and expanded so that its waxy green waters ambled along silently. Around its periphery but not oppressively close great mountain peaks stood sentinel far enough away that a man could see their tops without getting a crick in his neck from tilting his head back. At any time Tête Jaune Cache was a spot in which to relax, but to the tired and bruised Overlanders it appeared an oasis in a vast desert of mountains. Moreover, it afforded two apparently gentle routes of exit, one down the Fraser, and the other up the open valley to the south.

Hitherto, in all their four-month trek there had been but one route to take. Hitherto, as they had pulled pack horses out of muskegs, goaded oxen across swift streams, or chopped their way through windfall, though their toil had been excessive, they had but to follow the guide and had no decisions to make. Here they had to decide whether to float down the Fraser or to head up the McLennan in search of the waters of the North Thompson River.

For Tête Jaune Cache, as it had been in the days of the Nipissing, as it had been when Tête Jaune the Iroquois had passed, and as it was to be in the distant future when railways came blasting their way through and in the even more remote future when paved highways came into existence—Tête Jaune Cache was the parting of the ways. Having reached that point they had become the first significant party to travel today's Yellowhead route from Portage la Prairie to where it forks at the Cache. There too, like modern tourists following the pavement, some chose to follow what was to become one leg of the future highway to Kamloops and others chose the other leg to Prince George.

Into the northwest flowed the Fraser, a navigable stream—navigable by supermen. Down it 150 airline miles and, as Henry John Moberly had found, more than twice that many by canoe, lay Fort George, just beyond the great bend where leaving the Rocky Mountain Trench the river swings south towards Quesnel and Fort Hope and the Pacific Ocean. For some forty years before the Overlanders camped at Tête Jaune Cache, occasional parties of fur traders had traveled the 315 river miles down to Fort George. As a means of communication between the prairies and that post it had proven impractical and consequently had been left to wind its way through its cedar forests only rarely disturbed by the rap of the white man's paddle or the ring of the voyageur's laugh. A few Indians lived here and there along it, but unlike the Peace River or the Columbia, or even its own reaches below Fort George, its upper 250 miles were almost untraveled and unknown. And as an unknown river it came to be regarded with suspicion.

A vigorous growth of cedar found the rainfall of its valley congenial, but the deep shade of the forest floor, relieved only by the fresh green or yellow of devil's club, lent a gloomy aspect to the whole area. The dark forests, combined with the river's risky rapids and its death-dealing canyon, all united to produce its reputation of a stretch of dismal and dangerous river which it was not advisable to travel.

In spite of that, as they wound interminably back and forth, these 250 miles of the upper Fraser had their own languid if somewhat monotonous charm. Strangely enough, while the stream continually meandered from one side of its narrow trough to the other, its valley was the arrow-straight gash of the Rocky Mountain Trench—the most continuous gash on the surface of the North American continent and one of the world's outstanding topographical features. For scores of miles south of Tête Jaune Cache the gash contains the Canoe and Columbia rivers, and much farther north holds the Parsnip and the Finlay. Flanked on the east by the steep wall of the Rocky Mountains and the Continental Divide, which rises to an elevation of 12,972 feet at Mount Robson, and on the west by the Cariboo Mountains towering 6,000 feet above the village of McBride, its floor, in which the upper Fraser runs, has an elevation of 2,400 feet at Tête Jaune Cache. By the time the river reaches Prince George it has dropped more than six hundred feet, and most of the descent is in occasional rapids and the Grand Canyon. A very lamb of a river it is for long, milky green stretches, as wimpling and simpering around its invariable bends into unbroken coniferous forests, it fawns deceptively. But a rampaging ram of a river it is too, as suddenly throwing off its mask of friendliness, it reveals white water ahead at various minor rapids and at the worrisome Goat Rapids. And a roaring lion of a river it becomes at its awesome Grand Canyon some one hundred miles above Prince George, where the level forested valley is suddenly heaved up into transverse ridges through which, dropping swiftly, the sizzling waters go ranting and swirling down between rocky cliffs.

The Overlanders, of course, did not know the river's dangers, and the Indians, prophets of gloom and doom, provided little useful information. One thing the Overlanders knew; the river would lead them to the gold fields, and no matter how risky it might be, rafting was better than driving oxen through marsh and deadfall.

In the other direction, to the southeast, up the McLennan River valley, they knew even less of what faced them. For that matter, neither did the Shuswap they met, or at least they did not want to stick their necks out by venturing any opinions. Originally the Overlanders had felt sure that there must be some way to cut across from Tête Jaune Cache to the Cariboo, which after all was less than a hundred miles straight west. At Tête Jaune Cache they realized that any such direct route was entirely out of the question. Those who preferred proceeding by land would have to ascend the McLennan valley to Cranberry Lake, just west of modern Valemount, and then cross the Canoe River and ascend its tributary, the Camp River, to the summit of Albreda Pass. There they could start the fifteen-mile trip along the Albreda River to where it ran into the North Thompson. After that they could follow the larger stream all the way to Fort Kamloops.

But they had no one to advise them. André Cardinal, who had earned everyone's gratitude by the manner in which he had carried out his undertaking to guide them to Tête Jaune Cache, was too honest to pretend to know the route from there on. He and the Overlanders had hoped that from the Cache the Shuswap could supply a guide, but while they knew all the details of the region for a couple of days' march away, they had no knowledge of the area beyond that.

The Overlanders had to make their own decision. It was to split up into two parties; one to take the horses across the country to the south and to make its way to Kamloops, and the other to build rafts and other craft and take the cattle down the Fraser as far as Quesnel. Having made up their minds, they set to work immediately, for not only was the season advancing rapidly, but equally rapidly their food supply was running out. Some of the groups killed an ox or two and others did some trading. "Euphriam Harper Paid $20.00 for 20 lbs of flour from Fortune," and "Big Smith gave his horse today for 20 lbs of flour."

Fortunately, among the dozens of men milling around Tête Jaune Cache in September, 1862, many kept journals. The Overlanders were not only the first significant party of miners from the east to head for the Cariboo but the first ones from Tête Jaune Cache to descend the Fraser on the one hand and the North Thompson on the other who have left a good record of their experiences.

Those who went down the Fraser did so in a variety of vessels. A few made dugout canoes of cottonwood logs and embarked sometimes singly and sometimes with two canoes lashed together. One party collected the hides from the oxen they had killed, stretched them together, fastened them to a frame and went bowling down the river. Most of the men, however, rearranged themselves into crews and built rafts—the first large rafts to carry freight from Tête Jaune Cache. They averaged twenty feet by forty feet, and one party lashed two of them together end to end. Most of the rafts carried oxen carefully tethered, but some of the men preferred killing their beasts and carrying the meat to having an ox for a shipmate.

On the afternoon of September 1, amid cheers and sighs, the great exodus started down the river. The Overlanders cheered, but the Shuswap Indians shuddered, saying: "Poor white men. No more!" In any event, except for the thirty-six who were taking horses up the McLennan River and some groups which were still in the Yellowhead Pass, in canoes, bullboats and rafts, men and oxen set off down the swift river.

Of the first day's run, A. L. Fortune wrote:

"We were much cheered that first day's run, having had no serious interruption in the river and making so long a run with no fatigue to animals or men. This was a great change from the labor of walking, cutting a trail, or making bridges. We tied up at night where we could find feed for our stock."

During the whole of their trip to Fort George the weather was wet, cold, and uncomfortable, but in spite of that they made rapid progress. Those on the rafts cooked their meals as their crafts, passing and repassing each other, ran from daybreak till dark. The canoes, of course, soon outdistanced the larger, cumbersome rafts. The steady, milky green current swung them at a reasonable speed around so many loops and hairpin bends on their way to Fort George that they traveled nearly three miles of waterway for every mile of headway. With the Cariboo Mountains to their left, peering over the unbroken ranks of spruce trees and cedars, they slipped around bend after bend, quickening their heartbeats now and then as they darted and bounced down a few stretches of rapids. Once in a while, long, dark vistas, hemmed in by cedars and ending in a snow-capped mountain, showed them the river for three or four miles ahead. For five or six days till they came to the Grand Canyon they had little to do but enjoy the ease of floating along.

The men in the dugouts, of course, reached the canyon first. The swirling waters, hungry for victims, drowned one man, abetted the death of another, and snatched away the canoes. W. McKenzie, E. Pattison, and a man named Carroll in the first canoe stopped to study the canyon and then decided to lower the canoe by means of a lariat. Almost immediately it foundered and they lost everything, and wet, cold, and hungry, had to wait to be rescued. Pattison, already a sick man, died a few days later from exposure.

Before they were aware of the canyon, A. C. Robertson,

R. Warren, and a man named Douglas, slipping downstream
in two canoes lashed together, were caught in an eddy. The
canoes capsized and separated, and while Robertson, a good
swimmer, struck out for shore, the others clung to their craft.
When it had drifted onto a bar and they had time to look for
Robertson, he had drowned. Fortunately for the survivors, W.
A. Sellar's raft came along within a few hours and picked them
up.

While those events were taking place, the crew of McMicking's raft successfully ran the canyon. McMicking's group had
not been caught unaware, and they tied up to examine the situation. They lightened the load by having everyone walk except
for the ten men who were needed to control the raft. McMicking
was one of the men watching from the shore and his description
is well worth quoting:

"Onward they sped like an arrow. They seemed to be rushing into the very jaws of death. Before them on the right rose
a rocky reef against which the furious flood was lashing itself
into foam, threatening instant and unavoidable destruction, and
on the other side a seething and eddying whirlpool was ready
to engulf in its greedy vortex any mortal who might venture
within its reach. With fearful velocity they were hurried along
directly towards the fatal rock. Their ruin seemed inevitable.
It was a moment of painful suspense. Not a word was spoken
except the necessary orders of the pilot, which were distinctly
heard on shore above the din and tumult of the scene. Now
was the critical moment. Everyone bent manfully to his oar.
The raft shot closely past the rock, tearing away the stern rowlock,
and glided safely down into the eddy below. The agony was
over. The gauntlet had been· run, and all survived."

The main batch of the Overlanders all passed through the
Grand Canyon about the same time and it impressed on them
a deep respect for the ferocity of the Fraser. With similar thrills
but no fatalities they threaded their way through the Giscome
Rapids and practically all were on hand at Fort George to bury
Pattison, who died there on September 8. "A small canoe was
split and shaped into a coffin, there being no boards. We had
a short funeral service after the grave was dug and there committed to his last resting place young Pattison from England. He
was modest and refined in manner . . . We now knew of two
of our party who were gone to their long home."

As soon as possible the McMicking and Sellar parties and

a few others left the Hudson's Bay Company's fort, and after further thrilling adventures passed through the Fort George Canyon. Not long after getting through that gorge they came upon the first actual miners they were to see—some Chinamen working with rockers. Upon asking them what luck they were having, they got the rather guarded reply: "Oh, some day four bittee, six bittee; one day, long time, two dollah." Then, after navigating the wild waters of China Rapids and Cottonwood Canyon, that batch of Overlanders reached Quesnel on September 11.

A significant fraction of their associates, principally the Symington, Whitby, and Redgrave parties, were still behind them, still feeling their way down the Fraser. They too were to experience its fury. On September 6 the Symington party arrived at Tête Jaune Cache in an emaciated condition. The Whitby men who had just slaughtered their oxen and were loading the meat on their raft, stopped everything to prepare some of it for the famished men. The Redgrave party was still making its way over the Yellowhead Pass.

Bright and early on September 7, the Whitby men cast their raft loose, and with a cheer went whirling away down the stream. By evening they were back at Tête Jaune Cache. Seven miles down the river their raft struck a rock and wedged upon it. The rushing water swept everything away, tools, baggage, and provisions, as well as one of the men, leaving the rest clinging in desperation, knowing that sooner or later the raft must break up under the punishment the water was giving it.

Fortunately the man swept off, a good swimmer, reached the bank, and after turning to enjoin the others to hang on, set off for the Cache for help. Struggling through the forest, stumbling along the bank of the river, running, panting and hurrying desperately, he finally burst in upon the Symington party with the news. They dropped everything, jumped into canoes, and set out to help. A few hours earlier the Whitby men had shared their food with the starving Symington party and now the shoe was on the other foot. After the rescue both groups made common cause and built canoes which they eventually navigated to Fort George and on to Quesnel.

About September 20 the last of the Redgrave party got away from Tête Jaune Cache. All of them descended the Fraser in canoes during a spell of cold, rainy weather and reached the Grand Canyon about ten days later. It treated them just as roughly as it had their predecessors, and took one man's life. Even without any knowledge of what the other Overlanders had experienced, the Redgrave party approached it with caution. R. H. Alexander, who accompanied J. Carpenter and Dave Jones, stated that the three of them walked along to try to decide how to get their canoe down and then, having let it down the first part with a line, decided that it could not be lined down the next section and that the three men would have to paddle through. Alexander described his experience in his narrative:

"As we thought it rather dangerous, I took off my boots and buckskin shirt before we started. We went at a tremendous rate for a short while, when we got among some big waves, and the canoe filled over the stern and went down. When it came to the surface again, Carpenter was holding to the stern and I to the bow, the canoe then turned broadside to the current and rolled over and over. I then let go and swam for it. Carpenter I never saw again, nor yet the canoe. I was carried a long way under water by the under-current, but I kept thinking it was not all up yet and resolutely kept my mouth shut till I could come to the surface and get another gulp of air, and down I would go again. Sometimes I would be so long under water that I could scarcely hold my breath. At last I got down out of the boiling surf, and the water, though rapid, was smooth. I then began to keep myself better afloat, and began to swim for shore. At first I was under water so much that all my exertions had been to keep my head above water. I was so exhausted that I had to swim on my back and lay gasping for breath, but I was quite cool all the time (the water was remarkably cold) and managed to pull my shirt up out of my pants so as to let the water out. I had on heavy Canadian cloth pants. At last, after swimming a distance of about three quarters of a mile I touched the shore but was so benumbed with the cold I could not hold on to it but drifted off again. Soon, however, I made the shore again and dug my hands among the pebbles and pulled myself out of the water and lay there.

". . . I forgot to tell you that Carpenter wrote something in his diary just before starting, which on examination proved to be the following, as near as I can recollect, 'Arrived this day at the canon at 10:00 a.m., and drowned running the canoe down; God keep my poor wife!' Was it not strange? He was not much of a swimmer . . . Well, here we were without a canoe and at least 200 miles from Fort George, with very little provisions, only eight ground-hog between us; flour we had run out of before we reached the river. We went at once upon rations, the allowance being one ground-hog a day, each man getting a piece about the size of your hand. We calculated this would last us eight days in which time we expected to reach Fort George."

Then after several cold, wet days of semi-starvation and many hardships, they reached Fort George on October 8. Five days later, after descending the canyons lower down the river, they finally reached Quesnel. In April they had looked forward to a trip of sixty days; they had reached the entrance to the Cariboo gold fields after an heroic struggle which had lasted 180 days.

But four men who set out down the Fraser never reached their goal. The Grand Canyon had claimed three of their original number; E. Pattison, J. Carpenter, and A. C. Robertson, and a man named Leader whose death was recorded, although no details of his drowning have come down. After enduring the six-months' trip with its hunger, hardship, and tremendous exertion, those four, even when skirting one flank of the Cariboo Mountains, died almost in sight of the fabled gold field they had come so far to see.

While those who floated down the Fraser endured a drastic drubbing and lost four men, those who went by way of the North Thompson suffered equally and lost two men. That group, which included Mrs. Schubert, her husband and children, set out from Tête Jaune Cache on September 2, driving over one hundred head of cattle and horses up the valley of the McLennan River. When the Shuswap either could not or would not guide them, they persuaded Cardinal to go along even though he had not traveled in the area.

For two days the adventurers were able to follow a good trail past Cranberry Lake and on to the Canoe River. There it ended and André Cardinal had to use his judgment while the party chopped its way through the forest and advanced a mere five or six miles a day till they came to where the Albreda River flowed into the North Thompson. There, since all they had to do was to descend the main river, Cardinal said that he might as well head back to St. Albert, and with mutual regret he left the travelers. They persevered for a few days, but their progress through the thick forest was so slow that at a point about sixty miles from Tête Jaune Cache, which they christened

Slaughter Camp, they decided to make rafts and float down the river. They killed all but a few of their cattle, dried the meat, and turned most of the horses loose to fend for themselves.

On September 22, in small groups, most of the party set forth down the river. Like their colleagues descending the Fraser, they ran into rapids and driftpiles and bars. On the North Thompson the most formidable obstacle to navigation was the nine-mile stretch of the Murchison Rapids, which reached a climax in Hell Gate Canyon. In the rapids at least one raft was taken unawares and one of its crew, a man named Strachan from London, Ontario, was swept overboard and drowned.

The rest of the groups abandoned their rafts and spent three or more days slipping and sliding through the snow which fell as they climbed and descended the rocky portage trail. Below the rapids they had to choose whether to walk the estimated one hundred miles to Fort Kamloops, or to make more rafts. Most of them chose to float. Shortly after setting out from the foot of the rapids, one of the parties met the first of the Cariboo miners they were to see. Those men were familiar with the river and were returning to a location upstream which they had previously prospected. Eager as the Overlanders were to hear news of pay dirt, they obtained little information from those tight-lipped, practical miners.

Somewhat farther downstream the adventurers landed at an Indian village and were overjoyed to see a flourishing patch of potatoes. The place was strangely silent, so the men approached the keekwillies cautiously. To their horror they saw several dead bodies, which a quick glance indicated had been the victims of an epidemic of smallpox which had decimated several Indian camps. The villagers who had survived had fled.

The Overlanders dug a supply of potatoes on which they subsisted for the next few days till on October 13 they reached Fort Kamloops. There, where the Hudson's Bay Company fort and a few residences provided the only semblance of civilization which they had seen since they had left Fort Edmonton eleven weeks earlier, the tired travelers rested a few days.

They had earned their rest. For endless weeks, over endless prairies, through miles of bottomless muskeg, and over or around foothill after foothill, they had fought their way forward. Day after day, hungry and nearly exhausted, they had struggled through windfall and forest or gambled their lives in roaring rapids and fearful canyons, and now they rested. Now, in something resembling civilization, they could just sleep and eat and wonder why they had ever been so foolish as to start on the venture and what they were going to do next. All the glamour had gone out of the gold fields. And for a few days, while they recuperated, they did not care.

But even though they were weary and discouraged, there was not a quitter among them, and in a few days they started out in canoes, on rafts or on foot to make their way to the Cariboo road. Even that close to the Cariboo death struck one of their number when in descending the rapids below Kamloops, Frank Penwarden of the St. Thomas party drowned. On October 25 the rest of the group which had gone down the Thompson River reached Lytton where it debouched into the Fraser.

Once they reached the Fraser they experienced the same discouragement which had confronted their colleagues, the main body of the Overlanders who had descended that river from Tête Jaune Cache. They met hundreds of hungry and disillusioned miners who were on their way out from the fabled Cariboo. There, all but a handful of the easterners decided to head for the Coast, where, hopefully, they might find work. A few actually started up the road from Quesnel to Barkerville, and one or two reached it. The rest turned back and joined the tide of disappointed miners leaving the diggings.

Their great overland trek had proved a costly, difficult, and dismal failure.

And yet, so long as Canadians honor hardiness, courage, and fortitude, the memory of the Overlanders' expedition of 1862 across the prairies and through the Yellowhead Pass will form an inspiring chapter in Canada's history. Even though the Cariboo failed them, even though west of Tête Jaune Cache six of their companions died, their heroic exploit will always shine forth from the pages of the country's history.

And perhaps more heroic than any of the men who had crossed the Yellowhead Pass or camped at Tête Jaune Cache was Catherine O'Hare Schubert, who, heavy with child, accompanied her husband and tended their three children until the evening of October 13, when the family arrived at Fort Kamloops. There, in a hastily erected tent her labor pains commenced. There, early next morning, assisted by an Indian woman from the fort, she bore the first white girl to be born in the interior of British Columbia. "It is related that the Indian woman stepped outside the tent with the babe in her arms and, holding it aloft, cried out: 'It's Kumloops, Kumloops!' At first the parents felt inclined to call the child by that name, but later decided to name her Rose.''

In his memoirs, Thomas McMicking expressed the praise which all the Overlanders felt. ''In performing this journey Mrs. Schubert has accomplished a task to which but few women are equal; and, with the additional care of three small children, one which but few *men* would have the courage to undertake. By her unceasing care for her children, by her unremitting and devoted attention to their every want, and by her never-failing solicitude about their welfare, she exemplified the nature and power of that maternal affection which prompts a mother to neglect her own comfort for the well-being of her child, by which she rises superior to every difficulty, and which only glows with a brighter intensity as dangers deepen around her offspring.''

7

THE RAILWAY THAT MIGHT HAVE BEEN

THE TREK of the Overlanders marked a turning point in the history of the Yellowhead Pass. Prior to their passage in 1862, the few hardy souls who had ventured through Tête Jaune's pass, either on their way to the Albreda Pass and Fort Kamloops or bound up or down the Fraser as far as Fort George, had been engaged almost entirely in the fur trade. By that year, however, prospectors were swarming over the gravels of the Cariboo and hiving off to start new colonies of bearded, red-shirted miners all over southern British Columbia. And in their wanderings little groups of men made their way up or down nearly every watercourse and valley in British Columbia, and, for that matter, in western Alberta. Some worked up the Canoe River toward Tête Jaune Cache, some tested gravels on their way up the North Thompson, and some, like Love, Clover, and Perry, whose experiences influenced the Overlanders, had ascended the Fraser to Tête Jaune Cache. As a result, the Yellowhead Pass began seeing its share of adventurers passing east or west in their endless and often aimless search for gold.

Although they were not prospectors, the next interesting travelers to pass through the Jasper valley were a pair of English tourists who had been sufficiently attracted by the fame of the Cariboo to want to visit it. Those two, successors to Paul Kane as tourists, were Lord Milton, a young man of indifferent health and character, and his physician and tutor, the able and energetic Dr. W. B. Cheadle. With them they took the first hitchhiker to cross the Yellowhead Pass, Felix O'Byrne, an Irishman and one of the most fascinating fools of a long line of tenderfeet who have visited western Canada.

According to Dr. Cheadle, O'Byrne was "between forty and fifty years of age, of middle height and wiry make. His face was long and its features large, and a retreating mouth, almost destitute of teeth, gave a greater prominence to his rather elongated nose. He was dressed in a long coat of alpaca, of ecclesiastical cut, and wore a black wide-awake, which ill accorded with the week's stubble on his chin, fustian trousers, and highlows tied with string."

After much wandering around the world, Felix O'Byrne had found himself at Fort Garry and there had attached himself to the Overlanders, who had cast him off at Fort Carlton. Before long he had advanced westward as far as the Victoria mission in Alberta where the Reverend Mr. Woolsey looked after him until he seized the first opportunity of sending him to Fort Edmonton. There Dr. Cheadle found him and, to his great misfortune, took pity on him.

How often and how much the generous doctor was to rue that action is all spelled out in the two classic travel books he wrote, *Journal of a Trip Across Canada 1862-63* and *The North-West Passage by Land,* that any condensation of the report of the doctor's suffering would only spoil his masterful narrative. Moreover, Felix O'Byrne's story from the time he entered North America until he parted from Dr. Cheadle and left its shores, has been told so well in Esther Fraser's *The Canadian Rockies — Travels and Explorations,* that it would be redundant to dwell on it here.

Since Mrs. Fraser's excellent book also touches the highlights of Dr. Cheadle's adventures on his way to the Cariboo, I have thought it sufficient to mention only those of his comments which throw additional light on the story of the Jasper valley.

As the party left Edmonton House on June 3, 1863, with twelve pack horses, it consisted of Lord Milton, Dr. Cheadle, and the hanger-on, Felix O'Byrne, together with Baptiste Supernat as guide, and Louis Battenotte, a one-armed half-breed as general factotum. Louis, known also as Assiniboine, the most capable man of the lot, was accompanied by his equally capable wife and their teen-age son. Acting on the advice of both John McAulay, who was on the point of returning to his post in the Jasper valley, and André Cardinal, who had guided the Overlanders, the cavalcade took the trail by way of Lac Ste. Anne. After enjoying Colin Fraser's hospitality there they pressed on, and a month after leaving Edmonton found Roche Miette towering over them. Because the river was in flood, they had to take the pack trail over Disaster Point. As soon as they stopped at the top of the steep climb to breathe their horses and to get their own wind, the beauty of the view astounded them. As Cheadle said: ". . . even the woman and boy cried out, 'Aiwarkaken!' with delight and admiration at the magnificent scenery around." From the same vantage point they got their first view of Jasper House, which lay two or three miles away across the river and far below them. Cheadle described it as "a neat white building, surrounded by a low palisade, standing in a perfect garden of wild flowers, which form a rich sheet of varied and brilliant colours, backed by dark green pines which clustered thickly round the bases of the hills."

Although they did not go to the house, John McAulay, who had charge of it during 1863 and 1864, met them and helped them cross the river higher up at the cold sulphur spring near the site of the modern highway bridge. At the same time, Dr. Cheadle, feeling that hiring an additional guide might be a good investment, arranged with a local Iroquois to join their party. From a blaze on a tree at the river crossing they learned that three miners who were on their way to the Cariboo had camped on the spot three weeks previously. That night Cheadle slept somewhere south of the mouth of Snaring River, and by noon next day, on a prairie richly carpeted with flowers, came upon the remains of an old house. While he commented on it in both books he wrote, he was not certain of its identity. In one book he referred to it as " 'Petite Maison' . . . I presume it is the site of the former Jasper House." In the other he called it "the old Rocky Mountain Fort, Henry's House." Actually it was La Rocque's House, on the west side of the river.

The fifth day after leaving the vicinity of Jasper House the party crossed the almost imperceptible divide of the Yellowhead Pass. Next day they camped on the shores of "Buffalo-dung Lake" (Yellowhead Lake), which Cheadle understood to be well stocked with trout, "and several Shuswap slants of bark, and frames for drying fish, bore out this assertion."

While they were camped on the shores of Yellowhead Lake, Dr. Cheadle admired the majesty of the mountains which hemmed in the narrow valley. The Iroquois, noting his interest, "assured us that they should be known from that time forth as 'Le Montagne de Milord' and 'Montagne de Docteur.' We, however, took the liberty of naming them Mount Fitzwilliam and Mount Bingley."

With his usual magnanimity, Dr. Cheadle named the larger one to the south (elevation 9,538) after his companion, Viscount Milton of Fitzwilliam. Although he refrained from using his own name, he called the smaller mountain (elevation 8,064) to the north after his birthplace, Bingley in Yorkshire. These names are still recorded on maps. The mountain on the north side of the valley, however, had two peaks, and some fifty years later some wag of a surveyor, probably one employed by the Grand Trunk Pacific Railway and familiar with Cheadle's story, named it. Yielding to temptation, he bestowed on the second and higher peak (elevation 8,400) the name of the helpless hitchhiker who had been such a trial to the good doctor—Mount O'Beirne. Milton's mountain, however, was not to escape unscathed from a surveyor's attention, for a second peak on it received the name of one of the pack horses which with a woeful lack of acumen found itself carried down the Fraser for some distance —Bucephalus.

After many adventures, some grave and some made ridiculous by the antics of Lord Milton and Felix O'Byrne, the travelers passed and named Rockingham Falls and had to follow the mere scratch of a path across the face of the slate cliffs. There, according to Cheadle, "a large rock had slipped down, probably since the Yankee party passed, & overhung the road in such a manner as to render it impossible for a pack-horse to pass without the almost certainty that the pack would catch & probably hurl the horse from the narrow footing into the river below. The American party last year had lost a horse & all contained in the pack, viz. guns, ammunition & flour, by an accident of the kind at this very place. Assiniboine, the guide, & I therefore set to work with pine poles for levers, & after some ¼ hour's work loosened the rock & hurled it down with mighty bounds & crashes into the stream below. We then led the horses across singly, & without mishap; the path was about a foot broad, of hard rock covered in most places with loose slate . . ."

On July 14, shortly before reaching the Grand Forks of the Fraser, the wanderers paused to marvel at the sublimity of one of the world's more majestic mountains. "On every side," wrote Cheadle, "the snowy heads of mighty hills crowded round, whilst, immediately behind us, a giant among giants, and immeasurably supreme, rose Robson's Peak . . . When we first caught sight of it, a shroud of mist partially enveloped the summit, but this presently rolled away, and we saw its upper portion dimmed by a necklace of light feathery clouds, beyond which its pointed apex of ice, glittering in the morning sun, shot up far into the blue heaven above, to a height of probably 10,000 or 15,000 feet."

Moving on, they came to the forks, of which in his *North-West Passage by Land*, Cheadle said: "This Grand Fork of the Fraser is the original Tête Jaune Cache, so called from being the spot chosen by an Iroquois trapper, known by the *sobriquet* of the Tête Jaune, or 'Yellow Head,' to hide the furs he obtained on the western side." The doctor must have obtained his information from his Iroquois guide, but apparently even that early the name had been transferred a few miles down the river to the vicinity of what is now Tête Jaune Cache at the head of navigation on the Fraser.

On the score of where the original cache was there is no better authority than Cheadle's Iroquois. The doctor was there thirty-six years after Tête Jaune had been murdered, but the guide, who as a youth was almost certain to have known his compatriot Tête Jaune, would indicate the location of the cache as a piece of local knowledge falling within his own experience.

It is unfortunate that Cheadle did not query the Iroquois about the identity of the man who left his name associated with what he called Robson's Peak, or, if he asked, did not record the answer. H. J. Moberly as an old man explained that he had always understood that Robson was a trapper or freeman who at one time had lived near the mountain. Such a man must have been a Hudson's Bay Company employee, who, when his term of employment was over, had gone trapping or trading on his own account, and yet a search of extant lists of the company's employees does not reveal any likely candidate for the honor. It has been suggested, and perhaps with some merit, that the Iroquois, such as Tête Jaune or his companions, might have honored Colin Robertson, the Hudson's Bay Company man they reported to at St. Mary's House at the mouth of the Smoky by calling this the most majestic of all the Rocky Mountains after him and that in the course of time or on the Iroquois tongue his name might have been contracted to Robson.

On the evening of July 16 Cheadle's worn-out wayfarers camped at Tête Jaune Cache and saw some Shuswap on the south side of the river. From them they learned that three days previously two of their number had been induced to take the three Cariboo-bound miners of Hutchinson's party down the Fraser in their canoes. They also learned that five men who had started down the Fraser some months previously had all been drowned and that the Indians had found their bodies a short distance below Tête Jaune Cache.

From the Cache the party started south toward the North Thompson River along the route one branch of the Overlanders had taken. When they finally reached what their predecessors had called Slaughter Camp and found that they had rafted down the river, Milton and Cheadle were on the horns of a dilemma—too small a party to raft and too weak a party to cut a trail through the heavy forest. They chose to push on through the forest of wet fern and giant cedars, obstructed at every step by devil's club, of which Cheadle said: "The swampy ground was densely covered with American dog-wood, and elsewhere with thickets of the aralea, a tough-stemmed trailer, with leaves as large as those of the rhubarb plant, and growing in many places as high as our shoulders. Both stem and leaves are covered with sharp spines, which pierced our clothes as we forced our way through the tangled growth, and made the legs and hands of the pioneers scarlet from the inflammation of myriads of punctures."

Under those conditions they persevered for days, until on August 7 they ate their last scrap of food. Occasionally they had procured a few small rodents, but their only hope now lay in killing one of their hard-worked horses, and unless they found some game, they resolved to do that on the morrow. Next day, except for having killed a marten, Assiniboine returned empty-handed but with a tale of a macabre discovery which he had made a few hundred yards from their camp—the corpse of a starved Indian.

When they went over to inspect it, Cheadle wrote, "it was in a sitting posture, with the legs crossed, and the arms clasped over the knees, bending forward over the ashes of a miserable fire of small sticks. The ghastly figure was headless . . ." Broken parts of a horse's skull told the story of starvation and of a man who had killed his horse and even then had come to the end of his food. Did that headless, starved corpse point to their own fate? "The similarity between the attempt of the Indian to penetrate through the pathless forest — his starvation, his killing of his horse for food — and our condition, was striking."

Next day Cheadle's party shot one of its horses and then pressed on in a desperate attempt to reach Kamloops. Perhaps the men were sustained by their ignorance of the fact that it was to be two weeks more before they saw another human being and nearly an additional week before, exhausted and starving, they dragged themselves into the fort.

Dr. Cheadle was a modest man with a rare sense of humor and the ability to write one of the most fascinating travel books ever published. Incidental to that, his book throws some light upon the history of the Jasper valley and records the naming of a number of natural features. Four mountains overlooking Yellowhead Lake bear witness to their trip, as do Mount Milton near Albreda, Mount Cheadle some twenty miles farther along Highway 5, and Mount St. Anne across the river from it. Moreover, Dr. Cheadle named the Murchison Rapids.

Even though the logistics of the fur trade had left it behind, the Yellowhead Pass continued to fulfill its role as a transportation route. In 1864, a year after Dr. Cheadle had patiently borne the impositions of Jasper's first hitchhiker, another Briton came striding into the valley. Neither gold nor furs had sent him through the mountain passes. He came on a reconnaissance mission for another form of transportation; the idea of a wagon road and telegraph line which would connect the new colonies in British Columbia with the Canadas was under consideration. A combination which involved the Hudson's Bay Company, the Imperial and Canadian Governments, and the Grand Trunk Railway, had decided to take up the idea and sent Dr. John Rae to make a hasty trip along the proposed route. Several years earlier during the search for Franklin, Dr. Rae had won the reputation of being an intrepid and resourceful traveler and now he set off alone on foot to cross the prairies and the mountains. In due course, unaided and unencumbered by horses, he marched up the Athabasca and at Tête Jaune Cache procured a dugout and descended the Fraser to Fort George.

For the time being, however, the projected telegraph line did not materialize and the Yellowhead Pass was left to languish while Canadian statesmen forged the bonds which were to make Canada one country, *A Mari usque ad Mare*. One of the bonds they planned was a transcontinental railway, which, according to their promise to the province of British Columbia, they would complete by 1881.

In 1871 John A. Macdonald, Prime Minister of the new Canada, appointed Sandford Fleming as engineer-in-chief of the transcontinental railway. He in turn employed his old friend Walter Moberly, an engineer and a brother of Henry J. Moberly, to make detailed surveys for the new railway in his mountainous province of British Columbia. In the course of that work Moberly took charge of a party examining the Big Bend of the Columbia and sent Roderick McLennan to make a reconnaissance up the North Thompson and over the Albreda Pass to Tête Jaune Cache and the Yellowhead Pass.

Leaving Kamloops on August 19, 1871, McLennan made his way to Tête Jaune Cache. In October he decided to winter his party in that vicinity and built a camp four or five miles upstream from the Canoe River on what consequently came to be named Camp Creek. Traveling with McLennan, A. R. C. Selwyn of the Geological Survey of Canada came to study the strata of the area. Though his trip along the sketchy trail up the North Thompson was beset with the usual difficulties, Selwyn nevertheless made careful notes of the geology in his field book until, somewhere in the Albreda Pass, accident befell it.

Wishing to examine an outcropping a few yards off the trail, he tied his hungry horse, left the book on a nearby rock, and taking his hammer, went down to look at the strata. When he came back with his samples, intending to enter information about them in his book, it was missing. The covers lay nearby, but the pages with all his precious notes had disappeared. Suspecting that some wild animal had carried them off, he searched about for a few moments until his eyes, falling upon the hungry horse, clouded over with conjecture. The look of injured innocence with which the horse returned his suspicious scowl did nothing to reassure him. Seeking confirmation of his theory, he dived into one of his pack sacks, pulled out several loose sheets of paper, left them lying on the ground within reach of the animal's large sensitive lips, and walked away. Turning around within a few yards he was in time to see them crumpled and disappearing in the direction of his servitor's throat.

By April, 1872, Moberly had sent a party under Edward Mohun to carry on the work in the Yellowhead Pass and was about to leave Victoria to join the larger parties he was sending to continue his own survey along the Big Bend of the Columbia when he was instructed by telegraph to divert all his forces to the Yellowhead Pass. Though he was dumbfounded and felt that Sandford Fleming's decision was an incorrect one, he nevertheless obeyed orders, and with amazing energy and organizing ability redirected his crews to the new area.

The railway surveys created a demand for experienced packers, and referring in his notes to the head packer who worked for Mohun in the Yellowhead Pass in 1872, Moberly revealed some of the facts of life on a frontier where most of the engineers and employers were Scotsmen. "I asked the head packer his name, and he told me MacBrown; this struck me as a peculiar name.

I asked him how he came by it, and he told me that in the previous year, wishing to join the parties under Mr. Roderic McLennan on his expedition to Moose Lake, he found nearly all the parties were Macs, so he thought he should have a better chance of employment if he were a Mac too, and therefore substituted MacBrown for Brown.''

After talking to MacBrown, Moberly went to see Mr. Mohun and learned that Sandford Fleming, who was crossing the continent on a tour of inspection, was expected to reach Yellowhead Pass very soon. In the meantime Moberly continued east, checking on his parties and trying to determine the exact route for the railway. Near the mouth of the Miette he saw the site of what he called Henry House and recorded that it had "entirely disappeared" except for the hole of what had been the cellar and a pile of stones where the chimney had been. "The old fort was at the junction of the two routes," that is, the Yellowhead Pass route and the one up the Athabasca Pass. Undoubtedly this was La Rocque's House.

Continuing down the valley, Moberly met Sandford Fleming and his party. Rather naturally he queried the Engineer-in-Chief about the wisdom of selecting the Yellowhead Pass route, and they parted on strained terms.

Amongst others accompanying Fleming through the pass was Rev. George Grant, who later wrote a fascinating book about his experiences, *Ocean to Ocean*. The party left Edmonton on August 28, 1872, and beyond Lac Ste. Anne proposed to follow the rather sketchy route which the Overlanders had taken as far as Tête Jaune Cache. As far as Lac Ste. Anne they traveled with Mr. Adams, the new factor at the Hudson's Bay Company's post there.

Colin Fraser, who for so long had helped so many travelers along their way, had died in the spring of 1867, leaving "a large family . . . some of them yet young and several daughters grown up and married." Perhaps as a faint indication that change was coming over the land, he was not buried at his post but his body was brought to Edmonton and laid in the graveyard of the new Methodist mission (McDougall Church). Nancy, his wife, lived to be eighty-seven and died in 1900. Several of his sons rose to prominence as employees of the Hudson's Bay Company or as individual traders in the North.

By dusk on September 9, Fleming's party camped on what appears to have been Hardisty Creek, which flows through the modern pulp mill town of Hinton. Then, according to Grant:

"While hacking with his axe at brush on the camping ground, just where our heads would lie, Brown struck something metallic that blunted the edge of the axe. Feeling with his hand he drew out from near the root of a young spruce tree, an ancient sword bayonet, the brazen hilt and steel blade in excellent preservation, but the leather scabbard half eaten as if by the teeth of some animal."

Although Rev. Mr. Grant probably did not realize it, the party spent the night at the spot which for a hundred years the natives have called "The Cache Picote" — the Smallpox Camp. In 1870, when the dread disease swept the prairies, carrying away families and even whole camps, it ascended the Athabasca River and crept into the Jasper valley. When a few of the Iroquois there contracted the disease, several families decided to move to the mission at Lac Ste. Anne for help. By the time they reached Hardisty Creek the loathsome disease had fallen upon many of them. Sparing neither the hardy hunter, the chattering crone, nor the toddling child, it laid its clammy hand on the camp and the group decided to travel no farther. In two or three days many were dead, but in the meantime the others detailed some of the best travelers to hasten to the Catholic Fathers 150 miles away and bring back help.

One reached there, but long before his return, the disease had run its course, and the living had moved back to Jasper. Only stark teepee poles stood as temporary memorials to those the dread scourge had swept away at the Cache Picote.

On their way from the Cache Picote to Prairie Creek a wonderful array of mountains ahead of them thrilled every member of Fleming's party. Their amazement and pleasure increased as day by day they advanced farther into the Jasper valley. Finally, on September 12, fifteen days after leaving Edmonton House, they came to Jasper House of which Rev. Mr. Grant said: "Now there are only two log houses, the largest propped up before and behind with rough shores, as if to prevent it being blown away into the River or back into the Mountain gorges. The houses are untenanted, locked and shuttered. Twice a year an agent comes up from Edmonton to trade with the Indians of the surrounding country and carry back the furs." According to the Hudson's Bay Company's records, Jasper House had no official incumbent from 1865 to 1877.

Going on from there along the west side of the river, Fleming's party finally rounded the end of the Colin Range and could look south for miles up the valley to a mountain which "Valad said, was 'La montagne de la grande traverse . . .'" (Mount Edith Cavell).

Continuing south on the west side of the river, Grant was told that old Henry House was on the east side near the mouth of the Miette but did not see it. A short distance up the Miette River the party met Moberly, who turned back and accompanied them as far as Mohun's camp at the west end of Moose Lake. At the summit of Yellowhead Pass he formally welcomed them into British Columbia. "Round the rivulet running west, the party gathered, and drank from its waters to the Queen and the Dominion." Next day, after a long, hard trip, the party reached Mohun's camp.

From there Fleming's party was able to follow the reasonably good pack trail first cut out by McLennan's party in 1871 and recently improved by the current year's parties even to the extent of minor bridges and an occasional raft. Before reaching Tête Jaune Cache Grant stopped to read an inscription on a tree, which indicated that in spite of the heavy toil the pack horses endured, the processes of nature continued to follow their course.

"Birth
"Monday, 5th August, 1872
"This morning about 5 o'clock, 'Aunt Polly,' bell-mare to the Nth Thompson trail party's packtrain, was safely delivered of a Bay Colt, with three white legs and white star on forehead. This wonderful progeny of a C.P.R. survey's packtrain is in future to be known to the racing community of the Pacific Slope as Rocky Mountain Ned."

As they approached Tête Jaune Cache Grant repeated the version of how the place got its name: "An old Iroquois hunter, known in his time as Tête Jaune or Yellow Head, probably from the noticeable fact in an Indian of his hair being light coloured, had wisely selected this central point for caching all the furs . . ." It is significant that the early travelers, such as Dr. Cheadle and Rev. Mr. Grant, who crossed the Yellowhead Pass at a time when some Iroquois who had known Tête Jaune would still be living, identify him correctly.

Eventually, after Fleming's party had ascended the river named after McLennan the surveyor, and started descending the Thompson River, it came to the spot where Dr. Cheadle had seen the headless Indian. In many quarters Cheadle's story had been regarded as a fabrication, but Grant found that it was indeed true. On what he called Goose Creek not far above the Grand Canyon of the North Thompson, he saw another inscription made by some of Mohun's men a few months earlier, saying:

"Here lie the remains of the 'Headless Indian,' discovered by Lord Milton and Dr. Cheadle, A.D. 1863. At this spot we found an old tin kettle, a knife, a spoon, and fishing line; and 150 yards up the bank of the river we also found the skull, which was sought for in vain by the above gentlemen.

T. Party, C.P.R.S.

June 5th, 1872."

By searching, Dr. Moren found some souvenirs of the headless one. His interest in the case had been whetted by one of the packers who a few days earlier at Mohun's camp had presented him with the hapless Indian's spoon and fishing line which he had appropriated some months earlier.

Finally, on September 28, Grant and his associates reached Fort Kamloops. Moberly, who had left them near Moose Lake, went back east to complete the work he had planned in the Jasper valley. He arranged to have a camp built below what he called Henry House and spoke of it as the Athabasca Depot. That depot, which consisted of a large building for the men's quarters, a storehouse and a barn, was at the edge of the west bank. Its site is almost one and one-half miles downstream from the bridge which carries traffic into Jasper Park Lodge from the north.

Leaving there Moberly worked his way down the valley and by Christmas was camped at Fiddle Creek. There he built another depot in which to winter his party and sent his pack horses to graze on the rich pasture at Brulé Lake. Early the next spring he decided to carry a reconnaissance survey farther east and shortly after setting out had another adventure.

His party was assisted by Louis, one of the Iroquois hunters, who set a couple of his buxom daughters to carrying some of the surveyor's goods. As evening was drawing on Moberly came to a long pond, two hundred yards wide, on which the ice was covered by six inches of water. There was no alternative but to cross it, but before doing so he sat down to have a smoke. The rest of the party waded to the far side and began preparing supper. Soon he saw one of the huge girls coming back toward him and found that her father had instructed her to carry him across the pond. He protested but "she insisted, saying that I was much lighter than the load she had just packed over, and if she did not take me her father would be very angry so I resigned myself to my fate, and was ignominiously packed over. Louis was very proud of the girl's strength, and that evening, as we were smoking a pipe, he pointed out the great advantage of having such a powerful girl, and, as he wished to get a horse I had, he made me an offer to make an exchange — I to give him the horse and a few other things, and to take the girl instead, to which she did not object . . ."

Eventually Moberly continued his line to the west bank of the McLeod River. Shortly after that he severed his connection with the CPR and made his way back to Victoria, British Columbia. In reporting to Fleming on the work he had accomplished during the 1872-73 season in the Jasper valley, Moberly wrote:

"We have not sustained any loss of life nor had any accidents, not a single pound of the supplies has been lost in transit, and out of nearly two hundred and fifty pack animals employed, only seven have died in all; nearly all the pack animals on this route travelled back and forth last season about twenty-seven hundred miles, and almost invariably averaged loads of three hundred pounds each . . . Not a single quarrel has arisen, not a single article has been stolen, and without exception the most friendly feeling is now existing. The Indians have rendered us much and valuable assistance."

Organizing and co-ordinating the activities of the many pack trains was a heavy task in itself. Those supply trains, working behind the scenes and traveling back and forth, often clearing their own trails, made it possible for small parties of surveyors to function. When any particular route or valley had to be examined they brought the survey parties in from the nearest point of civilization and often traveled several hundreds of miles to do so. Then, once the surveyors were actually working, the pack trains had to dance attendance upon them and move their camp every few days as the work advanced. As well as transporting them they had to set up depots of supplies and caches of food, and then undertake to replenish the supplies in the caches as they were used up.

Pack horses were expected to forage for themselves, and at the end of a day's trip were turned loose to graze. The packers had to govern the length of their day's trip so as to stop at some meadow or creek bottom where the horses could find good grass. Next morning they had to get out and round up the horses and load them up. During the first days of a long trip, when the horses were fresh, one or another was constantly darting away from the main route or bumping into other horses or trees along the way. The packs shifted and the ropes slackened, and delays occurred while the loads were tightened or repacked. Finally the pack train settled down and then the packers got time to draw a free breath, to roll a cigarette, or to light a pipe.

Grant, in his *Ocean to Ocean,* commented on the support the pack trains gave the surveyors and of the make-up of the trains. Near the Grand Canyon of the North Thompson he met a train which was on its way to Tête Jaune Cache and it "consisted of fifty-two mules led by a bell-horse, and driven by four or five men, representing as many different nationalities. Most of the mules were, with the exception of the long ears, wonderfully graceful creatures; and though laden with an average weight of three hundred pounds, stepped out over rocks and roots firmly and lightly as if their loads were nothing." The mules aroused Grant's interest and he noted: "A bell-horse is put at the head of the mule train, and the mules follow him and pay him the most devoted loyalty. If a strange dog comes up barking, or any other hostile looking brute, the mules often rush furiously at the enemy and trample him under foot, to shield their sovereign from danger or even from insult."

He went on to relate the adventures of one mule who lost his footing when going along a precipice and fell down the cliff. "The packers went down to the river side to look for him, but as there was no trace to be seen, resumed their march. Five days after, another train passing near the spot heard the braying of a mule, and guided by the noise looked, and found that he had fallen on a broad rock half way down, where he had laid [sic] for some time stunned. Struggling to his feet, fortunately for him the apparaho [aparejo, packsaddle] got entangled round the rock, and held him fast till he was relieved by the men of the train from his razor bridge over the flood."

As early as 1821 when the Hudson's Bay Company took it over, Fort Kamloops had been important in connection with the pack horse route from Fort Okanagan on the Columbia River to Fort Alexandria on the Fraser. Horses found its climate congenial, and for decades before the arrival of the CPR surveyors, the fur trading company had maintained a large herd there. When the surveys commenced, Kamloops was not only ready to supply horses but could also provide most of the packers needed to handle them. Kamloops then was a logical point at which to assemble and fit up survey parties to send out on their assaults on the mountain passes of eastern British Columbia. The relatively few pack trains needed on the eastern approaches to the Rocky Mountains, however, were assembled at Edmonton and manned in the main by frontier types there.

For years after Fleming's interesting trip through the Yellowhead Pass in 1872, the pack trains had plenty to do, because he kept parties busy studying all possible routes across Canada, and especially the difficult mountain passes. By 1876 he had spent over three million dollars on surveys and his crews had examined six main passes by way of the headwaters of the Peace, Pine, Smoky, Miette, Athabasca, and Saskatchewan rivers. One by one those were eliminated until only Howse Pass at the headwaters of the Saskatchewan and the Yellowhead Pass were left as contenders for the honor of carrying the railway. Finally, Sandford Fleming reported that "beyond question the advantages of the Yellow Head Pass, — every consideration being taken into account, — outweigh those of the other passes . . ."

During 1876 and 1877 he sent out definite location surveys which resulted in staking a line from the mouth of the Miette River over the pass and west as far as Tête Jaune Cache. Over the years several other surveyors besides Moberly, Mohun, and McLennan took parties into the general Tête Jaune Cache area. Among the more interesting were: H. P. Bell, who passed the winter of 1875-76 studying the upper Fraser above Fort George, and George A. Keefer, whose party wintered at Tête Jaune Cache and worked down the Fraser to link his line with Bell's. Another was E. W. Jarvis, who, accompanied by C. F. Hanington and a few Indians, carried out a reconnaissance across the Continental Divide from Fort George to the headwaters of the Smoky River. They ascended the McGregor River, crossed the divide and descended the Kakwa River into Alberta. After a grueling trip, during which they lost dogs and nearly starved and were not sure which way to go to reach Jasper House, "Alec caught sight of a, to him, well known feature in the landscape, the 'Roche à Miette', whose peculiar and distinct profile was plainly visible about twenty-five miles south of us." Eventually they arrived "at the Fiddle River depot [built by Mr. Moberly]. We were cordially received by the Iroquois Indians camped there. An immense dish of boiled rabbits set before

us disappeared in quick order, and after this good meal we were
more reconciled to hear the Company's post at Jasper House
was abandoned.''

Other survey parties which had to overcome complicated
problems were those which approached the Jasper area from
the east. They could get packers at Edmonton but it was more
difficult to get enough supplies for large parties. In 1875 Edmonton was an insignificant hamlet stretched along a mile or so
of the river bank with a total white and half-breed population
of about two hundred. While the palisaded Hudson's Bay Company's fort was its focal point, another nucleus of settlement
was growing around Norris and Carey's store, which was perhaps
a quarter of a mile north and west of the fort, while another
knot of shacks centered around the Reverend George
McDougall's mission. The latter group contained John Brown's
and Frank Oliver's stores and the homes of Daniel Noyes and
Colin Fraser, junior. As merchants and suppliers, Norris and
Carey, John Brown, Frank Oliver, and Colin Fraser traded in
furs and provided considerable competition to the Hudson's Bay
Company. While at any time any one of those was capable of
rounding up a pack train and hiring it out to travelers, hunters,
or surveyors who wished to make an expedition into Edmonton's
hinterland, the outstanding packer was the frontiersman, Dan
E. Noyes.

Because the trails for hundreds of miles east of Edmonton
were very poor and the one from there west to Jasper was barely
discernible, the problem of provisioning the survey parties of
1875-76 was a most difficult one. Access to Edmonton was limited
indeed. The first steamboat ever to ascend the Saskatchewan
River as far as Edmonton had arrived there on July 22, 1875.
The telegraph line being built along the Canadian Pacific Railway
right of way had not yet reached that hamlet. The old cart trail
from Fort Garry had been in use for some thirty years and
a newer but poorer one wound around the sloughs along the
recently located CPR survey line. Only three other trails radiated
out of Edmonton and they were all difficult to travel; the Victoria
Trail, the one to the newly established North West Mounted
Police post at Fort Saskatchewan, and the one to Fort
Assiniboine which was good as far as St. Albert. From there
a cart trail branched off to Lac Ste. Anne but west of its mission
became little more than blazes on the trees. By means of those
dubious trails and an uncertain steamboat which had difficulty

in reaching Edmonton at all some years, it was proposed to help provision the survey parties approaching Jasper from the east. It was a risky venture.

One of the surveyors who proposed to go west from Edmonton was H. A. F. McLeod. His first experience in the area came in 1875 when, without undue difficulty, he included a reconnaissance survey up the Maligne River with his other tasks. After checking some of the survey work between Edmonton and Jasper, he started up the Maligne River on September 8, 1875, to see if a favorable route for the railway might be obtained by ascending the Saskatchewan and Brazeau rivers and descending the Maligne to the Jasper valley. After noting Maligne Canyon and the underground outlet of Medicine Lake, his party went up the river until it reached Maligne Lake, which McLeod called Sore-foot Lake. By that time he realized that there was no hope of running a railway up the Maligne River, so he headed east over the divide to the Rocky River and descended it to its mouth. That river also proved unsatisfactory, and McLeod returned to Edmonton.

During 1876 he also worked out of Edmonton and experienced an assortment of difficulties with the logistics of transportation. That year he had two parties, about seventy men in all, working under Messrs. Lucas and Ruttan, along that part of the proposed railway. From Ottawa in April 1876, via the United States, he had wired the company's purveyor in British Columbia to send three months' provisions for his two parties to the Athabasca Depot in the Jasper valley. He hoped that they would be delivered from Kamloops by July. In September at Sandstone Creek, near present-day Pedley, as McLeod was proceeding west, he met Thomas Trapp, who was in charge of the long-overdue party from Kamloops. Trapp reported that he had cached the goods at the Athabasca Depot and planned to take twenty-four horses and twenty-one cattle to winter at Edmonton.

Persuading Trapp to go back with him to take charge of the depot for the winter, McLeod found the cargo of provisions stored there and learned that another train load was expected to arrive daily. At the first crossing of the Miette when he was making his way west he met the other train bringing supplies from Tête Jaune Cache. By the time it was unloaded at the Athabasca Depot the supplies stored there amounted to twenty thousand pounds, most of which was flour. After McLeod had worried about the late arrival of pack trains from British Columbia, they had eventually come in and delivered an excessive amount.

Thomas Trapp kept a diary of his trip and of his activities when during the winter of 1876-77 he took charge of the Athabasca Depot. Starting from near Kamloops on July 11, Trapp pushed his pack train along and every day or so met other trains coming or going. By August 5, when his outfit was crossing the North Thompson, he nearly came to grief on the horns of an angry steer which turned back from the water, "made for Joe, Loue, and myself in quick succession. Joe managed to jump into the bush and let him by. Loue fell down and rolled over, hitting him alongside. The steer made for him but did not catch him. I being next, he came full pelt after me, but leaping behind a tree near, got away from him. As he passed his horns just struck me on the thigh, but not to hurt me. He next made for Dan, who also dodged him behind a tree. One of the Indians then lassooed him from here, then takes him to a tree where we tied himself, and after a while took him again on the raft."

Trapp reached Tête Jaune Cache on August 19, and still driving the cattle, headed east over the Yellowhead Pass to reach the Athabasca Depot eleven days later. When he assumed charge of that large cache he had his friend Michael O'Keefe as his assistant. Having little to do, he spent the next twelve months trapping martens and hunting. He seems to have had a talent for reciprocating the friendliness of the native inhabitants, most of whom he mentioned by their first names only. He found their ideas and way of life considerably different from those of the Shuswap he had known in the Kamloops area.

In November his companion, Mike O'Keefe, had a close call when all alone he crossed the river towards the depot "with no one to catch the rope (of their raft), and consequently was driven back to the other side and away down, and had also lost his paddles. I went down to him, when he made another paddle out of wood on the raft and made another attempt, when the strong current landed him with the raft on some large rocks in the centre of the river, where he was unable to move it, and also broke paddle in trying to do so . . .''

Trapp tried various ways of helping him but one after another failed, and meantime Mike, wet through, nearly perished on his rock in the middle of the stream. Trapp went back to the depot and "with part of floor of cabin made another raft and in due course, about 1½ hours awful hard work, managed to get her afloat and started off to the rescue. Managed to steer close alongside, within about four feet, and was going to throw out rope, but current so rapid took me quicker than expected, so called out to Mike to jump, which he did, and got right on the raft, leaving rifle etc. in the middle of the river on old raft. By this time Mike was so overcome with cold he declared he could not have held out another ½ hour. He had three fingers and three toes frozen in spite of his frantic efforts to keep warm.''

Once he got into the depot Mike recovered quickly. Fortunately, a few days later the raft, which had hung up on the rock, floated off and stranded on the far side of the river, making it possible for the two men to retrieve two of their very precious possessions, which had remained frozen to the raft — Mike's ax and rifle.

On one occasion when Trapp and his native friend Pierre had been successful at their hunting, the local man had remained at the scene of the slaughter while the white man went back to tell Pierre's wife, Marie, how to get there. Trapp reported in his diary: "Shewed her the way across river to my tracks; where she could follow them and reach Pierre all right. She presented a rather novel picture, with her four dogs following her, two of which were packed pretty heavily, and she having a very large butcher's knife stuck in her belt, and an axe in her hand, going off in a trot and calling her dogs after her, which followed on in a string, she calling them with a Boo-oo-oo.''

Early in January, 1877, everyone, including the two white men, ran short of ammunition, so Trapp and Pierre and another Iroquois, Paulette, decided to snowshoe to Tête Jaune Cache to replenish their supply. The weather was mild and the three and a half feet of soft snow made traveling hard and their progress so slow that about twenty-five miles from their destination they found themselves out of food and nearly exhausted. If only the weather would turn cold and put a crust on the snow they knew that they could soon reach the western depot. At that point Pierre produced a trick from his store of Indian lore: "Pierre in evening made a snow rabbit and set him out on the snow, telling him to fetch cold and hard snow, so that we could get to our destination without suffering.'' Next day they made an early start and "the snow being hard and good for travelling we got along nicely . . .''

Unfortunately, although Trapp remained at the Athabasca

Depot until the following fall, his diary closed at the end of January, 1877, probably because he had run out of paper. He was still there, however, when on August 27 Marcus Smith, who was in charge of all the mountain surveys, reached there. He found such a surplus of supplies at the depot that he had John Brown, a packer, take some clothing and other articles back to Edmonton to be sold. He felt sure that the purveyors had deliberately shipped excess material for which in the end the government would have to pay. In any event, he locked the depot, discharged Trapp and O'Keefe, who were being paid a total of $1,440 per year for guarding the depot, and arranged with a native to do so for a fraction of that amount. Then Smith went on to the Tête Jaune Cache depot, where he likewise found a large surplus of goods. Although CPR survey parties had haunted the pass for years, most of them had now been taken off the work and the government found itself stuck with large surpluses in those two depots.

When in 1876 McLeod's surveyor, H. N. Ruttan, had set out west from Edmonton, he had hired the outstanding local packer, Dan Noyes, who was in a postition to provide sixty-four horses. From then on for decades Dan played a large part in any activity taking place in the Jasper area. Dan, who had been born in 1838 in Vermont, took part in the California Gold Rush and then moved on to the Cariboo in 1859. Finally he crossed the Rocky Mountains and in 1866 came to try his luck at panning the Saskatchewan River's gravel bars. Liking the looks of the country, he decided to throw his lot in with it. Within two years he married Adelaide, daughter of J. E. Brazeau, the well-known Hudson's Bay Company trader who had spent the years 1850-54 and 1861-62 in charge of Jasper House. Shortly after that Noyes established Edmonton's first stopping place on a site in the vicinity of today's Macdonald Hotel. It soon became famous for the quality of its seventy-five-cent meals, of which the staples were buffalo and bannock.

By marrying J. E. Brazeau's daughter he found himself in the select circle of Jasper-oriented frontiersmen. Two years earlier Mary Jane Brazeau had married John McAulay, who had been her father's successor at Jasper during 1863-64, while in 1869, the year before her father's death, Sophie Brazeau married Simon Fraser, who had been born at Jasper House in September, 1847, while his father Colin was the post master there. Before long, Dan Noyes became familiar with the Jasper valley and the crude trail leading west from Edmonton.

Undoubtedly Dan was not far away when in 1878 the Hudson's Bay Company at Kamloops decided to get rid of its large surplus of indifferent horses and send them to Edmonton. For years they had been multiplying on the rich pastures of Kamloops until they had become a drug on the market. Even at that, in 1878, the company, in a decision it was to regret, turned down an offer of eight thousand dollars for the lot of them and instructed John Tait, its Kamloops factor, to take them across the mountains.

Out of the herd on the range Tait and his helpers finally rounded up 425 and began to drive them along the pack trail up the North Thompson. Before he was well started many of them escaped and returned to their familiar range. The rivers were high that season and Tait's cavalcade moved so slowly that by the time he reached Tête Jaune Cache he was out of provisions and had to buy some at what he considered an exorbitant price from the CPR depot there. Striking east over the Yellowhead Pass and the broad Jasper valley and through the muskegs of western Alberta, he finally reached Edmonton months after leaving Kamloops. There he sold the 221 horses he had left at eighteen dollars each. Having deducted the drovers' wages and the cost of the supplies they had consumed, the company netted about a dollar a horse delivered.

By 1878, even though Sandford Fleming's parties had spent several years surveying various lines through the Yellowhead Pass, no grading was ever begun. When the election of September, 1878, reinstalled John A. Macdonald's Conservative Government, however, he was eager to get the railway started and equally eager to get the millstone of a government-owned railway off the people's necks. Tackling one problem at a time he achieved both objectives. By October, 1880, he had unloaded the transcontinental railway onto a group of capitalists which came to be known as the Canadian Pacific Railway. The new company decided to abandon Fleming's route through the Yellowhead Pass and began laying steel west of Winnipeg along a line which took their railway through the Kicking Horse Pass. The company immediately concentrated every available survey party onto that route.

As the clang of the last survey pack horse's bell receded in the distance, the Jasper valley returned to the isolation it had known when about twenty-five years earlier the fur trade brigades had forsaken it. Though grass grew knee-high in front of their doors and pack rats found their way past their guard, the sturdy log buildings of the Athabasca and Tête Jaune depots settled down to their silent task of guarding their stores from the instrusion of inquisitive bears. The CPR had no use for the old log buildings and the extensive supplies they contained. The supplies had cost thousands of dollars, but any move on the part of the railway to salvage them would have cost more than they were worth.

Businessmen of Edmonton, however, had not forgotten the contents of at least the Athabasca Depot and the merchants, Norris and Carey, offered the railway an amount said to have been one thousand dollars for them. When the company accepted their offer, those merchants contracted with Dan Noyes to bring the goods to Edmonton, and once more for a short time in the spring of 1879 or 1880 the old depot saw a brief burst of activity. With ax, auger, and saw, Dan and some helpers soon fashioned sturdy scows, loaded them with everything except an anvil, which, though it had entered the valley on a pack horse, he deemed not worth taking to Edmonton, and entrusted the scows to the rough waters of the Athabasca. In due course they successfully descended to Fort Assiniboine, where Dan had a string of pack horses waiting to forward the goods to Edmonton. By that time, according to the noted geologist, G. M. Dawson, the abandoned buildings of Fort Assiniboine had been burned. In passing there in 1879 he recorded that a fire "not long ago" had reduced the ruins to heaps of stones and charred wood.

With Dan Noyes's departure, the CPR's rejection of the Yellowhead Pass was complete. For some years its surveyors, studying and sighting and slashing lines, had rung echoes from all the rocks of the Jasper valley. Then the valley's second venture into the realm of becoming a main transportation route had fizzled out. Before long, growing brush filled in the surveyors' cutlines, rising gum oozed out to heal the axmen's blazes, and running rabbits knocked over the chainmen's rotting gray stakes. In a few years all of the railway effort that was visible to casual eyes were the depots; one at Tête Jaune Cache, empty, and another beside the Athabasca River, empty except for an anvil.

8

THE LONG WAIT FOR
ANOTHER RAILWAY

As COMPLETELY as Dan Noyes had taken the flour out of Athabasca Depot, the diversion of the CPR through Calgary took the starch out of the hamlet of Edmonton and out of the transportation route through the Jasper valley. Their prospects for a railway had faded; Edmonton's for over ten years and Jasper's for thirty. Despite that, as a few of the earliest home-steaders straggled in, Edmonton's population of 263 in 1881 continued to creep ahead. For the next two decades, except for Jasper's natives who continued to make their annual pilgrimage to Lac Ste. Anne, and a few prospectors, the old trail leading west towards the Yellowhead Pass saw little activity.

During the fall of 1880, however, one interesting band of settlers on its way from New Westminster to Alberta traveled it. Hearing of the fine farming land around Edmonton and enticed by the belief that the transcontinental railway would soon reach Edmonton, Tom Henderson decided to hurry from the coast to be sure of getting some of the rich soil before it was all taken up. Teaming up with three similarly minded young men, Tom set forth with his wife, Margaret, and six children between eight months and thirteen years old.

Deciding that for the trip over the rough road to Kamloops his family should travel on wheels, Tom cut growing trees and made a wagon. At the same time, out of green rawhide from which they did not bother to remove the hair, the young men riveted together a set of harness. For the first part of the trip through the moist coastal climate the rawhide stretched and gave them endless trouble, but the wagon worked well. As they ascended the Fraser into drier regions, the green harness dried out and proved fairly satisfactory, but the fresh lumber in the wagon wheels shrank and they wasted much time trying to keep them from falling apart. At Kamloops, the end of the wagon road, the men at least were relieved to get rid of the harness and wagon and changed over to traveling as a pack train.

From there on everyone, including the three older children, Olive, Robena, and Percy, rode horseback and hazed the pack horses forward. Mrs. Henderson carried Walter, the baby, in her arms, but Charles, aged two and a half, and Annette, aged five, made the journey alternately standing or slumping in gunny sacks hung from the saddle horns.

Following the pack trail up the Thompson River used some years earlier by the CPR surveyors and continuing through Tête Jaune Cache and Jasper, the party lived mainly on bannock and some supplies the men obtained from the railway caches. To sustain her breast milk for her baby, Mrs. Henderson, carrying a tin drinking cup, nibbled frequently at oatmeal from a bag which she kept slung over her shoulder. Reminiscent of Catherine Schubert of the Overlanders' party, who eighteen years earlier had traversed the passes in the opposite direction, she had a nerve-racking and hazardous trip as day after day the cavalcade crossed rushing streams or clung precariously to the rocky ledges along the pack trail.

Fortunately, the party had a tent but its shelter did little to offset the misery of sleeping in the sodden saddle blankets dragged off the ponies at each camp. Everyone suffered discomfort, but Margaret carried the heavy load. To the men it was just another trip on another trail, but each of them had only his own problems to solve. To the mother who had to care for and comfort the brood of six, most of them infants, the madly conceived trip was one more uprooting in a life that had known little leisure and scant pleasure. Like all pioneer women, she had no choice but to follow meekly or rebelliously, but nevertheless to follow from one harebrained adventure to another, and meantime to continue bearing children and caring for them.

Leaving Kamloops late in June the cavalcade reached the mission at St. Albert sixteen weeks later. There, where the Sisters at the mission extended Mrs. Henderson and her children every kindness, they stayed for the winter. In the spring when he became one of Edmonton's very early farmers, her husband moved to Belmont, a couple of miles northeast of the hamlet, and filed on the first of his two Edmonton district homesteads. Only then Tom Henderson found out that all his hurry and all the hazards to which he had exposed his family had been of little avail; the CPR had been diverted through Calgary and for years to come Edmonton's rich lands excited little interest.

In a similar manner, Jasper also lay dormant. James Kirkness, who was in charge of the company's Lac Ste. Anne house as well, visited Jasper House and kept it open for a while late in 1877, but it was closed again. It remained so until W. R. Brereton, whose main responsibility was Lac Ste. Anne, reopened it in 1881. Acting in a dual capacity he saw to it that in a desultory fashion Jasper House was open for business till the spring of 1884 when the company finally severed its connection with the old post.

After that one or two independent traders, finding the buildings empty, occupied them for a winter or so. Starting in 1884 and continuing for two or three years, John A. McDougall, a prominent Edmonton merchant, stationed a man in the Jasper valley but the beautiful approach to the Yellowhead Pass, like the hamlet of Edmonton, had been swept out of the mainstream of the increasingly busy white man's activities in the West. That stream now occupied a narrow streak across the southern prairies, which passed through Calgary and the Kicking Horse Pass and went on to Kamloops and the coast.

The natives of the Jasper valley, the self-reliant mixture of Métis, Cree, Stoney and Iroquois — the Cardinals, Caracontés, Callihoos, Plantes, Gautheirs, Finlays and the Moberlys — were probably relieved that outsiders' activities in their valley had subsided. Through winters hard or mild they continued the ways of their ancestors, losing a few horses when the snows were deep but gaining them back as new foals when the summer breezes swept the pass. In the vast friendly wilderness of the valleys of the McLeod, the Athabasca, and the Smoky rivers, those remnants of ancient tribes dwelt together, if not in entire harmony certainly in peace — an honest, hospitable, and kindly people. Indian blood predominated but the languages they used interchangeably were French and Cree. While it was possible to find rare individuals untainted by white blood, their native blood was gradually being depleted, always by the same route — white fathers who spent a year or so in the area, and Indian mothers who took their fair-skinned offspring back to the teepees to be raised in the praiseworthy native ways.

While little family groups considered one small area having good pasture to be their home and built a shack or two there, some at Grande Cache, some at Solomon Creek, some scattered along the Jasper valley, they moved about through the seasons, depending upon where the best big game were at that time of year, so that there were trails known only to themselves leading up every valley and over every pass — tracks few white men had ever seen. At times, to take their furs out to sell, to pay homage at the Ste. Anne shrine, or just to visit their kin, they pitched off along the pack trails for a brief reunion. For they were a sociable folk. And as the years rolled along, the older folk died and the younger intermarried, until finally everyone was related to everyone else.

Feeling his way into that civilization in the Jasper valley in 1890 and groping his way into the mountains, came Lewis John Swift. Born February 20, 1854, in Cleveland, Ohio, Swift as a young man set out for the West. He worked in many of the early mining camps in the Denver area, spent some time in the Black Hills, and for a spell drove the stage from Bismarck to Deadwood. After years in the mountain states, he turned up in the embryo Calgary of 1888 and soon moved to the less-crowded outpost village of Edmonton. There or at Lac Ste. Anne he met many of the natives from the Jasper area and in 1890 traveled west with the Moberlys, till in the valley of the Athabasca he was once more in the shadow of the mountains. But he was still on the move and before long passed west through the Yellowhead Pass to emerge in due course at Mission Creek in the Okanagan, where he appears to have spent the next two years.

But Swift was drawn to the Jasper valley and in 1893, bringing a six-inch grindstone and a supply of trade goods, he returned to it. For two years he lived in the only building that was left of old Jasper House which had been abandoned about ten years earlier. Having plenty of time on his hands he studied the whole valley for two years before he built a new home in the shadow of the Palisades on a piece of land which he thought would make a good divisional point whenever the rumored second transcontinental railway would be built.

He cultivated a little patch of soil and in due course, by irrigating some of it from the stream which flowed past his door, he grew potatoes, wheat for flour, and oats for his horses. He continued trading in a small way and on one trip to Edmonton brought out some cattle and loaded his pack horses with a few domestic chickens.

In 1897, at the home of his friends the Wylies, away out in the country and along the Namao trail about half a mile north of Edmonton's Jasper Avenue, he married Suzette Chalifoux who was of mixed blood. She was not only a compatible bride but a resourceful one who quickly tidied up his household. She also helped him sow and reap their garden and their small grain field. While she took care of his domestic needs, he set to work and built an ingenious little waterwheel which, except for the nails, was entirely of wood. It turned out only one or two sacks of flour in a day, so that when he operated it he consumed more time than energy. He also made a one-horse cart of which the wheels were solid discs sawn from the end of a large Douglas fir log. He did his blacksmith work on an old anvil which Dan Noyes had failed to take away from Moberly's Athabasca Depot, not far from Swift's house.

Of much the same background was Jack Gregg, who in his youth had been a scout under General Custer but left the army before the Battle of the Little Big Horn in 1876. Later on, in the early eighties, he fought against the Apaches who were led by the famous Geronimo. Some time after 1894 he settled down on a choice piece of land along Prairie Creek. To add to his income he started a small store and traded with all who came along the old Jasper Trail. While he was a shrewd trader, he was well liked by all oldtimers.

He gave varying explanations to account for his scars, but none could doubt the dozen bullet holes he could display. Shand-Harvey, the oldtimer who recently died at Entrance and who knew him well, vouched for his scars, saying: "Well, maybe it wasn't a full dozen, but I saw them many times, and the number could not have been more than one or two short of that total."

Like Lewis Swift, Gregg wed one of the local girls, and in Mary Cardinal found a fit partner for pioneering in the foothills. As the years slipped by and travelers and pioneers in increasing numbers began making their way over the trail past Prairie Creek, she grew into one of the most highly respected characters in the whole foothills area, where her memory is preserved in the name of the Mary Gregg River.

In the nineties, H. J. Moberly's sons had become two of the leading men in the valley. Of these, Ewan (pronounced Ee-wan, possibly a revamping on Indian tongues of his Scottish name) was perhaps the more prominent. About 1898, on the flat below Cobblestone Creek and on the left side of the Athabasca, he built a well-constructed and comfortable house. His brother John built his home on the opposite side of the Athabasca, a short distance below the mouth of Maligne River and fairly close to that of Isadore Finlay.

After the Hudson's Bay Company abandoned Jasper House,

a few independent traders began trying their luck in the valley and in other spots within the general area where the company's former native customers roamed. When in the fall of 1897 Inspector A. E. Snyder made the first of the NWMP patrols into the area, he commented on some of those traders: Pierre Grey, of mixed blood, who had a post at Lake Isle and another at the "Fishing Lakes" and a dozen miles straight north of Brulé Lake; Derr and Craig in the vicinity of Grande Cache; Swift and another trader named G. Cowan in the Jasper valley, and Dan Noyes and his son at Whitemud Creek (modern Marlboro). He did not mention Jack Gregg at Prairie Creek or H. Rosling, in the same area.

But white men's activities in the area were not confined to trapping and trading. Even though over the years the Yellowhead Pass and Tête Jaune Cache were to prove disappointing to prospectors, a few optimists kept trying to search out the secrets of the creeks and valleys. Most of them came from the Cariboo goldfields either around by Fort George or by Fort Kamloops and the Thompson River. As early as 1876, G. M. Dawson, when working in British Columbia and reporting on its mining areas, stated that thirteen miles up the McLennan River from Tête Jaune Cache a handful of miners were finding traces of gold which paid them four to five dollars a day. Since those were little pockets here and there in a stream where heavy boulders made the work most arduous and since the cost of getting supplies in was prohibitive, they abandoned the area.

The next find of possible significance came in 1883 when James McKinlay, of Kamloops, after working his way up the North Thompson, found a deposit of mica at what came to be called Mica Mountain, some ten miles south of Tête Jaune Cache. That fifteen-foot-wide vein of fair grade, light green muscovite was to tantalize various miners for the next several years. Five years later an enterprising negro by the name of John Fremont Smith, from Kamloops, organized an expedition which included Louis, Chief of one of the Shuswap bands, and a number of his retainers, and took them in to open up the mine. With ever-changing crews, Smith pegged away at what he called his Bonanza Mine for several years.

A year earlier, in 1887, it was rumored that gold had been found on Goat River, some seventy miles down the Fraser from Tête Jaune Cache, and forty white miners from the Cariboo rushed there. After panning up and down the stream for a week or so and finding nothing but worthless traces of gold, they decided to try their luck farther up the Fraser. As soon as they could build boats, they ascended the river and dispersed into various side valleys, but all of them returned to Kamloops empty-handed.

While most of the prospectors who tried their luck in the Tête Jaune area came from Kamloops or the Cariboo, a few Edmontonians kept making the long trip through Jasper to the Fraser River. In 1894, three Edmonton prospectors, Harry Anthony, J. Graham, and George Purches, who were all to head for the Klondike three years later, went prospecting near Tête Jaune Cache. As well as meeting Smith, who was still working at his mine, they staked some mica claims nearby. Anthony reported that Smith was getting some splendid samples in pieces eighteen inches by twenty-two inches and had loaded several pack horses with the mineral and sent them back to the railway at Kamloops. By 1899, while Smith was still working his mine, a few other Edmonton prospectors were reported as filing claims on the headwaters of Canoe River, fifteen miles south and east of the Bonanza Mine.

About that time other venturesome men, not having the slightest interest in furs or minerals or even railways, began directing their attention towards the Jasper area. They were the forerunners of the Alpine Club mountain climbers, and they approached from the CPR at Banff. Following parts of the route now taken by Highway No. 93 and ascending the Bow and Saskatchewan rivers and then descending the Sunwapta and the Athabasca, those tourists became the first white men to leave written records of traveling by that route. Some of the earlier fur traders, such as Klyne and Brazeau, who had both been stationed at Jasper House, had traveled at least some of the passes leading from the Athabasca River to the Saskatchewan River at Kootenay Plains. Their names had been bestowed upon the Klyne and Brazeau rivers and Brazeau Lake, but they failed to leave any written records of their discoveries.

The first of the mountain climbers to pay serious attention to the peaks in the general vicinity of the old Athabasca Pass was Professor A. P. Coleman, of Toronto, who in 1892 led a party which left the CPR at Morley and worked its way northward till it crossed the Saskatchewan and ascended to Brazeau Lake. Coleman had set his heart on climbing the famous mountains Brown and Hooker, which David Douglas had described in 1828 and which he had estimated to be about 16,000 feet high. Ever since Douglas's trip, those two remote mountains had been considered the highest in Canada and Coleman was eager to scale one or both of them.

From Brazeau Lake he led his party across Poboktan Pass and down to Sunwapta Falls, which he knew to be in the Athabasca watershed. The group descended the Sunwapta to its mouth, started up the Athabasca and discovered Fortress Lake. They climbed several mountains in its immediate vicinity, hoping to see the two famous peaks. If they did see them, they did not recognize them, because nowhere could they see any that approached Douglas's estimate of 16,000 feet. Finally they had to descend to the mouth of the Sunwapta and return to Morley disappointed.

But Coleman was persistent, and during the following summer (1893) he returned to the Sunwapta River and with his associates made his way down to Athabasca Falls. There they noted that, by felling six spruce trees and tying them together, someone had made the first bridge over the canyon. They had hoped to ascend the Whirlpool River but as they descended the Athabasca they failed to notice its mouth and pressed on till they came to the mouth of the Miette, where Jasper is now. Assuming it to be the Whirlpool, they ascended the Yellowhead Pass for two toiling days before they realized their mistake. In reaching the Miette, however, they had become the first of the mountain-climbing tourists to make the trip all the way from the CPR to the Jasper valley.

Turning back down the Miette they ascended the Athabasca and that time recognized the Whirlpool. They were surprised to find the old fur traders' trail so well cut out and from the frequent relatively fresh blazes on the trees they concluded that some time since the days of the CPR surveyors someone else had chopped out the trail. Before they reached their second night's camp on the Whirlpool, Coleman met with a serious accident which prevented him from climbing any mountains for several years.

While Coleman could not climb, he could still ride, and a few days later, according to his journal: "I climbed on my own horse ready for the start, keen to see the giants Brown and Hooker, which should loom up just round the bend of the valley ahead." Later that day the party arrived at the Committee's Punch Bowl, but as Coleman said: "Where were the great mountains Brown and Hooker?'' They had expected to see magnificent summits rising ten thousand feet above the pass. "Instead, we saw commonplace mountains with nothing distinguished in their appearance, undoubtedly lower than half a dozen peaks we had climbed as incidents along the way for the fun of the thing, or as lookout points from which to choose our route . . . We had reached our point after six weeks of toil and anxiety, after three summers of effort, and we did not even raise a cheer. Mount Brown and Mount Hooker were frauds, and we were disgusted at having been humbugged by them. Personally, I found some solace in the disappointment, as I hobbled round camp, in the thought that if I could do no climbing it did not really matter much, for there was no glory to be got in climbing Mount Brown.''

The party spent a few days at the Committee's Punch Bowl during which some of the others climbed Mount Brown, and by means of their barometer determined that it was slightly over 9,000 feet high. While they noted the much finer peak of Mount Hooker (10,782) some miles to the east, they did not climb it. As Coleman wrote: "What had gone wrong with these two mighty peaks that they should suddenly shrink seven thousand feet in altitude? and how could any one, even a botanist like Douglas, make so monumental a blunder? . . . That two commonplace mountains, lower by two thousand or three thousand feet than some of their neighbours to the south-east, should masquerade for generations as the highest points in North America seems absurd; and it is not surprising that Dr. Collie ten years later should wonder if he had not reached the wrong pass, and should make a new search for these high mountains.''

Though Coleman had been disappointed in the two mountains, he had led the first party from the vicinity of Banff to Jasper. And yet even he who had seen those two mountains was still baffled by their spurious reputation. It is not surprising then that they still puzzled the equally great mountain climber Walter Wilcox, who resolved to go and see for himself. Consequently, leaving the CPR at Lake Louise, during 1896, he approached by way of the Bow River and eventually crossed the pass which was subsequently named after him and entered the Sunwapta valley. From there he went to Fortress Lake, but also failed to find the answer to the riddle, and so returned to civilization with his puzzle still unresolved. In spite of his disappointment, however, he and his party established a record of which perhaps they thought little at the time — they had been the first party, other than possibly some unrecorded fur traders, to cross from the headwaters of the Saskatchewan River to the Athabasca along a route nearly the same as that now taken by Highway No. 93.

The riddle of the mysterious Mounts Hooker and Brown also bothered two other famous alpinists, and in 1898 J. N. Collie and H. Woolley went north from the CPR intent on solving it. They too failed, but before they returned they had discovered the Columbia Icefields, climbed Mount Athabasca (11,452), and identified Mount Columbia (12,294), the highest peak on the Alberta-British Columbia portion of the Continental Divide. In spite of that magnificent achievement, Collie was still left wondering about the whereabouts of Mounts Hooker and Brown and how, if indeed Coleman had seen the right mountains, David Douglas could have been so far wrong in his estimate of the height of these two peaks.

Not until he returned to England and looked up Douglas's report did he come to understand how the famous botanist had made the mistake which for seventy years had enthroned two very ordinary mountains adjacent to the Athabasca Pass as the highest mountains in the Canadian Rockies. The explanation was that Douglas, accepting the idea current in his time, had believed the altitude of the pass to be of the order of 11,000 feet and had climbed what he thought to be an additional four or five thousand feet to the summit of Mount Brown. As a result he recorded its total height above sea level as about 16,000 feet. He did not report how long it took him to climb it, but he stated that about 1,200 feet of his ascent was most difficult and fatiguing. It must have taken him six or seven hours to make the trip up and down. When Collie actually read Douglas's journal he easily perceived how the misconception of Mount Brown's altitude had come about. Before Collie's time, the CPR surveyors had crossed the pass with their fairly accurate instruments and had reduced its elevation from the 11,000 feet which it had been believed to be to the much more prosaic figure of 5,700. Thereby they had cut over five thousand feet from the height of the pass and in the process had cut the altitude of Mount Brown by the same amount. Coleman's party recorded it as slightly over 9,000 feet high, and recent more accurate measurements place it as 9,156.

For seventy years, however, due to their remoteness, Mounts Brown and Hooker had been enshrined in the mystery with which Douglas's quite innocent statement had clothed them. Because of that and because they were so difficult to get at, they had set several parties of alpinists off on expeditions which in the process of their search had pioneered the route which Highway No. 93 now follows.

While the alpinists had been looking for Mounts Brown and Hooker and while miners searching for gold, silver, and copper were wandering all over British Columbia, a few devoted geologists employed by the Geological Survey of Canada were dispersing their forces to try to look at the various strata and to work out the geology of the tangled maze of mountains. In the seventies the earliest of those, Dr. Dawson and Dr. Selwyn, had done much preliminary work. During the nineties men like McConnell, Dowling, and McEvoy spent what time they could working in the vicinity of the Continental Divide. Not only were they concerned with the search for precious metals, but the growing towns of the prairies looked to the eastern slope of the mountains for a coal supply, and the Geological Survey concentrated much of its effort into studying some of the large coal fields which were soon to burst into prominence.

One of the geologists was James McEvoy, who in 1898 hired two Edmonton packers, F. A. Jackson and S. Derr (after whom Derr Creek was named) to take him west into the mountains. The report of his trip gives a good idea of the conditions along the trail from Edmonton to Tête Jaune Cache. By that time Pierre Grey had extended the wagon trail from Lac Ste. Anne to his post near the head of Lake Isle. Going on from there McEvoy noted the coal exposures in the banks of the Pembina. When he came to the vicinity of Dan Noyes's post on Whitemud Creek he saw half a dozen half-breed cabins (the beginnings of modern Marlboro). After commenting on the coal exposed on the McLeod River, he noted that for miles west of the Leavings of the McLeod the country had been burned over during the recent past and that it was a mere wilderness of bare trunks. Many trunks had fallen over what traces there were of the trail and his packers made slow progress cutting the wind fall to let the horses through. As others had noted, the corduroy placed by the CPR crews was rotten and dangerous.

Turning up the Miette and continuing to a point twelve miles west of the summit, he saw another area extending to

Tête Jaune Cache where for miles fire had desecrated the valley. Within that burned-over area he found a few gold miners hopefully scratching entries into Rainbow Mountain. His report is probably the first one to mention Mount Robson's Indian name. A combination of the form of the strata and the processes of erosion make it appear that a road winds up and across its lofty face, and the Indians called it YUH-HAI-HAS-KUN — the Mountain of the Spiral Road. Reporting on other mountains in the area he mentioned and named Mount Geikie and said it was fifteen miles south and east of Yellowhead Mountain.

During the time he spent at Tête Jaune Cache McEvoy went to see the Bonanza mica mine still being worked by J. F. Smith, his new partner, S. Winter, and ten men. That summer some of the blocks of mica which they took out weighed from twenty-five to three hundred pounds, and on one occasion four men mined three tons in eleven working days. From this material they split out and cut 650 pounds of finished material, which they sent out by pack horse. From there McEvoy went over to another site on the headwaters of Canoe River, some fifteen miles south and east, where several Edmonton men had staked claims.

Having completed his work in that area he retraced his steps to the Jasper valley and took his party up Jacques Creek and across to Rocky River where once more he found large areas of fire-killed timber. He noticed that he was following the route which the Jasper valley Indians used when they wanted to make a trip to Rocky Mountain House on the upper Saskatchewan. Having reached the area where the headwaters of the Brazeau, the Pembina, and the McLeod rivers are all close together, he descended the McLeod and noted several outcrops of coal in what was later to become the famous Coal Branch mining area.

McEvoy left the Tête Jaune Cache area too soon to hear the news that some of the miners had made a placer strike on Swiftcurrent Creek which comes swirling down to join the Fraser a mile or so below the Grand Fork and some ten miles from Tête Jaune Cache. As soon as the news reached the outside, several parties, all well provisioned and equipped, flocked in. Then, group by group, after working for a season without finding enough gold to pay their expenses, they slipped away to answer the call of some other siren stream. Though the very name of the Tête Jaune Cache area and its remoteness from settled regions

Father P. J. De Smet, 1801-1873.

Sir George Simpson, 1787-1860.
Governor-in-Chief of the Hudson's Bay Company Territories

Jasper-Yellowhead Historical Society

Lewis Swift's ranch in the Jasper valley, 1909. Photo taken by Fred Seibert, DLS.

Old Indian suspension bridge at Hagwilget, B.C. Constructed originally of poles, spars and cedar withes, the bridge spanned the Bulkley River canyon 100 feet above water. It was reinforced with telegraph wire by a construction crew about 1866 and still in use when the Grand Trunk Pacific Railway was built.

British Columbia Archives

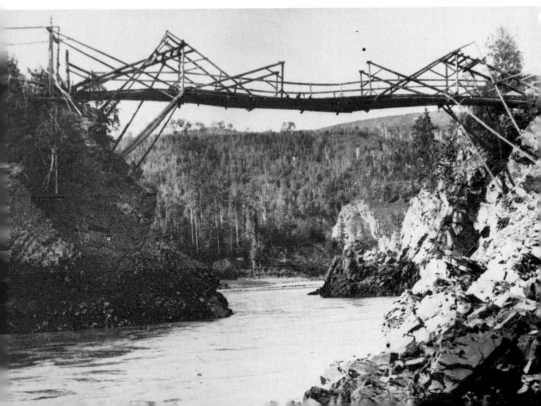

The Mission at Lac Ste. Anne in 1852, eight years after its founding.

Father Jean-Baptiste Thibault, founder of the Mission.

Stephen Redgrave, 1831-1903.
Organizer and leader of one party of
Overlanders in 1862, and sheriff of
Kootenay from 1884 to 1903.

Mrs. Catherine O'Hare Schubert.
Only woman in the party of Overlanders
of 1862, and mother of the first white girl
born in the interior of British Columbia.

Some of the oldtimers of the Jasper valley. L-R: Jack Gregg, Mrs. Lewis Swift (Suzette
Chalifoux), Lewis Swift, and Bob Jones (Gregg's partner in coal mining).

Kamloops Museum Association

John Fremont Smith, 1850-1934.
Adventurer, world traveler, prospector
and prominent citizen who settled in
central British Columbia and opened up
the Bonanza Mica Mine.

In the Jasper valley, looking west, showing Jasper House in foreground, cemetery (enclosed
by posts) the teepee poles in background. Photo taken in 1872.

Public Archives of Canada

Glenbow-Alberta Institute (H. J. Green photo)

Pack horses of Grand Trunk Pacific on summer trail in Yellowhead Pass, c. 1910-11.

Grader on GTP construction, 1911, Frontier College instructor driving dump cart.

Glenbow-Alberta Institute

Eight-mule team on grader during GTP construction west of Edmonton, c. 1910-11.

General view of GTP camp at Mile 1, B.C. near summit of Yellowhead Pass, 1911. In the group is A. S. Cummings, who later became Registrar of Wesley College in Winnipeg.

Glenbow-Alberta Institute (H. J. Green photo)

Buster stopping house at Tête Jaune Cache, c. 1910-11. Holes in stumps were used as a resting place for oars during carving.

Street scene at Tête Jaune Cache, 1911.

Jasper-Yellowhead Historical Society (D. S. McCready photo)

Jasper-Yellowhead Historical Society (Bickersteth collection)

The Big Eddy trestle in the Edson district, built up to about half its final height, c. 1911. It was at this same location that the Hornbeck tragedy had occurred in 1907.

Jasper Park Lodge, probably in the early 1920's. "Tent City" closed in 1919 and was officially opened as Jasper Park Lodge in 1922, with a few cabins. This photo was taken by F. A. Jackman, Jasper druggist about this time.

Jasper-Yellowhead Historical Society

Building scows at Tête Jaune Cache for the Grand Trunk Pacific, May 1913.

Track layer operating at Tête Jaune Cache, July 1912.

Tree lobbed by Michel Gauthier in 1872 for meeting of Sandford Fleming and Walter Moberly during survey by CPR through Yellowhead Pass; still standing on bank of Athabasca River across the highway from Jasper Cemetery.

Glenbow-Alberta Institute (H. J. Green photo)

Grand Trunk Pacific Railway bridge over Prairie Creek, near Jasper, c. 1911-14.

Mine buildings at Pocahontas, looking north across the Athabasca River.

Jasper-Yellowhead Historical Society

Pack train heading west, crossing Disaster Point, 1909. Photo taken by Fred Seibert, DLS.

Smuggled whisky found by the provincial police at Tête Jaune, B.C., 1912.

Track layer or "Pioneer" laying track on a temporary trestle over the McLennan River in 1912. Piers for permanent bridge may be seen to left of trestle. This was Mile 50, B.C. near Tête Jaune Cache.

Base camp during railway construction in B.C., 1911. From this point supplies for about 5,000 men were shipped down the Fraser River. John Moore, Frontier College instructor, worked here as camp builder.

Summit City, the GTP construction camp at Yellowhead, just inside the B.C. border. Looking south, with Mount Fitzwilliam in the background, 1911.

Hinton, Mile 62, during construction days; establishments like the "Pool Hall — H. W. Bennett — Beds — Beer," and "Dad's Lodging House" were an integral part of all such towns. The owner of the latter business, "Dad" Renshaw, moved along with construction crews to Wolf Creek, Bickerdike, Tête Jaune, and McBride as well.

A scow in the Grand Canyon of the Fraser River, 1908.

S. S. *B.C. Express* and S.S. *B.X.* tied up at the pier at South Fort George, 1912.

Alberta Archives (Ernest Brown collection)

Daniel Noyes and son, Jasper frontiersmen.

A. O. Wheeler, 1860-1945.
Founder of the Alpine Club of Canada.

Jasper-Yellowhead Historical Society (C. G. Peterson photo)

John Moberly buildings on south side of Athabasca River, across from Jasper Air Strip; built in 1898 and abandoned in 1910 after the creation of Jasper National Park.

Charles Neimeyer, driver of the first car to travel from Edmonton to Victoria by way of the Yellowhead Pass and Kamloops, receives a good-luck handshake from Charles H. Grant, president of the Edmonton Automobile and Good Roads Association, upon the departure of the Neimeyer-Silverthorne party from Edmonton, June 17, 1922.

Yellowhead Highway Association

Neimeyer car on the old railway grade west of Edson, Alberta.

Neimeyer car in rock slide near Lucerne, B.C.

continued to lure a few prospectors, its performance fell far short of its popularity.

Perhaps because the area was too poor in pay dirt to retain swarms of miners, Tête Jaune Cache was a peaceful place. During all those early years only one known murder marred its tranquillity and that, involving traders not miners, took place in the spring of 1899 at the mouth of Swiftcurrent Creek. During the winter Alex McAuley, a half-breed said to have come in from the east, teamed up with a bachelor of about forty years of age named J. Hughes, who had come from Kansas. McAuley was accompanied by his young native wife and two small children.

Relations between the two men became strained and their hard feeling came to a head when they decided to part company and divide up the furs. Finally, as his wife was taking down the teepee and McAuley was loading his pack horses with what he claimed was his share of the fur, he bent forward to reach for the pack rope. When he was in this half-stooping position with his face turned toward his partner, Hughes shot him with his 44-90 rifle. The bullet entered his head, carried away his jawbone and ended up in his lung. While his wife moved the teepee poles over him and re-erected it, Hughes busied himself by digging a grave a dozen yards away.

For six days, while Hughes came to the teepee each day to find out if McAuley was dead yet and until a couple of Edmontonians happened along and the woman called them, the unconscious victim lay in the lodge. The two Edmontonians hastened up Swiftcurrent Creek to fetch two other men, Price and Evans, who previously had been associated with Hughes.

They could do nothing for the victim but Price went back to get the Edmontonians Hostyn, Derr, and Hollings who were working at Swiftcurrent Creek. When they arrived the lot of them took Hughes into custody and a few of them set out with him for the nearest police station at Donald. During their seventeen-day trip the party first met a group of eleven men and thirty-five pack horses on its way to Swiftcurrent Creek, and a few days later met a similar party also heading for the diggings.

On the ninth day after the shooting McAuley died, and Price buried him in the grave his murderer had prepared. Then Mrs. McAuley and her two children made the two-week trip up the Canoe and Columbia rivers to the upper end of Kinbasket

Lake, where she remained with some relatives. The police at Donald kept Hughes until his trial the following November, at which, because there was some doubt about the circumstances, he was acquitted.

In 1900 Edmontonians became interested in one of the resources of the Jasper valley which was neither mineral nor fur. Because farmers were flocking into the area adjacent to Edmonton and creating a market for horses, George B. McLaughlin and Frank Armstrong decided to capture some of those which were running wild on the plateau around Pyramid Lake. Their success hardly justified their effort. After studying the movement of the horses and the area in which they pastured, the men discovered that they were in the habit of using fairly regular paths to and from the lake. Well inside a large copse the hunters erected a strong corral across one of those paths and from its mouth ran two diverging wing fences. Then, when the horses headed along the path, they closed in behind them and tried to rush them into the corral. Most of the time the animals were too smart for their pursuers, but finally McLaughlin and Armstrong captured seven horses and two colts and took them back to Edmonton.

For several years, except for the passage of a few hopeful prospectors and the more or less regular coming and going of a handful of fur traders and Indians, the Jasper valley and Tête Jaune's pass were left to enjoy their seclusion. The fur trade companies of the olden days had forsaken them, the CPR builders had rejected them, and the majority of miners had passed them by. Each time such traders as Lewis Swift or Jack Gregg came out to Edmonton they discussed the prospect of another railway seeking to use the Yellowhead Pass, but did not lose much sleep over the matter.

When they came out to Edmonton in the fall of 1900 they heard of Mrs. Colin Fraser's death there at the age of ninety-two. She had died at the home of her daughter, Mrs. Phillip Tate, on August 25 and had been buried in the Protestant cemetery. Of her descendants, ten of her offspring survived, fifty grandchildren were alive and twenty-seven had predeceased her. Thirty-nine great-grandchildren were living and ten had passed along ahead of her. Another link with the Jasper of the early days had been severed.

During 1901 Jack Gregg got tired of cutting his hay by hand, bought a mower in Edmonton, and in some manner packed it out to Prairie Creek. The same fall Lewis Swift decided to try raising more of his own meat and nearly worried the life out of his pack horses by burdening them with an unstated number of small pigs and poultry which he took home from Lac Ste. Anne. Though this endeavor must have taxed his patience and the horses' forbearance to the utmost, he succeeded in introducing the squealing of his porkers to the valley which for so long had resounded to the squeaking of Colin Fraser's pipes. And every morning of his trip as he tied the pigs onto his pack saddles Swift muttered about it being high time that some of the daydream railways which everyone talked about came down to earth and started laying steel towards Yellowhead Pass.

All at once everyone had begun talking about a second transcontinental railway — the press, the politicians, and the pioneers; Winnipeg people, Edmonton people, and even the moneyed people of the East. First with the talk had been the Grand Trunk Railway, which back in 1864 in its embryo era had sent Rae through the Yellowhead Pass but then had averted its eyes. By 1900, however, the Grand Trunk was a major railway corporation with so many miles of roadbed that, when it talked, politicians listened. Once more it began to dream of its long-delayed transcontinental, and even while Swift was packing his porkers west it was propositioning the politicians and pointing west.

But other dreamers, William Mackenzie and Donald Mann, both with experience in building railroads and rare genius in financing, had fought their way into the select circle of moneyed men, and now hoped to dip into the overflowing pot of gold available to railroad builders. Before long Canada was to hear much of the magicians William Mackenzie and Donald Mann, contractors, railroaders, and capitalists extraordinary. Before long, out of small beginnings, they organized another transcontinental, the Canadian Northern Railway, pointed it toward the Yellowhead Pass, financed it with Dominion Government subsidies of some 65 million dollars and government-guaranteed bonds of 245 million dollars, and sent surveyors swarming all over western Canada.

For the next few years, to the great satisfaction of Edmonton's businessmen and its suppliers of pack trains, several GTP or CNR survey parties worked north and west and northwest out of the ambitious new town. For the next several years, glowing with pride in his town which was to be a key point first on one new transcontinental railway and then *two* new transcontinentals, the editor of the *Edmonton Bulletin* reported the comings and goings of survey parties. Out of the perpetual breezes which swept over the West, breezes invariably redolent with seductive hints of railway surveys, his perceptive nose sniffed out every last rumor and his panting pen recorded each one. In August, 1900, he relayed the information that Mackenzie and Mann were ready to start building the CNR from Port Arthur to the Yellowhead Pass. Some months later, in bated-breath style, he announced that the GTP was also on its way to the city. Edmonton was to rejoice in *two* transcontinentals.

Then blowing away from the mass of rosy rumors came one which spoiled the editor's day. It hinted at the possibility that the CNR and the GTP might amalgamate so that both could concentrate on building just one transcontinental. The idea was so sensible and yet so depressing that it gave the editor a bad turn. Even then, however, he was sanguine and wrote: "It is to be fervently hoped that the talks indulged in so freely as to the amalgamation of the Canadian Northern and the Grand Trunk schemes will not prove to be correct."

His hopes were justified. In the speculative atmosphere of the time such a breath of sanity stood little chance of survival. Although Collingwood Schreiber, the chief engineer of the Federal Department of Railways, opposed building two railroads side by side for most of the three hundred miles from Edmonton to Tête Jaune Cache and some other civil servants questioned the duplication, the politicians failed to listen. At that point Ottawa could have prevented what turned out to be utterly wasteful duplication, but it paid no attention.

And so the surveying went on and the pack trains continued to form up at Edmonton and to head for the Pine, Peace River, Smoky, and Yellowhead passes. Judging from the number of survey parties the GTP had on the headwaters of the Peace River and working toward Fort Assiniboine, everyone assumed that that company was going to head northwest from Edmonton and that it intended to leave the Yellowhead Pass to the CNR. The GTP officials took no steps to correct that assumption and thereby may have deceived the CNR management into a false sense of security in believing that they would have the Yellowhead Pass to themselves.

As far as Edmonton was concerned, it, like every other embryo town in the West, dreamed of being a railway center out of which a host of railways would radiate. And indeed, in every respect, Edmonton's prospects were rosy. Its own transcontinental was on the way, settlers were flocking in, urban property values were soaring, and the streets burst into a new busyness. Nothing escaped the vigilant eye of the *Edmonton Bulletin*, which in October, 1903, in reporting a minor accident, took occasion to point out how busy the town was.

Evidently, at one of its most congested corners, a steam tractor in turning off Jasper Avenue to go north on 100 Street ran into the ditch and got stuck. From somewhere the driver procured another steam engine to pull his machine out. The conjunction of the two puffing monsters struck terror into a team of horses which approached the intersection from the east. The team ran away, and at the same intersection collided with a farmer's wagon, "one of the teams turning a complete somersault," and tore off the wheel and part of the rear axle of the wagon.

No one was seriously hurt, but the editor was impressed by the result: "This temporary blocking of the street served to show how really busy Edmonton is. All this took place in a few minutes, but in this short time over a score of heavily laden rigs were blocked in the street." Edmonton was beginning to experience traffic jams.

Some months later, in May of the following year, the town's first automobile made its appearance. According to the *Bulletin;* "The credit of bringing the first horseless carriage to Edmonton belongs to Mr. J. H. Morris who on his return from Winnipeg last evening brought (by train) a two cylinder auto car. The new carriage created quite an excitement on Jasper Avenue last evening especially among horses and small boys."

The very next day, somewhere on the town's outskirts, Edmonton's first car ran out of gas for the first time, and as the *Bulletin* reported: ". . . the predicament was a serious one. It was finally solved by securing a bottle of benzoine from a neighbouring house and the car came back to town burning the clothes cleaning liquid, with one cylinder in operation."

Unlike Morris's car, the town was operating on all cylinders as the events of the next year or so were to show. On November 7, 1904, with a population of 8,350, it was proclaimed a city. Less than a year later, on September 1, 1905, Canada's foothill region was raised to the rank of a province. At the same time Edmonton assumed the role of Alberta's capital city. Then a

few months later, on November 24, to add another triumph to
its many successes, Lieutenant-Governor G. H. V. Bulyea
". . . drove home with unerring blow the silver spike which held
in place the first rail of the Canadian Northern Railway to reach
the station in Edmonton." Train bells rang, corks popped, and
champagne fizzed.

Finally, the new transcontinental railway had reached the
new capital city of the new province.

But even as the silver spike of one transcontinental was
quivering in the tie, another transcontinental, the GTP, was
clawing its way across the prairies to the east, rushing to reach
Edmonton. Moreover, the CNR engineers, well ahead of their
rivals, had already swept on west through the city and were
rushing their railway grade to Stony Plain on its way toward
the Yellowhead Pass.

At last Edmonton's oldtimers could travel by train along
much the same route over which when they had come west
decades earlier they had driven their Red River carts from Portage la Prairie to Edmonton. For miles at a stretch portions
of either the Canadian Northern Railway or the Grand Trunk
Pacific grades swept along parallel to the old Winnipeg-
Edmonton Trail. In 1905, however, a number of thriving towns
and cities were springing up at strategic points along the railways;
Neepawa, Yorkton, Saskatoon, North Battleford, Lloydminster,
and others.

At last too, over the old trail which Henry John Moberly
had pioneered, over the trail by which Lewis Swift had packed
his pigs, through the Jasper valley where William Henry had
built his house and where David Thompson had struggled, and
finally through the pass where Tête Jaune had built his famous
cache, a real railway, and perhaps two of them, were to run.
Across the creeks, around the cliffs, and through the canyons
where for interminable years surveyors had come and gone,
first for seven years in the seventies, then for more than seven
years since the late nineties, at last actual construction toward
the Yellowhead Pass had started.

Edmonton's cup, brimful of successes, started running over.

9

TWO RAILWAYS START TOWARD THE PASS!

NEARLY ten years were to elapse, however, before the CNR completed its line to Vancouver. Long before that it found out that the GTP feint towards the Peace River passes had been a bluff designed to give its surveyors time to get ahead of their rivals and to select the best route through the defiles of the Yellowhead Pass. Meanwhile, by June, 1907, the CNR laid its steel as far as Stony Plain and left its transcontinental dead-end there while it allowed its attention to stray to other branch lines on the prairies.

Not so the GTP; with men, mules, and machinery it fairly swarmed into the narrow 235-mile-long strip of the old packers' trail to Jasper. Months before its first train reached Edmonton in August, 1909, the GTP organization had started working west of the city.

Fortunately for its efficiency the company was able to let contracts for all of the grading from Edmonton to Aldermere (beyond Prince George), 723 miles away, to one firm of contractors, Foley, Welch and Stewart. More capable contractors could not have been found because all four of the firm's partners had years of experience behind them. The two Foley brothers, who came from Minnesota, had each worked on the construction of the CPR and several other lines. Patrick Welch was well known for his major building ventures around Spokane. J. W. Stewart was a hard-boiled, fair-minded and at times generous man who had grown up in eastern Canada and had had railway experience there.

Before the grading contractors took over, however, the GTP engineers had to show them where to build by chopping out a cutline winding through the forest and studded every hundred feet with a surveyor's stake. Sometimes in a straight line for five or six miles at a stretch the evenly-spaced stakes, stepping off so individually at first, soon merged to a blur in the distance. But whether they could be seen or not, always marching ahead for a hundred miles, these stakes pressed on down a straight line through the trees, curved around this lake, or swung around that timbered hill, and on and on.

Following the stakes, Foley, Welch and Stewart sent in

the forerunners of that company's army of railway builders, a small but skillful contingent. Armed with axes and saws, cant hooks and chains and taking along light camping equipment, those specialists were to hew an avenue one hundred feet broad out of the forest. As mile by mile they chopped their way along, felling trees, saving appropriate ones for lumber, piling and burning the rest and grubbing the stumps, the advance of the clearing crew left a trail of smoke and smoldering brush piles along the winding gash they had opened through the solemn woods.

At last, after years of rumors, the railway toward the Yellowhead Pass had really started. At last, after years of surveying, something tangible had been accomplished, and now a cleared strip one hundred feet wide wormed its way ever westward through the forest.

But the cleared strip was only one of the earlier steps in the costly and complicated construction processes. As the clearing crews gnawed their way west they triggered a host of associated activities. The survey crews and the clearers themselves had called into being a few temporary camps and a few depots to which pack trains, dancing attendance upon those relatively small crews, carried food and supplies. However, now that thousands of men were on the point of descending upon that broad streak through the forest, a whole new organization had to come into being to support them. And this was where Foley, Welch and Stewart excelled; they provided the organization by which a score of smaller contractors did the actual work.

First they built a tote road and dotted it with dozens of camps and depots. In many cases the trees cut down sufficed to provide the logs for the various buildings; cookhouse, bunkhouses, and stores or caches, some roofed with shingles but most covered by canvas. Those half-tented camps were intended to care for the temporary needs of something over a hundred men and whatever horses were necessary. Tied here and there about the clearing, close to great piles of hay, those patient animals took up any space not covered by parks of wagons, dump carts, scrapers, and other horse-drawn earth-moving machinery. Around the official construction camps sprang a sprawling temporary and unofficial hamlet of cafes, flop joints, and barns to cater to the needs of freighters and their beasts. Other institutions grew up too, for wherever there are hundreds of men there will be liquor, gamblers, and women.

The job of bringing in the enormous quantities of food and

material needed was contracted out to freighters. Foley, Welch and Stewart paid a fixed amount for transporting a hundred pounds one mile, and everyone owning a wagon and a team of any kind was free to bid. To each of the end-of-steel towns — Entwistle, Wolf Creek, Bickerdike, and Prairie Creek — as many as a thousand freighters constantly came in empty, loaded up, and pulled out for destinations many miles to the west. Except for rails, they carried every conceivable article needed to build a railway: lumber, bridge timbers, dynamite, canned goods, sacks of flour, beef, pork, bacon and beans. All their destinations had the fabulous ring of the far-off places: The Big Eddy, Mile 129 (Wolf Creek), Fiddle River, Henry House, Fitzhugh, Roche Miette, Mile 1 (the British Columbia border), Mile 28 (Resplendent), and Mile 53 (Tête Jaune Cache).

Winter was the time for carrying the heavy loads, when over the slick snowy trail the teams pushed on to pile supplies into sheds at advance camps. Except for the cold, which could be countered, winter hauling was easy on the drivers. But even in the rainy season the teams fought their way forward. Through sucking muskeg or endlessly recurring mudholes, as the drivers cursed and plied their blacksnakes, their poor beasts pulled their utmost.

But even their utmost was not always enough and in the midst of a mudhole the horses could flounder forward no longer and found themselves with their bellies resting on the mud, while the wagon settled into oozy muck to all appearances content to give up the fight and remain there forever. Exhausted as they were, the freighter and his helper had to unhitch the worn-out animals and, instead of leading them, had to drag them out of the hole to relatively dry land and await the arrival of another freighter. When, possibly an hour later, he came on the scene, both teams would be hitched in tandem and with the horses straining to their limit and all the men up to their knees in mud, pushing and turning the wheels, another hour would probably see the wagon literally sucked out of the slough and hauled to dry land perhaps fifty feet ahead. Then, by combining their efforts, they dragged the second wagon through the mess. After that, while the horses stood by recovering their wind, the men would take off the wagon wheels one by one, flick out most of the mud and regrease the axles.

In such service many a horse died from exhaustion or broke

a leg and had to be shot. Its carcass was pulled clear of the tote road and left to taint the air until nature's processes finally disposed of it. Near such mudholes the bleaching skeletons of many a fine horse or mule became signposts showing the sacrifices the progress of the railway had exacted.

Most freighters made some money and enjoyed the life. Neither the hardships, the filthy stopping places, nor the dubious meals could deter those hard-bitten, determined men who, through rain or shine or snow, pressed on. All day long, in bitter competition with other teams or in friendly rivalry, but always traveling in the open air and at night entering into the camaraderie around the campfires, they kept moving their loads forward. Regular freighters, men for whom driving a team was a way of life, did their work in an orderly way, expected risks and hardships, and generally made a satisfactory profit. Some greenhorns, dreaming of carning easy money, soon dropped out of the service, others stuck with the job and in time counted themselves among the well-known characters of the tote road. Freighting was no job for sissies.

But freighting was only one of the preliminaries to the main bout with mud and muskeg which produced the railway grade. It was men and horses and mules, thousands of men, hundreds of horses, and scores of the cow-tailed, long-eared, small-hoofed, hardy and cantankerous mules whose toil wheeled and scraped and dragged the earth out of the cuts and piled it into fills and brought into being the finished grade. Seeing the giant modern internal-combustion-propelled, dirt-moving machines, it is perhaps hard to realize that when the Grand Trunk was built muscle power alone moved dirt out of the cuts into the fills, shoveled it into place or pushed it in wheelbarrows up hand-hewn planks. Shovels, in the hands of a generation of Swedes and Galicians, Irishmen and Italians, Scots and Cornishmen, built the early railways.

Many of the laborers on the GTP were Alberta homesteaders toiling to get a grub stake to maintain their families until they could make their 160 acres produce enough to keep them. A large share of them were Ukrainians who were recent immigrants. As F. A. Talbot, who in his *The Making of a Great Canadian Railway,* marveling at how hard those "foreigners" worked, said: "They subsist on the plainest and cheapest of food, invariably pork and beans, thereby cutting down their living expenses to the irreducible minimum compatible with keeping body and soul together. Yet as workers they cannot be equal-led . . . His home was a small wooden shack barely eight feet square, and was noisome to an extreme degree. His entire ward-robe consisted of a pair of tattered nether garments and a dis-coloured, mud-stained flannel vest, while his feet, from which socks were absent, were encased in a pair of heavy boots. He was up with the sun in the morning, and four o'clock saw him slaving away as if for dear life. It was a monotonous round; his shovel swung regularly to and fro until the wheelbarrow was loaded, then there was a short run up a narrow plank, a dexterous tilt, and the vehicle was discharged; then he ran quickly back with it to the site of excavation, and the cycle of operations was repeated. He made no pause for meals, but hurriedly swallowed some of the pork and beans, an ample supply of which he carried in a tin pail. They were devoured while cold, because they would have taken more precious time to eat had they been hot! He kept himself glued to his task until the shades of evening had fallen and the gathering mantle of night prevented him from seeing more than a yard before him. He was making between £10 and £12 a week clear at this slavery, and yet he was as happy in his own little world as if he were revelling in the lap of luxury.''

A variety of carts, scrapers, slushers, and graders were used on the larger cuts and fills, including elevating graders which were propelled by as many as eight horses pulling in front and eight more pushing from behind. Steam shovels were reserved for major cuts only as, puffing and groaning, they gnawed at dirt and clawed at loose rock and dumped their loads onto flatcars or dribbled them down the sides of cliffs. Steam shovels, locomotives, and hoists were the only true machines on the whole job.

In due course, with the creeks and valleys bridged by tres-tles, a stretch of grade some one hundred miles long would be declared ready to receive the rails. Along what had once been merely a surveyor's line, over marsh and muskeg, green timber or fire-killed waste, through cuts and over fills and trestles, the finished grade wound its way as a great raw gash.

At that point, as fast as the rails could be received from the hard-pressed steel mills, the railway company brought its track layer into operation. Noisily lurching forward, it spewed ties onto the grade from one side and rails from the other. A huge machine with winches and small steam engines in its body, with jibs and booms projecting like antennae, jerking erratically forward, attended by sweating, cursing men who called it a gibbet, it resembled a great grasshopper laying its eggs and crawling forward over them.

Though the track layer was the effective part of the procession, its efforts were supported by special flatcars loaded with rails, spikes, and fish plates and other flatcars piled high with ties, all pushed forward a rail's length at a time by a work locomotive. Along with it came its hundred-man crew, some taking ties off a flatcar and dropping them on an endless conveyor on the right side of the track layer, or hoisting rails from other flatcars to a conveyor on the left side. As the conveyor pushed their ties or rails forward, many other men were waiting to seize them, lay them in place and spike everything down temporarily so that the machine could advance another rail's length. In that way the machine and its crew could usually lay two miles of track in a day — a long and a hard day. In doing so, the men would have handled six thousand heavy green ties and spiked over 500,000 pounds of steel rail to them. Later on the rails would have to be aligned more carefully and carloads of gravel would have to be spread over the grade and tucked under the ties. But after the passage of the track layer the railway line could be used.

By the fall of 1909 the grading was finished to the Pembina canyon at Entwistle. The steel was laid soon after, and by December 10 the bridge, started a year earlier, was completed. Meanwhile, crews had pushed the grade to the Wolf Creek bridge, so that as soon as the track layer could cross the Pembina it could continue its remorseless crawl forward. Its progress, however, had been made possible by men — men with all their sturdy strength and their human weaknesses. Only their strength enabled them to endure the toil, the mud, and the primitive accommodation. Only their weaknesses sucked them into the toils of bootleggers, gamblers, or strumpets. But in spite of their weaknesses and the fact that a bootlegger's arrival in camp presented them with the relief of going on a binge, they were good men. Far from being a lot of devils, they were in all matters that counted remarkably generous in outlook and openhanded, and men on whom, except during their binges, one could always rely.

At any time during the years when the GTP was building west from Edmonton, rarely less than two thousand men were employed somewhere along the grade. Many of them came from Edmonton and many were prairie homesteaders, but even though by the hundreds the contractors brought men from Toronto and Winnipeg, or advertised for them in the labor exchanges at Edmonton, they rarely had enough laborers.

At Winnipeg or Toronto, after signing one of Foley, Welch and Stewart's *Contract to Work* forms, they were given railway tickets, crowded into the poorest of obsolete coaches, and hauled to Edmonton. From there, like cattle, they were shipped to the end of steel. Seventy or eighty men were jammed into a battered old coach, having neither lights nor water, a coach without seats, standing room only. By turns men stretched out on the floor for an interval and then stood up to allow others to lie down, taking care that the jolting train did not make them step on the faces of the reclining men.

Many of the men, having been transported to Edmonton free of charge, simply deserted the train, and, therefore, the company's service. On the witness stand during the course of a legal action at Edmonton brought against some of those deserters, they declared that as their train drew into Edmonton the crew had locked the cars, but some men in the yards had jimmied the lock and let everyone out. As a side issue in the case, another witness claimed that he and most of the rest had not left the car at Edmonton but had gone on to Edson. There, he alleged, they had looked around for two days at their own expense but could find no one to put them to work, and consequently several of them had returned to Edmonton.

Glad indeed were the laborers of all nationalities to reach the end of steel and to set out on foot along the grades to the camps to which they were assigned. Their walk might continue for two or three days until the men arrived at whichever camp they were needed. There they would be allotted space in a bunkhouse.

In his *Land of Open Doors* the Reverend J. B. Bickersteth described one such bunkhouse as follows:

"Imagine a long low building of lumber, covered with black tar paper; it looks dingy enough. The door when opened lets out an atmosphere reeking with coal oil, bad tobacco, and wet socks. On the right are two tiers of wooden bunks, each tier consisting of two bunks side by side. The men are pretty closely packed. A bench runs along by the bunks, and this, with several boxes and tree stumps, forms the sitting accommodation. The floor is covered with mud and slush, brought in by many pairs of boots — the said boots, with the socks which belong to them, are hung up in various advantageous positions near the central heater in which a huge wood fire is roaring . . . When you see the conditions under which these men live, you could hardly be surprised if the outlook which many of them have on life is little better than a beast's. They work like horses, eat like pigs, and sleep like dogs. Is it to be wondered at that after months of this they go wild when they reach the lights and glare of a city, and that the height of enjoyment is to be found in the whisky bottle? . . ."

The living conditions, coupled with an upsurge of labor unrest, which with good reason was sweeping the continent, made them truculent and very often unfair to their employers. Independent observers, noting a good deal of ill-feeling and fault on both sides, concluded that the contractors did not treat their men any too well and that often the men treated the contractors shabbily.

One legitimate grievance against the contractors was that they paid the men by cheques or time slips payable at Edmonton hundreds of miles away from where they had worked. In order to get money the laborers had to have them cashed by scalpers in the construction towns, who charged 10 per cent for that service, or else by train crews who also made a profitable practice of exacting a discount. If a man leaving the job refused to accept that levy, he was faced with returning to Edmonton to get the cash — often without a cent in his pocket and depending upon the charity of camp cooks or restaurant owners for meals along the way. Then, on enough occasions that it became a much-talked-of scandal, the paying officers in Edmonton would be unable to cash vouchers because the proper papers had not been received from the timekeeper hundreds of miles away on the grade. On several occasions the men took the matter to court and in one instance in the fall of 1910 Magistrate Byers commented that it was "not the first time the disgraceful treatment of the GTP towards its employees has come to my attention."

If men working for Foley, Welch and Stewart had cause to complain about their pay cheques, they perhaps had less to complain about in the way of hospital services which the company provided. From the vantage point of modern medicine and extensive health services, it is hard to understand the callousness or the fatalism with which employers and laborers alike viewed accident, disease, and death sixty years ago. Death or crippling for life fell to the lot of scores of fine men working on the grade.

By the time the GTP came to be built the Federal Government had passed legislation insisting that contractors on such jobs had to provide medical and hospital facilities. On the grade west of Edmonton the company's senior physician, Dr. Richardson, had general supervision of the hospitals, which as well were in charge of a resident doctor. As the construction progressed the GTP operated hospitals at Entwistle, Big Eddy (Mile 14), Prairie Creek, Mictte River (Mile 111), and Tête Jaune Cache.

Some of the smaller hospitals such as that at Miette River (Fitzhugh) were of frame construction. The one at Prairie Creek was a long, rambling log shack, unprepossessing on the outside but spotless inside with its operating room and its rows of cots and its white linen. One ward was kept for accident cases, while the other was reserved for contagious diseases.

The most feared disease was typhoid and rarely was one of the hospitals free of a case or its nearby graveyard without its quota of its victims. Typhoid, though not nearly so common as it had been a decade earlier, nevertheless exacted its toll everywhere. During October, 1910, the Edmonton hospitals cared for sixty-four typhoid patients, of which sixty-one had been brought in from outside the city, and of them, twenty-eight had come from the GTP grade.

Notwithstanding hospitals, however, most men preferred to treat their ailments with a remedy which at times was hard to come by and at other times flowed like water. Federal Government legislation prohibited the sale or even the possession of alcoholic liquor within a specified and generous distance of any railroad construction job. West of Stony Plain the federal authorities clamped down and no legal liquor could be had beyond there until the GTP construction had moved well on toward the mountains and the railroad began operating its regular trains, first to Wolf Creek and then to Prairie Creek, and so on.

Drink was a curse of construction camps. The Mounties did a good job of halting the flow of bootleg liquor, but in spite of all that the two or three men they could assign to that service could do, some bootleggers sneaked into the camps. For perhaps two or three weeks when no liquor was in sight, the clink of shovels and the bumping of wheelbarrows went on at a regular rhythm and a fast pace. But then some bootlegger would get in and the whole camp seemed to go mad. If drink were available the men just had to have it, and the contractor, not concerned with moral issues, shut his eyes to the legality of the liquor the men consumed. Very often indeed, the hard drinkers were the best workmen when sober.

Yet the proscription of alcohol by legislation tended to defeat its own object, for it was available in other forms besides the distillers' shiny bottles, the bootleggers' dubious services, or even the moonshiners' barbarous brew. Rubbing alcohol sold for laborers' sprains, red ink, which would have been used on the contractor's books in case of a deficit, and even the cooks' harmless-looking lemon extract, could all on occasion be used to "get a jag on" and innocent-appearing grocery stores did a thriving business selling extract at ten times its landed cost.

Out of dried apples, peaches, or other fruit, here and there well back in the bush "Blind Pigs" stewed many a wondrous concoction. Boiling the fruit with sugar, capturing the liquor and dosing it liberally with tobacco juice, opium or other narcotics, produced all degrees of a diabolically intoxicating drink known up and down the grade as rotgut.

In his book *The New Garden of Canada,* which contains a vivid description of building the GTP railway, F. A. Talbot gave his impressions of that rotgut whisky. Curiously enough, perhaps because of the interest he took in blasting the railway through tunnels and cuts or perhaps because of an ear hardly attuned to Canadian accents, he referred to it as "rock-cut." In any event, he gulped one drink of it, which he claimed was potent enough to last him a lifetime. Describing his reactions, he said:

"Within ten minutes of swallowing the liquor every part of the human engine sprang into active revolt. My head spun round faster than any teetotum yet designed, throbbed like a steam-hammer, and felt as if it were bursting in all directions. The abdominal muscles were contracted to the uttermost limit, while the whole frame vibrated with an intense chilling sensation. One could not walk; the limbs were as if paralysed, and one simply blundered and groped along. Some days elapsed before the effects of that glass of liquor wore off . . ."

So, to the accompaniment of moonshine and lemon extract, accidents and typhoid, and considerable hard feeling between contractors and laborers, thousands of men worked incredibly hard and lived under primitive conditions. At the end of the day or the week a large part of them, taking their vouchers to those who had amusement to sell, flocked into pool rooms, gamblers' tents, dance halls, or brothels, searching for relief from the bleak muddiness of their daily grind.

None of the temporary end-of-steel towns, Entwistle, Wolf Creek, Bickerdike, or any other, ever lacked enterprising characters offering relief at a price. While such shady pleasure vendors made up only a small portion of the town's citizens, who in the main were ordinary, decent people making an honest living by catering to the men's legitimate needs, the shysters nevertheless reaped a rich harvest. Moreover, they lent a life to the town out of all proportion to their numbers which but for them would have been as prosaic as a Presbyterian picnic on a drizzly afternoon.

Because of a spat between a RNWMP constable and an enthusiastic young missionary the *Edmonton Journal* has left a written record of the night life of Entwistle, the first end-of-steel town west of Edmonton. When in May, 1909, the ardent missionary first lifted the curtain on the little comedy, the grade had been finished but the steel had not reached the village. The bridge footings were under construction and gangs of men were still working on them, as well as at various points along the grade beyond there. Scattered here and there over the townsite, which J. G. Entwistle was developing and advertising but otherwise without much vestige of town planning, were a few small general stores, barns of a sort, a restaurant or two, and many log shacks, most of them with canvas roofs. The outstanding edifices were O'Grady's Pembina Hotel on the one hand and the somewhat isolated RNWMP barracks, first occupied in February, 1909.

Here and there, neither hiding their lights under a bushel nor flaunting their wares, were at least four houses of prostitution: one operated by Mrs. Campbell; one supervised by Lou Belle, a colored woman; a third one, and another with a canvas roof, occupied exclusively by Bessie, an independent young entrepreneur aged fifteen years. Gambling flourished in a few shacks and, although even the possession of liquor was a criminal offense, according to the missionary it was being sold at three and probably six places.

To maintain order in the best way he could short of locking everybody up in his new barracks, Constable Tyler kept an eye on the town, quelled its minor disturbances, and arrested bootleggers whenever he could get evidence. Anglican and Catholic clerics, wise to the failings of wayward mortals, came and went on their rounds, holding services, observing and regretting the excesses they saw and here and there lifting and encouraging a man who was slipping. Dr. Steele, a GTP physician, summing up the situation, said that the majority of the town's citizens who were on the side of law, order, and morality were seriously concerned about the wildness of parts of the town, but felt that no direct action could be taken or need be taken.

Entwistle, then, was not the type of hell hole of iniquity which had frequently existed in western America. It was a typical end-of-steel town where the large majority of good citizens saw many things they did not like and looked forward to better days. In Entwistle men and women, good and bad, led the kind of life they chose and were molested or unmolested as they chose. No shooting stained its record, no stabbings shook its serenity, and no killings marred the even, though bubbling, course of its days.

Then, at the end of May, 1909, a man we shall call Jones, the Methodist student missionary — a melodramatic soul — provided the color with which an Edmonton newspaper painted a lurid picture of Entwistle, calling it "the toughest town on the northwestern frontier." Jones, more wrapped in indignation than clothed in wisdom, was described as a squarely built, athletic type, "wise to the world" after having been several years in the "Secret Service on the Pacific Coast."

The reference to his being an athletic type should not go unnoticed, because he appears to have traded on his boxing ability. On one occasion, according to what a highly respected United Church minister told the writer, Jones goaded the Mountie into a fight in which the clerical gentleman won.

According to the Edmonton paper, Jones described Entwistle as a town where four hundred laborers "cut loose from authority, dropped the check reins from their passions and set up a wide open town after their own fashion, indulging in every form of vice and debauchery . . . In the face of threats of his extinction, he set up his tabernacle and held services every Sunday."

When the newspaper reached Entwistle the fat was in the fire. In real or feigned indignation, its more stable citizens, one and all, rose in their wrath, crying out for poor Jones's scalp. As they read further down the newspaper they discovered that on a Sunday morning as Jones was holding service in the Liberal

Hall, some men stood outside the windows "renting the air with ribald songs," and that bootleggers brought booze and sold it to the men as they came out from the service (no doubt assuaging the thirst after righteousness). Moreover, time and time again, Jones had unsuccessfully exhorted Constable Tyler to raid the liquor places. To strew thorns along Jones's dramatic path "several times his life had been threatened" and he had been told to get out. Someone had sent him a postcard depicting a winter view of the Pembina River and showing a hole cut in the ice. Written across it was the terse comment "The right opening for the right man — Rev. Jones."

By the time the townspeople read the newspaper article, which indeed revealed many truths, it was not the truth which hurt them so much as the fact that the man of God had laid bare their sociable little foibles to the world outside — the world hungry for gossip, the world ready to destroy reputations and ready to depress the price of Entwistle real estate. The aroused townsfolk held a meeting, roundly castigated Jones, and recorded a vote of confidence in the Mountie.

According to a later dispatch to the *Journal*, Jones had suffered in silence until February 21 when things got so bad he could stand it no longer. The previous night a dance in the Liberal Club had lasted until 8 a.m. Sunday morning. "That night two new prostitutes were brought out to Mrs. Campbell's dive. It just took Mr. Jones about an hour to get evidence and the place was raided Sunday night."

The RNWMP kept saying that they could not get evidence that would convict the offenders and Jones accused them of being willfully blind. The *Journal* carried more reports: "Gambling was going on regularly, liquor was being sold at three and probably six places. Four houses of prostitution were running. Drink was being manufactured out of tobacco, alcohol, molasses and drugs. Stores were running wide open on Sunday. Indecent photographs were being sold. . . .

"Bessie a prostitute of fifteen years lived in a tent, spreading disease broadcast. She claimed she had averaged $15 a day." Furthermore, one Sunday night about March 21, "the big negress of Mrs. Campbell's house of ill fame in a row bodily threw out three of the prostitutes." Then, perhaps in an effort to damn the hotelkeeper for a charitable act on a cold night, the correspondent continued: "They were given shelter in O'Grady's Pembina Hotel (unlicensed)."

Jones added fuel to the fire by declaring, "I could divulge the names of some of the business men of Entwistle whom I caught in a house of ill fame when I assisted Mr. Tyler to make a raid; but I consider myself more of a gentleman." When he was through with his charges, every man in the town, honest or dishonest, sincere or sly, would have taken an oath as to his absolute honesty, but on the score of popularity, all would have given him a wide berth.

In his enthusiasm Jones applied to J. W. Arnup, the J.P., and was given permission to carry a revolver, thus becoming one of the very few armed men in the town.

The uproar over the affair which, like bursting fireworks, threw sparks right, left and center, eventually set off an official investigation conducted by Superintendent Deane of the RNWMP, an inquiry wherein many witnesses, including Jones, were heard in their efforts to enlighten, confound, or confuse the court. Whatever Superintendent Deane's private opinion might have been and whatever he might have said to the Mounties on the side, they were exonerated.

On the stand as a witness, Jones, perhaps blushing a bit, revealed more of the cloak-and-dagger melodrama into which he had fallen. In an endeavor to get a conviction against the bootleggers, he explained, "On March 8, I went to Entwistle between eleven and twelve o'clock PM and disguised myself, and went into the Hub restaurant and the other between twelve and one AM." In the Hub restaurant, "pretending to be stricken with a violent attack of heart failure," he called for whisky. The keeper produced what in his innocence Jones supposed to be whisky. Jones pretended to partake of it and when sufficiently revived was removed to a bed. The druggist who had been summoned diagnosed his case, and upon the assurance that Jones had not been drinking for several days and that he did not get drunk only "once a year," suggested that the restaurant keeper sell him a bottle. In the presence of two witnesses, Entwistle and Marshall the druggist, he purchased a bottle for one dollar.

Evidently completely taken in by Jones's disguise, the restaurant owner, acting as any other charitable citizen would have, did what he could to comfort the stranger within his gates. Later in the evening Jones gave him an old purse containing about $2.40 for safekeeping.

Seeing his customer's apparently stringent financial condition the restaurateur offered him his dollar back. Jones refused, but in the morning the dollar was in the purse which was returned.

Leaving the restaurant keeper who had befriended him, Jones made straightway to Justice of Peace Arnup and laid a charge of selling liquor against his host.

During the investigation Jones admitted his unpopularity in Entwistle and attributed part of it to his action in deceiving the restaurant keeper, tricking him into selling liquor and then laying this charge.

Amid the raised eyebrows of the investigators, the Mountie, although soon to be moved to another detachment, was exculpated. Jones, perhaps somewhat wiser in the ways of the world, wandered away to other pastures. In spite of his dubious methods, his efforts undoubtedly had a salutary effect on conditions at Entwistle, which, pending the completion of the bridge, continued to be a busy place. Then as the steel advanced to Wolf Creek, many of its citizens, presumably including the druggist, the barber, the publican, and Lou Belle, the colored woman, moved west with it.

So, surveyors, droves of horses, and a crawling mass of laborers pushed the grade ever farther west. At the same time they dragged along a variety of camp followers, good and bad, honest merchants and restaurant proprietors, gamblers and bootleggers, and bringing up the rear, despairing missionaries and and watchful Mounties.

When in November, 1909, the first GTP train to carry commercial freight reached Entwistle, the town's boom was almost over. By that time Wolf Creek, sixty-three miles west at what everyone called Mile 129, was the focus of all attention. As the next bottleneck of contruction it promised to have an active, if maybe a short life. There, where the railway had to cross both the deep ravine of Wolf Creek and the canyon of the McLeod River and where along the half mile separating the two bridges the grade had to be excavated through a cut forty feet deep, the engineers anticipated a long delay before steel could be laid to the west bank of the McLeod River. Before that could be accomplished a total of 1,200 feet of bridging had to be erected and 130,000 cubic yards of material had to be shifted out of the cut.

Meantime, the temporary town of Wolf Creek came into being, and for many months hummed as the headquarters of all the exciting activity associated with building a railroad and catering to all the needs and whims of a thousand or so men.

Five separate construction camps, each with two to three hundred working men, were set up in selected spots in the deep valleys, or stretched out for a mile along the grade. Scattered about with little semblance of regularity were places of business, conscientious or clandestine, including one bank, half a dozen stores, and twice as many restaurants and stopping places. One popular "stopping place" was Dad Renshaw's, with its bunkhouses, kitchen, and dining room, where freighters could look forward to a copious and well-cooked meal. There were a few pool rooms, a drug store and barber and blacksmith shops; and with their rolls of maps, real estate men buzzed about.

For a few months a public school did its best to serve a floating population.

Set slightly apart from the main town were the two buildings of the Royal North West Mounted Police from where Inspector Tucker and three constables maintained order in the town and for miles along the grade. Considering their nature, Wolf Creek and the other construction towns as far west as the British Columbia border were remarkable for their lack of lawlessness. Devoted preachers visited Wolf Creek and the camps, slanting their services in the direction of a breezy bit of a sermon and advising the men to keep away from the wickednesses of this world. They held services in bunkhouses, cook tents, and pool rooms, sometimes with a quiet little poker game going on in the adjoining room, or even in sight, while as often as not a big grader stood just outside the meetinghouse drinking a bottle of rye and between gulps catching snatches of the sermon.

Such, then, was Wolf Creek, a jumble of shacks of all shapes, sizes, and materials, a town of perhaps two thousand souls at the height of its short active life. Its end-of-steelers were a rugged, stalwart lot who made their way by clinging to the edge of civilization and hovering on the verge of the unknown country beyond it. Perhaps it would be unfair to say that they reveled in roughing it, but they certainly made light of privation, and in doing so, removed much of the privation from the lives of the laborers. They were born hustlers, snatching opportunities from the town or from the preparations for the railway which were being made far ahead.

10

MOUNTAINEERS, GEOLOGISTS, AND SURVEYORS

ALTHOUGH the excitement of the decade of railway endeavor, which by the beginning of 1910 had laid the rails west to Wolf Creek, had eclipsed all other activity along the route leading to the Yellowhead Pass, nevertheless other ventures were afoot. For one thing, the mountain climbers had continued their attempts to scale new peaks in the Jasper area.

For a while after Coleman's 1896 attempt and Collie's and Woolley's in 1898 to solve the riddle of Mounts Hooker and Brown, the Yellowhead area had been left alone. In 1907, however, after wondering about what advantage he could get from the GTP grade west of Edmonton, Professor A. P. Coleman left the CPR at Lake Louise early in August with the hope of reaching and climbing Mount Robson that fall. He was accompanied by his brother, L. Q. Coleman, and Rev. George Kinney. On their way north after meeting Mary Schäffer near the headwaters of the Saskatchewan River, the party reached the Athabasca and descended it into the Jasper valley. Crossing the river in the vicinity of today's Jasper Park Lodge, they met three GTP packers on their way west with twenty-one horses.

From that point to Mount Robson the climbers had a well-cut pack trail to follow, but, although they did not have to use their axes, there were other drawbacks, which Coleman described: "In the soft parts it was too well beaten down by hundreds of hoofs into pools of foul mud with the odour of a dunghill, and sometimes just to one side lay the festering carcass of a beast that had gone that way once too often."

Eventually, after having been nearly six weeks en route from the CPR, the climbers reached the point on the Fraser River where the highest peak in the Rocky Mountains, Mount Robson, elevation 12,972 feet, made them gape in awe. But they had arrived too late in the season, and returning to civilization along the pack trail toward Edmonton, they met Lewis Swift and some of the Moberlys. Then Coleman's party hurried on to reach the "metropolis, Big Eddy, which at last was announced by a chorus of horse-bells. Its two tents and one log-house lay before us, with the fine ox-bow curve of the river below; and a picturesque medley of barking dogs and variously-coloured ponies showed that other travellers were there before us. The French storekeeper, white-haired but rather youthful in face, welcomed us and offered supplies at prices reasonable for the region . . ."

A few years before Coleman's visit, Ben Berthoux, a one-time chef in CPR hotels, had built a small post on the high bank overlooking the Big Eddy. Somewhat later on, Alex Sinclair came to keep him company by putting up a small shack on the flats below. In the fall of 1906 a young man named Ansell moved in with Sinclair, all unaware that within a few months he and his host were to be involved in a tragedy.

That fall a young rancher, named Hornbeck, from southern Alberta had planned to winter a small band of good Percheron horses on the far-famed grass at Prairie Creek. To help him, he brought a young companion named Harry Neergard. By the time the herd got as far as the Big Eddy, however, the infamous winter of 1906-07 had set in, so he decided to pasture his horses along Sundance Creek. There, about a mile from Ben Berthoux' store, he built a shack.

The fall and winter were extremely cold, with a heavy fall of snow, and early in February the horses began to die of starvation. Finally, only his favorite saddle pony remained alive and it became obvious that it could not last much longer. The dark, drear days had made their mark on Hornbeck too, and his loss and frustration became a heavier load than he could bear. When he had to shoot his pet pony, something in his brain died with the horse.

For weeks Harry Neergard had been worrying about Hornbeck and when he saw the turn his companion took, the young man fled to the safety of Alex·Sinclair's cabin. Hornbeck brooded all night and bright and early the next morning turned up at Ben Berthoux' store as a raging maniac, brandishing his well-oiled rifle. Ben talked him out of shooting and quickly abandoned the store and also ran for refuge in Alex's cabin.

For the rest of the day Hornbeck remained in the store. Next morning the men in the shack two hundred feet below watched him as he came out and then had to flatten themselves on the floor as he began firing shots which smacked into the logs of the cabin and punctured its stovepipe. Soon the demented man tired of shooting and went back into the store.

That night Harry Neergard strapped on his snowshoes and

headed toward Lac Ste. Anne, one hundred miles away, to fetch the Mounted Police. At daybreak Hornbeck reappeared and sent three or four shots smacking into the logs of Sinclair's shack and once more disappeared into the store. But in a few minutes he came out again carrying a sack of flour and his hunting knife. Ripping the sack to shreds and scattering the contents all over the snow seemed to please him so much that he went in and got a bag of beans, which he also dispersed over the drifts. Re-entering the store, he kept out of sight for the rest of the day. For the next two or three days he repeated the performance — lobbing a few bullets at the shack and destroying food.

By that time Ben Berthoux, Alex Sinclair and Ansell felt they had endured enough. Since it might be several days before the Mountie arrived and since, when he did, either he or Hornbeck might get shot, they resolved to take the situation into their own hands. Next morning before daylight, they crawled up the hill and concealed themselves at a point where they would be able to see the madman as he emerged. They had not been waiting long before he came out carrying his rifle. Ansell and Berthoux watched Sinclair, and when he nodded, their three shots rang out. Hornbeck crumpled on the flour-littered snow.

When the policeman arrived a few days later with Donald MacDonald as a guide drawing a flat sleigh on which to tie the madman for his journey back to Lac Ste. Anne, the three men told the officer what had taken place. Shutting up their cabin and the store, they lashed the corpse to the sled and accompanied the Mountie on their way to be tried for manslaughter. In due course, they were all acquitted on grounds of self-defense.

When in August, 1908, bound westward for another attempt on Mount Robson, the two Colemans and Rev. Mr. Kinney set out over the trail from Lac Ste. Anne, John Yates took them in hand. In the Jasper valley they met Adolphus Moberly, grandson of H. J. Moberly, and because of his knowledge of the area to the rear of Mount Robson, induced him to accompany them. With him he took his wife and young family. Of this young man, aged about twenty-one, Coleman said:

"He was the most typical and efficient savage I ever encountered, a striking figure, of powerful physique and tireless muscles, and thoroughly master of everything necessary for the hunter in the mountains. His fine black horse was like unto him, and quite ruled over our bunch of ponies, in spite of being a stranger among them. Mounted erect on his horse, with gay clothing and trappings, Adolphus was the ideal centaur . . .''

Once more Robson's cold, blue magnificence, calling upon its allies, cloudy weather, snowfalls, and blizzards, defeated them, even though Mr. Kinney, with immense pluck and a well-justified confidence in his powers as a climber, made one more fruitless effort. Three weeks they had spent making futile sorties from their base camp but finally they had to turn their pack horses east toward Edmonton, three hundred miles away. They did so, however, with the firm resolve of having Yates take them back to Robson's rugged base the next year.

The next assault upon Mount Robson came within a few feet of success, but in spite of its failure it stands out as such a supreme triumph of one man's courage and stamina that it ranks high amongst the epic achievements of mortal effort. When the Colemans and Rev. G. B. Kinney had returned to Edmonton in the fall of 1908 they had made tentative arrangements with John Yates to be ready to conduct them to the vicinity of Tête Jaune Cache the following August. But the fates and Kinney's all-consuming craving to be the conqueror of Mount Robson disrupted that expedition. In May, 1909, Kinney heard that the famous British climbers, Amery, Mumm, and Hastings, planned to try their gear on Mount Robson. Obsessed with his passion to be the first to master the mighty mountain and determined at all costs not to be beaten by "a party of foreigners," he advised Coleman in Toronto and Yates at his Hobo Ranch west of Lac Ste. Anne that in June he was going to set out, alone if necessary. Yates, however, wrote back protesting that normally June was far too early for such an expedition into the mountains, particularly so that year.

When, all alone, except for two or three pack horses, Kinney arrived at Yates's ranch, he found the packer away on some other venture which did not involve penetrating the mountain passes. Undaunted, Kinney set out alone, but in the Jasper valley met a kindred spirit, young Donald "Curly" Phillips, who was later to become one of the famous guides in Jasper Park. Although up to that time Curly had never climbed a mountain, the idea of challenging Mount Robson, the highest peak in the Rockies, did not deter him, and he threw in his lot with Kinney.

Ascending the north shoulder in much the same manner Kinney had done the previous year, the pair spent one night at the 9,500-foot level and continued their climb the next day, only to be forced to return to their base camp by ferocious storms. After delays due to weather and a few other attempts, they set out on August 12 on their last try, and by dark had reached the 10,500-foot level. Chopping away the ice and snow, they arranged a bed of stones for the night.

Next day, toiling for five hours after leaving their inhospitable couch, the pair reached an overhanging snow cornice five hundred feet from the summit. Moving slowly and cautiously, they worked their way upward until Kinney "struck the edge of the snow with the staff of my ice axe and it cut into my very feet, and through the little gap that I had made in the cornice, I was looking down a sheer wall of precipice that reached to the glacier at the foot of Berg Lake, thousands of feet below. I was on a needle peak that rose so abruptly that even cornices cannot build out very far on it. Baring my head I said: 'In the name of Almighty God, by Whose strength I have climbed here, I capture this peak Mt. Robson, for my own country, and for the Alpine Club of Canada.' "

For lack of material they were unable to build a cairn at the spot, which amidst whirling snows they took to be the summit. After a nerve-racking descent of seven hours, the wornout pair, alternating between exhaustion and elation, reached their base camp long after dark. The "foreigners" had been foiled. Mount Robson had been conquered by a Canadian!

Meanwhile, the Amery, Mumm, and Hastings party, the "foreigners," accompanied by the famous Swiss guide, Moritz Inderbinen, and John Yates, was making its way west toward the fascinating mountain. At Ewan Moberly's they met Rev. G. B. Kinney and Curly Phillips returning from what both believed to have been a successful assault on Mount Robson. As a matter of fact, later knowledge of the mountain indicated that the summit Mr. Kinney had scaled was lower by a matter of yards than a nearby peak. Until that came to light, however, he conscientiously believed that he had been the first man to stand on the summit of the great mountain. While disappointed that someone should have beat him to the top of it, Amery described Kinney's climb as "one of the most gallant performances in modern mountaineering history . . . they finally managed in the course of two days of continuous climbing to reach the top of the northwestern rock ridge." And as another member of Amery's party said: "Surely no mountaineering success was ever more richly deserved, or won by a finer exhibition of courage, skill and indomitable perseverance . . ."

Unfortunately for Amery's group, when they got to Mount Robson the weather was most unfavorable, and although they tried several times, none of the party got beyond the 10,000-foot mark — some three thousand feet short of the summit. Eventually Amery and Mumm realized that the bad weather and the lateness of the season had defeated them for another year, and they returned to Edmonton.

Though the mountain had proven difficult to defeat, its opponents, a dozen or so men, had turned out to be equally difficult to deter. At every opportunity they returned to the attack, and A. L. Mumm and some of his 1909 colleagues, with the addition of Norman Collie, did so the following year. Once more Moritz Inderbinen came to support them, and John Yates packed for the party, which was able to go as far west as Wolf Creek on the newly laid steel of the GTP. Assisting Yates were Fred Stephens and G. Swain, but once more Mount Robson, shielding itself in its mantles of cloud and storm, turned back their assault.

Much to the delight of A. O. Wheeler, head of the Alpine Club of Canada, all those assaults on the imposing peak, besides adding to the knowledge of the whole area, were instrumental in focusing world-wide attention on the Yellowhead Pass region. As a result, in 1911, he found it easy to launch a combined mountaineering and scientific effort aimed at unveiling more of the secrets of the Robson Massive and involving some specialists from the Smithsonian Institute. Obtaining monetary aid from the GTP and some assistance from the Alberta, British Columbia, and Federal Governments, Wheeler's party left Edmonton on July 1 and rode the train to where the rails ended at Brulé siding in the Jasper valley. Some of the party, however, including Fred Brewster and Byron Harmon, had chosen to reach the Jasper valley by coming direct from Banff along the trails which Coleman and others had pioneered.

Into his party Wheeler had concentrated men of many outstanding talents, including some who were to keep in contact with the Jasper area and in their devotion to the mountains were to become outstanding figures. Two of those were Fred Brewster, who later on, with his headquarters in Jasper, became world-famous as a guide and as the one man with an encyclopedic knowledge of the mountains, and Byron Harmon, who, although making Banff his home, was for decades the doyen of mountain photographers. Curly Phillips, of course, was indispensable in the transport department, and along with John Yates and Shand-Harvey, kept the pack horses dancing attendance on the climbers and scientists. Rev. G. B. Kinney, who was to play an assisting role, joined the group before it left the Jasper valley. Although Wheeler had not intended that any of the party should actually climb Mount Robson, he induced a young Austrian mountaineer, Conrad Kain, to join the party.

While Curly Phillips, Fred Brewster, and Shand-Harvey were moving the party west and while the Smithsonian people were scurrying about after voles, the climbers found the mountain peaks irresistible. Before leaving the Jasper valley Conrad Kain and Rev. Mr. Kinney practically ran up Pyramid Mountain, to become the first to stand on its peak. Meanwhile, A. O. Wheeler, looking at what is now known as Mount Edith Cavell from the site of what he called the government townsite of Fitzhugh, regarded it wistfully and referred to it not by the name the earlier voyageurs had used — La Montagne de la Traverse — but as Mount Fitzhugh.

In due course Wheeler's party left the slash of the railway grade some fifteen miles west of the summit of the pass and struck off along the Moose River toward Mount Robson. They enjoyed good weather, and eventually came away well pleased with the results of their efforts. Not only did the Smithsonian people leave the area with their bags well stuffed with specimens, but under Wheeler's eye the surveying men had climbed thirty peaks and mapped an area of about one hundred square miles.

Shand-Harvey reported that Conrad Kain also enjoyed himself: "He was just crazy about climbing mountains. One afternoon on that trip in 1911, when everyone else was resting, he set off alone and wasn't back by dark. We were all worried about him, but before breakfast he showed up and said that he had climbed Mount Whitehorn, which is five or six miles west of Mount Robson and something over eleven thousand feet high.

"Said he'd built a cairn on it and left a note in it. Now, everybody trusted him implicitly, but a story like that — going all alone and spending the night at some point on the way down — was hard to believe. Later on, of course, his story was confirmed."

In 1907, as mentioned, A. P. Coleman met the famous Mary Schäffer well up on the headwaters of the Saskatchewan River.

A most interesting woman, she was one of the first of her sex to penetrate the remote recesses of the mountains as a tourist, and was sufficiently entranced by the scenery to bear the extreme hardships of pack horse travel in the regions where pack trails were nonexistent. That year, on her first major trip, she heard of the existence of the mysterious Maligne Lake and resolved at all costs to visit it as soon as she could.

In 1908 after pausing briefly at Brazeau Lake, she crossed Pobokton Pass and then went on to Maligne Lake, which she found so marvelous as to justify all her effort and expense. "There burst upon us," Mary wrote, "that which all in our little company agreed was the finest view any of us had ever beheld in the Rockies . . ." After spending a couple of weeks enjoying its scenery, her small party tried to take their horses down the Maligne River, but four days of chopping their way forward convinced everyone that further progress in that direction was impracticable. Turning back, they descended the Sunwapta and Athabasca rivers to the vicinity of Jasper.

Because her guide was not familiar with the area, they took their horses over the hummock which is known now as Old Fort Point. Then in seeking a way to cross the Maligne River they ascended its left bank and crossed in the vicinity of the canyon. Coming down its right bank they could see Swift's place on the far side of the Athabasca, and then called at John Moberly's house but found it temporarily deserted. Looking across the river they could see two dugouts, and by firing two shots attracted Swift's attention. When he brought the crude craft over for them he was astounded at the presence of the two women, Mary and her companion. "Women in your party?" he said. "What brought you here, prospecting or timber cruising? I been in this valley thirteen years and you are the first white women I've seen around these parts."

Leaving Swift's next day to ascend the Miette River, the party soon met John Moberly and his family returning from some expedition. "It looked more like the moving of an orphanage. In all they counted eight, Mrs. Moberly bringing up the rear in a dignified manner, carrying a small infant under one arm. She smiled a pleasant smile at our greeting and we each passed on our way."

Following the atrocious pack trail west for six days Mary and her associates reached the foot of awesome Mount Robson. At Derr Creek they met several prospectors and at Tête Jaune

Cache found a Mr. Reading, from Philadelphia, sharing a shack and a small vegetable garden with his American friend, Finch. While there Mary was thrilled by spawning salmon swarming and splashing in the Fraser River. Reading took her over to old fireplaces and cellar holes which indicated where the CPR surveyors' depot had been during the 1870's. Not far from them he showed her the remains of a tiny cabin seven feet by ten feet, of which the logs were spongy and rotten, and she wondered if it could have been Tête Jaune's cache.

When she returned to the Jasper valley a week or so later, she went over to see what she called "Old Henry House," and commented: "Opposite us lay all that remained of Henry House, an old North West Fur Trading Company's post. Built as a rival to Jasper House, the site was close to the water's edge opposite the mouth of the Maligne. All that was left of it were the remains of two chimneys and a few scarred logs." In the case of these remains her information and speculations were incorrect but she allowed for that possibility by saying: ". . . perhaps they were the remains of Walter Moberly's CPR Depot."

Her observations on Lewis Swift's establishment are on much more certain ground. Her remarks of her 1908 visit, coupled with those of A. P. Coleman, who also called on Swift that year, give a good idea of Swift's farm in the shadow of the Palisades.

Lewis John Swift was one of that remarkable breed known all over the western States as "mountain men." Several of his kind had wandered into Alberta — Jack Gregg at Prairie Creek, Sam Livingstone, who finally settled down at Calgary, Dan Noyes, and others. Wandering about with a couple of pack horses, a few traps, a gun, and a gold pan, they would build a shack in some chosen spot and proceed to earn their living there for a year or so until the itch to wander would send them off in some new direction.

Thus it came about that Swift finally settled in Jasper. There he married and raised his small brood of healthy children. In the course of time, he added a Percheron stallion to his band of livestock. The forests and crags supplied most of his meat, his few acres provided his cereals, and except for sugar, tea and tobacco, he was independent of the outside world.

His wife, Suzette, like all the mixed-blood women of the era, kept a clean, tidy house. Cooking in copper kettles suspended in the fireplace and making most of her containers, such as milk pans, out of birchbark sewn with fine roots and gummed, she served fragrant meals. On the walls and rafters of her house hung many roots, herbs, and vegetables, as well as bacon, hams, and swatches of sphagnum moss. It served her in place of cotton for many purposes — to line the baby's bed, to use as diapers, to scrub with, and to wipe pots and pans.

With grease and wood ashes she made her own soap and with a broom tied from willow twigs kept her floor spic and span. With cloth bought at a trading post she made her family's fabric clothes and occasionally cut out and sewed one of the black dresses that were fashionable at the time and which she decorated with fine stitching and lace. She was proud of her needlework — a native art which she practiced with rare perfection. Most of the family's clothes, however, were made from buckskin, artistically ornamented with beads and embroidered with rich-colored silks.

Having a wife like that and living on his own land, surrounded by satisfactions of body and spirit, Swift was at peace with the present while he waited for the wealth of the future. By 1909 his vision of future wealth was beginning to dim. The Grand Trunk had surveyed through the valley without indicating more interest in his land than buying a narrow strip of right of way. "All right," thought Swift, "the other transcontinental, the Canadian Northern, is surveying towards Jasper, and surely it will need space for a future city and for its divisional point." But other clouds were drifting across his horizon. Back in 1907 the Dominion Government had set apart a vast area east of the summit of the Rockies as a national park and had selected an area some six miles south of Swift's ranch for its headquarters. Now it was rumored that all squatters and freeholders within the park were to be moved out. Swift began to worry.

Though he had lived on his land since 1895, he had never taken any steps towards officially recording his interest in it. Near the end of January, 1910, shortly after the boundaries of Jasper National Park had been established, J. J. Maclaggan came from Ottawa to buy out the claims of any residents who had homes in the area. They included Lewis Swift, the four Moberlys — Ewan, John, Dolphus and William — as well as Isadore Finlay and Adam Joachim. All the natives accepted the offer whereby the Government would pay cash for their buildings, corrals and other improvements, and would permit them to relocate on land outside the park. Swift, however, refused to consider the possibility of moving.

Most of the natives, including John and Ewan Moberly, went to Edmonton and purchased wagons and plows. John moved his family to Prairie Creek and took a quarter section which is still owned by his descendants. Ewan and his sons, as well as Adam Joachim, chose land at Grande Cache.

For a while it looked as though Swift would lose his land and only be paid for the improvements. After some correspondence in which the authorities were inclined to disregard his claim, he made a trip to Edmonton in August, 1910, to see what he could do. Fortunately he was successful and a month later he was granted title to the S.E. 15-46-1-6, the 160 acres which included his buildings. Once he had obtained that, he absolutely refused to sell out to the park authorities.

By the time the GTP had laid its rails to Wolf Creek railroad employees, park officials, and mountain climbers were not the only people interested in the Jasper valley and its eastern foothills. Concealed beneath the swaying forests lay seams of coal, a hitherto useless wealth, which in various cutbanks here and there were exposed, awaiting the prying eyes of geologists and prospectors.

When ascending the ice of the Athabasca River in the vicinity of modern Whitecourt in January, 1859, Dr. Hector, the geologist of the Palliser Expedition, noted strata of coal, and later when he spent some time at Jasper House mentioned other coal seams. Sandford Fleming's reports also mentioned coal in the vicinity of the Pembina and McLeod rivers. Finally, James McEvoy, the geologist who in 1898 had named Folding Mountain, confirmed the fact that the area which later came to be known as the Coal Branch had vast resources of the black mineral.

At the time this information was of merely academic interest; there was no demand for the coal and no way of moving it to any market anyway. When, however, in 1903 Sir Wilfrid Laurier announced that a new transcontinental had been conceived and everyone assumed that it would go through the Yellowhead Pass, the coal fields' prospects looked a little better. Then, when it was indicated that the CNR might also be built through the pass, they improved considerably.

During 1907, with the CNR already running to Edmonton and the GTP rushing its line across the prairies and with the knowledge that both of them would not only provide access to markets but in their own operations would be good markets for coal, the Geological Survey of Canada sent D. B. Dowling to make a more detailed study of the outcroppings at the headwaters of the Pembina and McLeod rivers. Approaching the Coal Branch area by ascending the Brazeau River and leaving it by descending the Rocky River to the Jasper valley, he reported the presence of large coal seams. On his way back to Edmonton he noted outcroppings of the coal near Prairie Creek.

But several enterprising individuals, including P. A. Robb, after whom the town of Robb was named, and R. W. (Bob) Jones, one of the divisional engineers on the GTP, could not wait for official geologists and prospected the area and staked claims. It was Bob Jones who bridged the gap between the white man's capital and the Indians' detailed knowledge of the secrets of the wild water courses. He asked Jack Gregg, who was ranching at Prairie Creek, if he knew of any good seams of coal. Jack's wife Mary was a half-breed girl by the name of Cardinal, whose ancestry, renowned for its faithful voyageurs and guides, stretched far back into the annals of the fur trade. She guided Jones and her husband to outcroppings in the Coal Branch area.

Before long, various companies, obtaining the support of capital from eastern Canada, the United States, Great Britain, and even France, had taken up claims. In 1909 the Yellow Head Pass Coal and Coke Company filed at Coalspur and began development. Twenty or so miles south of there, at what became Lovett, the Pacific Pass Coal Fields Ltd. began running entries into the seams, and soon many companies, including the Mountain Park Coal Co. Ltd., became interested.

When there was some likelihood of coal mines starting in what is known now as the Coal Branch, it was necessary for the Dominion Government's Department of Surveys to run some survey lines into the area. In 1907 A. H. Hawkins, DLS, did his best to extend the 13th Base Line west from the vicinity of the upper tributaries of Wolf Creek through what is now Coalspur until it crossed the Athabasca River near present-day Pocahontas.

The winter of 1906-07 was probably the most severe in white men's knowledge, and Hawkins had the bad luck to have to start into the muskeg west of Edmonton during the succeeding late, rainy spring. Bad weather delayed his departure from Edmonton until June 7, and then, hiring wagons, he reached the crossing of the Pembina River ten days later. From there he took to pack horses and found the trail "very bad indeed; in many places being merely a streak of mud through the forest rather than a horse trail, and constant showers did not improve its condition. Progress was accordingly very slow, as we were forced to relay over the worst portions, and unpacking and pulling horses from mud-holes was an hourly occurrence."

His tribulations had only started. From a point near Carrot Creek he followed a vestiginal trail south. After plunging through muskeg day after day, his progress was so slow that before he even reached the point where his survey was to start he had to find a way out to the Big Eddy to get more supplies. Not until September 5 was Hawkins in a position to set up his transit, "having occupied almost three months in getting to the work and making a trail over which we could get in sufficient supplies."

As rapidly as he could and in spite of five or six inches of heavy, wet snow, Hawkins ran the line west over the hill immediately north of modern Coalspur. By then the party was out of supplies again and had to cut a trail to the Big Eddy, which they reached on October 14. Not until two weeks later was he able to start producing the line west from Coalspur. On November 19, when he had carried it far enough to cross the McLeod River near the big sweep it makes towards the west, winter set in and he started for Edmonton, which he reached on December 20. It had taken him all season to survey some fifty miles of line.

Such was surveying in the muskeg of the foothills in pack horse days. None but the breed of men who devoted their lives to it would have endured it.

But Hawkins was not through with the 13th Base Line. For the balance of the winter he extended the 12th Base Line as far west as a point near the Brazeau River about twelve miles south of what became the coal mine at Lovett. Starting from there on May 14, 1908, he worked his way back to where he had discontinued the survey of the 13th Base Line near the McLeod River. In doing so he met a party which was prospecting for coal in the Coal Branch area.

Unlike his bout with muskeg, Hawkins enjoyed the work entailed in carrying the line west over the mountains to the Athabasca River. Crossing the summit of the Folding Mountains, his party pressed on west, but the going was not easy, according to his report: "Chaining was found to be practically impossible across Drystone and Fiddle creek valleys, and had to be accomplished by following the ridges around from one peak to another. From one of these ridges one could throw a stone into the valley of either the Drystone, Fiddle creek, or McLeod, all of which are timbered with stunted spruce and jackpine, with a large amount of windfall. The summit of Folding range at the time of my visit was covered with several varieties of beautiful wild flowers, forget-me-nots, white heather, and a very fine moss flower, besides several other varieties, which in a measure rewarded one for the rather arduous climb to reach them . . .

"The several branches of Fiddle creek were truly a fearsome sight, as in many places the gorge was cut through solid rock, that towers six or eight hundred feet above the bed, which is composed of boulders of all shapes and sizes, intermixed with logs as though hurled together by some Titanic hand into a most incomprehensible jumble. The climbing was so arduous and so wearing on shoe leather, that none of the party had the courage or ambition to go to the hot springs, said to be on the south or main branch of this creek, as by this time it had become necessary to devise all sorts of means to prolong the life of boots and shoes."

While Hawkins had been struggling through muskeg or clinging to cliffs, the CNR survey crews were also in the area trying to select the final route their railway should take through the valley. By midsummer, 1909, following up their trial surveys of three years earlier, they had picked out the exact line they wanted as far west as the summit of Tête Jaune's pass.

Even though they had hammered in a definite line of stakes leading up the Athabasca and the Miette rivers to the summit, they still found a discouraging lack of definiteness in the route by which their railway was to leave Edmonton. As early as 1907 Collingwood Schreiber, the Dominion Government railway engineer, had emphatically pointed out the sheer folly of allowing two transcontinental lines to build west from Edmonton, but no one, least of all the promoters and politicians, seemed to have heeded him. Also, in some manner the GTP had put the hex on the line the CNR had graded from Stony Plain to Wabamun, and in fact had torn holes in that grade and crossed it with their own steel. Although as late as March, 1910, the CNR officials announced that their transcontinental would continue west from Stony Plain, the survey parties sent out to look for a line from St. Albert to Lac Ste. Anne knew better. By June,

1910, the CNR had given up continuing west from Stony Plain and was assembling contractors and men and sending them out to work west of St. Albert.

11

TWO RAILROADS COMPLETED

BY AUGUST, 1910, Foley, Welch and Stewart had taken contracts for the grade from Wolf Creek to Tête Jaune Cache. As their first step they started the cutting and building of a tote road 184 miles long to the Cache. Before a single wagon load could be dispatched from Wolf Creek, that road, costing some $1,000 per mile, had to be built through the forest. With axes, picks, shovels, and horse scrapers, the crew assailed the terrain, gouging into hillsides, bridging creeks, cutting off minor humps, and filling up minor hollows. They installed ferries over the larger streams and for hundreds of yards at a time they corduroyed stretches of muskeg. For the first fifty miles west of Wolf Creek, through the dense timber and the tamarack muskeg, the road passed through Alberta's rainiest belt. In spite of the care spent on its building, the road soon became a series of mudholes.

Dotted along the road by the time it was finished, a hundred construction camps hummed with activity as they lived out their few brief weeks or months of existence. Crawling along the road freighters' wagons or sleighs carried loads of a wide diversity, including food, forage, timbers, and machinery. During the winter of 1910-11 the tote road saw the passage of thirty thousand tons westward out of Wolf Creek.

Its first eight-mile stretch brought the freighters to Edson, the spot in the muskeg which was destined to be the GTP divisional point. F. A. Talbot's description of its appearance in June, 1910, in his *The New Garden of Canada* is worth quoting:

". . . Imagine a stretch of densely wooded country, with the bush as thick as the jungle, and about 20 feet or so in height. A square mile of this is pegged off. The railway station site is selected, and immediately opposite extends what is to be eventually the principal thoroughfare. On either side, at regular intervals, are run parallel roads of uniform width. From each of these streets, at intervals of 300 feet, transverse highways are driven at right angles.

"At the time we rode into Edson one or two of the main thoroughfares had been defined, but the scrub had been cleared only just widely enough to permit a wagon to pass. As we looked down the main street, our view was obstructed by an ugly square-shaped black building. We turned towards it, and found that it was the hotel! Boniface was a Chinaman, and he had been the first to reach the place, had run up a wooden building of two floors, and had covered it all over externally with tarred felt to keep out water and for warmth. We could not see a soul in sight . . .''

Although Talbot did not see any other residents, many of the uncleared lots had already been sold, for like all new towns in the Canadian West, Edson experienced a real estate boom. Promoters in Edmonton put on a whirlwind campaign to sell lots to the wise as well as the unwary in this period when western Canada was swept with a townsite speculating mania. Europeans traveling through Canada or the United States rarely failed to express their amazement at what they called the new continent's strange "quest for the Almighty Dollar."

In the case of Edson with its railway divisional point and its adjacent resources, speculators, though often disappointed and frequently bankrupted, were on surer ground than a glance at the quaking muskeg of the railway yards might have indicated. Unlike many dream towns, Edson was destined to have a future. When about the end of July, 1910, the rails had been laid that far, merchants, tradesmen, and speculators moved in and transformed the hillside. In short order they stripped the bush off nearly a square mile, laid out several streets, balanced thousands of feet of siding tracks precariously on top of the muskeg, and ran up an amazing assortment of residences and commercial buildings opening on to uneven wooden sidewalks.

In spite of muskeg underfoot, the town was sitting on top of the world. Hundreds of men were working along the railway grade to the west. Other hundreds were rushing another grade from Bickerdike, seven miles away, toward the newly opened mines up the Coal Branch. Several settlers, not too well versed in distinguishing good land from poor, were homesteading all around the town. Moreover, the rush to homesteads in the Peace River country was under way, and since Edson was the end of steel closest to Grande Prairie, its newly formed Board of Trade took steps to cut out a trail to that destination. With such activities afoot, all centering on the new town, Edson's prospects looked good.

In the fall of 1910 the Alberta Government sent out one of its capable young engineers, A. H. McQuarrie, to do what he could to build a trail through the 250 miles of forest from the GTP grade to Grande Prairie. Settlers were clamoring for such a short cut, and in an effort to further the interests of their plan for town development on a site called Medicine Lodge, Kimpe, Smith and McDermid had put men to work forcing a trail north from their properties and had actually done some work on it all the way from Medicine Lodge to the Little Smoky River. McQuarrie, taking pack horses from Wolf Creek to Medicine Lodge and heading north, looked over the embryo road and in his report to his superiors declared that it would never make a practical route north.

Meanwhile the Edson Board of Trade, not to be outdone by the nonexistent Medicine Lodge, cut a trail north from their town to the Athabasca River. With the limited funds at his disposal, McQuarrie did what he could to improve that trail and by the spring of 1911 considered it fit for travel. One of the first to take it was a party made up of Harvey Switzer, Dr. R. Shaw, and E. Davidson, who set out in March with a team of oxen. In the winter it was a fair trail, but in the summer its endless miles of mud and muskeg, alive with mosquitoes, made traveling it a discouraging process. During the four years of its life before a railway reached the Peace River country, several hundreds, mostly heading north, traveled it, for it led to the fertile lands of Saskatoon Lake, Beaverlodge, and Bear Lake.

But Foley, Welch and Stewart, with scores of other matters on their minds, gave little thought to the Grande Prairie trail. So as to do away with bottlenecks interfering with the railway's construction, they took steps to eliminate them well ahead of the time when the grade should reach them. They had got work started on the Big Eddy trestle, the rock cuts, the long trestle near Marlboro, the Prairie Creek bridge, and finally the bridges over the Athabasca and Snaring rivers in the Jasper valley about a hundred miles west of Edson. And to take supplies to the camps and material to the bridge and trestle sites, hundreds of freighters drove their slobbering oxen, their jaded horses, or their unflappable mules over the tote road.

Less than ten miles west of Edson the construction town of Bickerdike, at Mile 17 from Wolf Creek, sprang up overnight. It performed a dual role. From that point in the forest in July, 1909, the GTP surveyors started staking their Coal Branch line, and Bickerdike became the headquarteres for its construction.

Furthermore, being a mile or so west of the Big Eddy, it served as the camp town while the famous trestle was built.

Though Bickerdike knew it had slim chances of any permanent future, it did the best it could with what present it had. With its log shacks roofed with boards or canvas and plastered with clay, perched in a row above the grade in front of the assorted buildings of a main construction camp, it was a busy place. Actually more pretentious than its buildings were the rakish, homemade signs indicating the type of business carried on inside: ''Dad's Stopping House,'' ''Short Order Resterant,'' ''Poolroom,'' ''The Old Man's Place.'' Perhaps the best stopping place and restaurant was that run by Dad Renshaw, who, when Wolf Creek folded up, moved his popular family west to continue in business. Most of the unsavory establishments which had followed the construction workers through Entwistle and Wolf Creek moved west also to be in constant contact with the graders. Commenting on some of the inmates of those places, Hulbert Footner, who passed Bickerdike in a construction train in June, 1911, and who later wrote *New Rivers of the North,* said: ''. . . Never will we forget the haughtiness of certain dames who, clad in sweaters reaching to the ground, and with innumerable puffs in their back hair, came languidly down to the cars to inquire if there were any packages.''

The summer was a rainy one, most discouraging to engineers and contractors and damnably disheartening for laboring men slipping around in the mud. But on many fronts the work had to go ahead; on the bridge footings at Prairie Creek and farther west in the stream beds of the Athabasca and Snaring rivers, on innumerable ditches which had to be dug to drain the surface water off the muskeg, on minor trestles and a longer one at Marlboro near the trading post Dan Noyes had operated for years, and beyond that, on one of the first rock cuts just west of there.

Tackling the excavation west of Marlboro with picks, shovels, crowbars, and dynamite alone was too slow for Foley, Welch and Stewart. They had to find some way to bring a locomotive and steam shovels to bear on that rock cut. So even before the bridges at Wolf Creek were finished or the curving trestle flung over the Big Eddy gap, those giant machines had to be landed at the cut.

The moment the steel reached Wolf Creek in February, 1910, a work train of gravel cars and the two shovels pulled into the siding there. A swarm of men descended on the locomotive, the shovels, and the cars, dismantled them and loaded the pieces on a large fleet of specially built wide-bunked sleighs. Pulled by scores of horses and mules, the train of sleighs set off down the bank, across the ice of the McLeod, and up the other side. Load followed load through the hoar-frosted pines, as wheels and rails, buckets and booms, and a thousand other bits and pieces slid along the tote road. The boiler of the locomotive was blocked and nailed and chained on to one huge sleigh, while its tender, shored up and tied down, followed on another. The whole train, pack, package, and caboodle, disappeared into the bush. In a few days it emerged at the rock cut where ringing hammers and clanking spanners re-erected it into a work train and steam shovels. Before long, steam was raised, the shovels swung their jibs, and a long cut along the side of the cliff began to take shape.

Mile by mile and curve by curve the grade snaked west, climbing steadily toward the Obed ridge. What pretentions Medicine Lodge had once had never caused a ripple in the railway's progress. Medicine Lodge had hoped to be a town, but the steel rolling west flattened the wood pegs marking the subdivided day-dream lots and killed that dream. At Obed station the grade reached an elevation of some 3,560 feet — a height not to be exceeded until months later when, beyond Jasper, the railway began ascending the valley of the Miette on its way to the Yellowhead Pass with its elevation of 3,728. From Obed, through miles of fire-killed timber, the railway pressed on, heading mainly downhill now and dropping into the deep trough carved out by the Athabasca River on the right. In front and to the left the vast wall of the Rocky Mountains loomed up larger and brighter with every mile the construction crews advanced west. In due course the grade reached the bottleneck of the Prairie Creek bridge and there, while it was under construction, the town of Prairie Creek had its bright, ephemeral existence.

Before work had started on the eight-hundred-foot steel span designed to carry the rails high above the trickling creek with its insignificant flow, the population of the area had consisted of a few people around Gregg's ranch and store a mile or so from the mouth of the creek. Now, what the oldtimers called "the new town" was springing up on the east bank of the creek immediately above where the contractors had started work on the bridge. The usual stores, cafes, and joints sprang into being all within the range of vision of Inspector Tucker and Constable Nitchie Thorne of the Mounted Police at their recently built police detachment. Down by the river the Grand Trunk contractors had built a long, log hospital, divided into two wards each containing fifteen beds. Dr. Shillabeer was in charge, and his hands were soon full, for typhoid fever was rampant. For a while the hospital overflow had to be housed in tents. In spite of a good physician and a hospital which for the time was very modern, the disease caused several deaths. A constant stream of freighters' teams fed overnight at each of the several large barns dotted about. Amongst the teams was one owned by a relative newcomer to the freighting and packing business, Fred Brewster, who for the next sixty years was to be intimately associated with the Jasper area.

In 1910 while Fred was a young man starting his career as an outfitter at Prairie Creek, Dan Noyes, the old packer who for forty-four years had been the authority on all the trails heading for the Yellowhead Pass, died at his home near Edmonton. Married to J. E. Brazeau's daughter and intimately associated with the story of the Jasper valley, he had gone on to become one of Edmonton's best-known outfitters and as such played a large part in the Klondike rush through Edmonton. For years he had maintained a trading post at Whitemud Creek (modern Marlboro). When Edmonton's businessmen began examining the marl which gave the creek its name and assembling the capital to start the Marlboro cement plant — capital it took them a mere decade to lose — Dan Noyes, the old frontiersman, had left the area, and leaving even his pack horses, had passed to the beyond.

Around 1910, however, Brewster was only one of the many outfitters working along the tote road. Another was Alex Wylie, then a tall rangy young man ready at any time to string out his pack horses to take any material anywhere or any party to any remote valley it wished.

J. M. Mullander was another of the more successful packers or freighters who operated a reliable outfit along the trails and the tote road. During the mild winter of 1910-11 he had many teams at work freighting in Jasper valley and up through the Yellowhead Pass. In an interview he gave an *Edmonton Journal* reporter about that time, he estimated that during that winter from one thousand to fifteen hundred horses were at work along the trail. There were so many of them that the cost of oats

and hay had soared, and in the Jasper area he was paying from
ninety to one hundred dollars a ton for hay and from ninety
cents to one dollar per bushel for oats.

All the freighting west of Edmonton was not confined to
Foley, Welch and Stewart's tote road. During 1910 the CNR
began pushing its long-delayed transcontinental west from St.
Albert. In general, it followed the old trail Father Thibault had
cut out as far as Lac Ste. Anne. That old hamlet which for
so long, with its mission and the Hudson's Bay post, had been
the headquarters for the country west of Edmonton and then
has been passed up by the GTP, took on a new lease of life.
By the fall of 1910 the CNR surveyors had laid out their line
of stakes west of it, following close to the north shore of beautiful
Lake Isle and heading toward a crossing of the Pembina River
at Entwistle. There, less than a mile north of the GTP, it crossed
the river on a wooden trestle.

At the Pembina crossings the needless duplication of two
railways side by side started and continued for some 225 miles.
For twenty-five miles west of Entwistle they were a mere stone's
throw apart. For the next forty miles they were never more
than six miles apart, and for 160 miles beyond that, until at
Tête Jaune Cache they diverged, the two sets of tracks were
practically on top of each other. The wasteful folly that permitted
the building of two rival lines through such difficult terrain in
an area nearly worthless from an agricultural point of view was
but a symbol of the times — when the North American
philosophy of the "pursuit of the Almighty Dollar" overruled
all other considerations. In this case alone, within a few years,
that philosophy was to saddle the people of Canada with debts
running into scores of millions of dollars.

The pursuit of dollars, however, was not restricted to major
moves on the part of remote capitalists. In his own way many
a local entrepreneur pursued dollars with whisky jugs. Some
of them prospered, some did not, but all of them tested the
vigilance of the RNWMP and provided a legacy of tall tales
which went rolling down the years. Many a time the bootleggers
delivered their wares successfully, many a time the Mounties
outwitted them, and probably, if one could know all the details,
the score remained about even.

On one occasion at Edson the forces of law triumphed.
About the end of October, 1911, out of the scores of boxcars
which were moving west carrying material and supplies for con-

struction, one filled with baled hay was spotted on the side track at Edson. By an odd coincidence, it was also spotted by the RNWMP, who found 350 quarts of a good brand of whisky artfully baled in with the hay. The Mounties, nonchalantly retiring to a discreet distance, awaited the arrival of the consignee coming to claim his hay. Undoubtedly hovering at an even more discreet distance while his caution fought back his anxiety, he never showed up. Failing to discover and arrest him, the police notified F. G. Forster, the chief license inspector, who came out from Edmonton and confiscated the joy juice. In the presence of a wistful mob of onlookers, the precious cargo was unloaded and sent back to the proper authorities in Edmonton. But to show that the law could also be lenient in a good cause, the inspector, in a gesture perhaps less munificent than magnanimous, aided the cause of the financially sorely pressed local hospital by donating two bottles to its dispensary.

Some time later, a Mountie, nosing around in the forest near a camp west of the Prairie Creek bridge, came upon a man dressed in "city clothes," carrying a brand-new suitcase. Few indeed of the men working on the grade bothered with suitcases and none tramped about in the bush all dressed up, carrying a shiny new one. Moreover, this one was obviously heavy. So, his ready curiosity aroused, Constable Hodgkins approached Clarence H. Rinchart and requested to examine his luggage. Discovering that it contained a dozen quarts of whisky, Hodgkins insisted that Rinchart accompany him the five or six miles to Prairie Creek and that for every foot of the way he carry the dolefully heavy suitcase. There, Inspector Raven, acting as magistrate, confiscated the liquor and fined the hapless and by now weary wanderer ninety dollars and costs.

Some months previously, in March, 1911, Prairie Creek became the end of steel and by May regular trains operated as far as Obed. By July the steel reached the bridge over the Athabasca a dozen miles west of Fiddle Creek. At last it had entered the Jasper valley — just over a hundred years since on December 3, 1810, David Thompson had struggled so painfully up the Athabasca River to shiver in some hunter's deserted windowless cabin at the upper end of Brulé Lake. Somewhere across the lake from the GTP station called Parkgate, Thompson and Thomas, his Iroquois guide, had built a log cache before the surveyor had pushed farther up the Jasper valley. Moreover, a couple of miles across the lake lay the cellar of Jasper Hawse's house.

It is doubtful if the railroad builders even knew of the existence of Jasper's house. What none could overlook, however, was Black Cat Mountain. Some three or four miles west of the lake and insignificant as compared to the peaks behind, nevertheless, because of the configuration of forest cover on its east side, it stood out as a landmark visible at least as far as Hinton. Covering most of its flank, the forest appeared at a distance to resemble the side view of a startled cat springing clear of the ground, with its back arched and its erect tail fuzzy with fright.

For weeks the builders had worked their way through the dismal defile of the Athabasca River heading west toward that landmark which each day barely came closer. Then, all of a sudden, by swinging the grade to the left at the shore of Brulé Lake the full glory of the Jasper valley burst upon them. In front of them to the south the blue expanse of the lake led their vision on to the blue of the mountain ridges, the nearer one the Boule Range on the right and the Fiddle Range on the left split at the end of the lake where the Athabasca had torn its way through them. Through the gap directly ahead reared Roche Miette's imposing block, the great guardian tower set beside the gateway to the blue mystery ahead.

Then, too, the terrain improved and to the men often toiling away in the mud up to their knees working on Brulé Lake's sandy east bank was like stepping into a new world. To the contractors, however, the seemingly easy stretch along the sand dunes posed a major problem. The winds racing down the pass gained their full momentum as they swept across the open expanse of the lake, swirling a blast of sand before them, which day after day settled into sifting dunes on the east shores. Through those dunes the grade had to run, necessitating a cut of some 90,000 yards in one stretch and a fill of 120,000 yards a little farther along. But as fast as the cut was dug, the gales filled it again. As fast as the fill was heaped up, the winds whipped it away. In the end, after much fruitless work, the contractor erected fences to break the force of the wind, and with brush and matting covered the exposed surfaces of the fill.

Eventually subduing their sandy adversary, the contractors carried the grade across Fiddle River and a little farther along on its west bank laid out station grounds. At that point the

GTP promoters, conscious of any tourist attraction, and the same men who brought into being the Fort Garry Hotel in Winnipeg and the Macdonald Hotel in Edmonton, resolved to build another edifice and one to fit the scenic grandeur of the valley. Knowing as others, including Hawkins the surveyor, had known, that Fiddle River drained away the steaming waters of Miette Hot Springs, they proposed to build the hotel where the steel crossed the stream and to call the station Carlsbad. The name which stuck to the spot long after the dream of a hotel had faded was finally changed to Miette Hot Springs station.

Continuing the grade another three or four miles the contractors came to the station which, because it was sitting over a seam of coal having many of the properties of the excellent coals of Pocahontas, Pennyslvania, they called Pocahontas. The seam which extends across the valley to modern Brulé was undoubtedly the same one which, when writing up his diary at Jasper House in October, 1824, Sir George Simpson had mentioned. Similarly, in 1907, D. B. Dowling of the Geological Survey had observed it.

On Dowling's heels came various entrepreneurs until by 1910 they had organized the Jasper Park Collieries Ltd. and done some development work on the seam. In 1912, the first full year during which the GTP was capable of carrying away their product, the mine employed 134 men who produced over a hundred thousand tons of seam coal. After Pocahontas was established on the GTP line, Mackenzie and Mann, who were busy pushing the CNR west toward the mountains, sent some mining men to examine the seam of coal in the vicinity of Brulé and as soon as the railroad got that far started another coal mine.

Three or four miles west of Pocahontas at Disaster Point (the toe of Roche Miette), Foley, Welch and Stewart's grading crews ran into some of their earlier rock work. Unlike the pack trains which always ran into difficulties at that point and had to sheer away, the graders had tried conclusions with that point of rock and had blasted out enough of it to squeeze the railroad in between the mountain and the Athabasca River.

During low water the pack trains had been able to ford the river, but for decades at times of high water their only alternative had been to climb hundreds of feet over the spur of Roche Miette. That precarious mile, the dread of every packer, had taxed every man's courage and had exacted its toll of horses.

The real danger spot was a few square yards at the top where the smooth rocks, polished to a glassy surface by the winds of centuries, appeared level. In reality they sloped, gradually at first, then more steeply, till finally they became almost vertical as they plunged into the rushing river hundreds of feet below. A horse straining up the steep path to gain the top invariably stopped on the level space to blow. The next horse and the next crowded up beside him, until finally the pressure of horses behind pushed the leading horses off balance and set them sliding along the smooth sloping surface, slipping faster and faster as they inevitably hurtled to their doom. Because of the many horses lost there, today's maps call this mountain spur "Disaster Point." Experienced packers who had been over Roche Miette before tried to prevent disaster at the summit by arranging that not more than three horses were on the treacherous rocks at one time. They saw to it that they started on their way down the other side before the next group came up.

During 1906 one horse, of whom Rod McCrimmon used to tell, achieved immortality in the memories of all packers and oldtimers of the foothills as the Grand Trunk Cheese Horse. Loaded with three large, flat Cheddar cheeses, he was jostled at the summit, lost his footing and went sprawling down the slope. Rod McCrimmon ran over to the edge in time to see him carom off one tree and wedge behind another about a hundred feet down. When the horse hit the first tree, the cheeses came loose and rolled. Then they bounced and then they flew down the mountainside.

It took several men with ropes and slings to get the horse back on the trail again, but in a few days he appeared as good as ever. Meanwhile someone retrieved one badly broken cheese, but for many a day the fragments of the other two must have provided tempting morsels for all the mice of Roche Miette.

When the tote road got as far as Roche Miette the contractors hauled in a cable and timbers and put a ferry across the river at that point. The old trail over the shoulder of the mountain was abandoned, leaving no vestige of regret on the part of any packer who had ever used it. A few years later, Foley, Welch and Stewart's crews set to work cutting away enough rock to scratch out a toehold wide enough for two steel rails to make their way between the rock cliff where the cheese horse had come to grief and the waters of the rushing Athabasca snarling around it. For a start, surveyors had to be let down from above with ropes fastened to a thick belt around their waists, and men dangling from ropes carried drills and dynamite so as to blast out a little notch above the swirling torrent where other men could stand to tear out a wider gap.

While all that work was going on at Disaster Point, Foley, Welch and Stewart had many a crew building the grade farther west. Shortly after getting around that point and crossing the nearby Rocky River, the right of way, keeping to the east of Jasper Lake, passed in sight of the spot where Colin Fraser and H. J. Moberly had spent so many years. Of old Jasper House, which for so long had been an important depot on the transportation route, little was left but a shack, some cellars, and a few graves.

Leaving those ruins to recede in the distance, the grade followed the sandy spit separating Talbot and Jasper lakes. Finally, after another tussle with a rock cut near the cold sulphur spring, it crossed the Athabasca near the spot where the packers had so often hazed their horses into the swift stream when making their way to Ewan Moberly's home. Ever since the Jasper Park authorities had moved the natives, Ewan's home on the left side of the river and on the flat below Cobblestone Creek had been deserted. Near it, standing sentinel in the silence, was the cross Ewan had erected over his mother's grave — one of the present landmarks in the Park. For in Ewan's house in May, 1905, Suzan Cardinal had died. She, whose memory had reached back to the days when as a young woman she had presented Henry John Moberly with his two strapping sons, Ewan and John, had lived to see the GTP surveyors coming and going.

Heading south away from the Moberly homestead the grade crossed the Snaring River, traversed Lewis Swift's land and headed for the site of its divisional point named in honor of Earl Hopkins Fitzhugh, one of the company's vice-presidents. The surveyors, paying scant attention to an oldtimer such as Swift and less attention to the remains of any old landmarks, were bent on maintaining an easy grade for their rails, which at all times had to keep climbing toward that distant point 3,728 feet above sea level which marked the summit of the Yellowhead Pass. As a result, they kept their grade above Moberly's depot and blasted a way for it through the shoulder of rock well above the site of La Rocque's House, which had been built near Cottonwood Creek. Along the creek on which the shack had stood the contractors built their construction camp.

At last the grade builders were ready to set out through the narrow glen which the old Scottish fur traders had called the Caledonia valley. At last they were ready to follow in the steps of so many valiant predecessors: Tête Jaune, passing and repassing to New Caledonia; the leather parties heading across the Leather Pass to British Columbia; the Overlanders prodding their oxen through the muskeg in the bottom of the dark glen, and many others.

Early in the construction process, Foley, Welch and Stewart's men had pushed their tote road farther west, corduroying muskeg, notching the way out of side hills, and shoring up the trail over which Alex Wylie and scores of other packers had struggled so often, the trail which, to avoid worse hazards, had crossed the Miette River seven times. Working west day after day the road builders had dropped construction camps at short intervals, with larger, more permanent ones at the cuts, the bridges, and the tunnel. At each camp they had left gangs of hardy men who had clawed their way around mountain shoulders and with their sledge hammers, drills, and dynamite had ripped or bored their way forward, leaving a smooth, gently curving way for the rails to follow; leaving some of their number beside the grade blasted into eternity in bits or swept more slowly to the cemetery near the tunnel by typhoid.

But at last the steel, advancing throughout 1911 and pulling up the remnants of construction camps as it went along, passed the typhoid cemetery and crept through the tunnel. Shortly after that it reached Dominion Prairie, which appears to have received its name when on a Sunday in 1872 Rev. G. Grant of Fleming's party held divine service there at McCord's CPR camp, where men from all the six provinces of the Dominion were represented. In GTP days that flat spot intersected by Derr Creek provided space for a construction camp. Some time earlier, graphite deposits along the upper creek had excited a number of prospectors. Those deposits, however, ceased to be of value when the area was declared to be within Jasper National Park, so the claims were abandoned. Four miles west of there, working its way up the nearly imperceptible grade, the track layer, pushing its rails ahead of it, enabled the first work train to reach the summit of Yellowhead Pass in November, 1911.

There, at Mile 129, at the summit, unnoticeable except for the surveyor's peg, the long construction division extending west from Wolf Creek ended. There, too, the railway grade passed out of Alberta and because at that point it entered the sovereign province of British Columbia, the invisible boundary became a barrier at which Mounted Police jurisdiction over liquor ceased. West of it liquor was law and speakeasies and bootleggers ruled the roost. The British Columbia Government, which had undertaken to police the line from there west, did little about what went on in the town at the summit or in the construction towns which succeeded it.

On the delightful flat immediately west of the summit moldering logs and long-abandoned cellars still mark the site where Summit City, the wide-open town, flourished. In it at least four saloons operated without let or hindrance, and in that one spot more drunkenness led to more fights than there had been in all the construction camps extending west from Edmonton to the boundary.

As W. Lacey May was quoted in the Fort George *Herald:*

"An 'end of steel' village is made up of booze, billiards, and belles. It is the home of the illicit liquor traffic of construction, the location of enough pool tables to stock a large city, and the residence of women who never elsewhere enjoyed so much freedom. Three-quarters of the shacks are restaurants in front — for about six feet. The restaurant is merely an outward plausible excuse for the existence of the shack.

"Back of the little counter is the pool room . . . and then through a small doorway, up a short flight of stairs that breathe exclusiveness and privacy is the real object of existence — the card room."

As Hulbert Footner, who visited Summit City in mid-summer, 1911, wrote in his *New Rivers of the North:*

"The first thing that struck us as out of the common was the sight of several inanimate bodies sprawled in the mud of the trail. No one paid any attention. 'Let 'em sleep it off,' was the general sentiment. The instrument of havoc was 'squirrel whiskey' at two bits a drink. One cynical traveler informed us that it was made out of gasolene: 'two shots and you'll explode,' said he."

No matter how bad or tough a town was, there was always someone who, either because he could hold more liquor than the rest or because he drank less, set himself up as guardian of the drunks. At the summit, according to Footner, was such a man who, joking all the time, laughingly or cynically kept an eye on them. His job was to "roll them there corpses out of the trail so that the wagons kin pass,'' and he would intervene in the affairs of each new drunk and call on the bystanders to "lay him out there to one side so's he won't git stepped on.'' Then taking the victim's watch and any money he had, he returned them when the man came to.

In spite of its rowdiness and in spite of rumors to the contrary and these rather exaggerated journalists' accounts, no one seems to have been killed in any brawl in that first construction town in British Columbia.

From Summit City, which was Mile Zero of the new construction division, to Tête Jaune Cache station at Mile 52, the GTP descended streams flowing to the Pacific and in doing so its grade dropped some thirteen hundred feet in elevation. Even though that stretch of the route was downhill, it bristled with construction problems and the grade progressed at a slow pace. Whereas work trains were running to the summit by November, 1911, the steel did not reach Moose Lake, some seventeen miles farther west, until March of the following year. By the end of that year it had advanced only to within shouting distance of Tête Jaune Cache station. Long before the steel neared it, Tête Jaune Cache was a major warehousing center to which an almost continuous line of freighting teams hauled an amazing variety of goods from the current end of steel.

As a result, after November, 1911, the narrow, dark valley of the upper Fraser swarmed with men building grade, blasting out cuts, erecting bridges, or freighting. The first three miles of their descent from the summit brought them to lovely Yellowhead Lake stretching ahead another three miles, a jewel in a delightful Swiss setting. For decades the fur traders had called it Buffalo Dung Lake and sometimes Cranberry Lake, and then in 1872 Dr. Grant suggested its present name. When the GTP engineers, men with an eye for beauty, ran their rails along its northern shore, they acknowledged its pre-eminence by calling their station Lucerne.

Still heading down the valley another seven charming miles the grade reached Grant Brook. For a few years there an enterprising man quarried marble of good quality not far from the railroad. It is sad, however, that in his eagerness he set off a charge of dynamite so large that by fracturing the rock it made it worthless.

A couple of miles farther west, where construction was held up while Foley, Welch and Stewart threw a bridge across

Moose River, the grade came to Moose City, Mile 17, another of the wide-open towns of the pass. It had several strings to its bow, of which bridge-building was only one; it was the terminus of the tote road and the center of a brief mining flurry. Although an execrable pack trail, sometimes on the hillside, sometimes in the lake, continued along the north side of Moose Lake, Foley, Welch and Stewart deemed it unnecessary to build the tote road along eight miles of lakeshore when they could move their freight on scows. For a while, then, Moose City was a transshipping point. Moreover, prospectors nosed around amongst the showings of gold, silver, and copper on the multicolored mountain nearby and for a while the seventeen-mile pack trail which started up Moose River was noisy with their comings and goings.

Amongst the many shady denizens of Moose City who for a brief hour provided some entertainment for everyone were one of the ubiquitous characters so often known as Baldy and a madam known as Dirty Mag. One day, by the time Baldy had already had two or three drinks too many and had entered Mag's place for another one, he insisted that she set up a round of free drinks.

"Come on, Mag," he said, "for old times' sake."

"Old times' sake don't pay no freight on booze," retorted Mag.

"Come on, Mag, you old—, set 'em up."

It grew to be quite an argument and finally Mag chased him out — nearly threw him out. She was quite a woman.

"I'll show you," said Baldy, "I'll put you out of business."

"You and how many more?" Mag flung over her shoulder as she went back into her joint.

Baldy went away muttering to himself and headed for the barn. Presently he drove his team over and hitched them to the corner of Mag's place. To illustrate what the team could do, he eased them into their collars and they gave the shack a preliminary jerk to show how nicely they could pull down the whole caboodle. Then, as Baldy held the team but stood ready to urge them forward into a real lurch, Mag gave in to his repeated request.

Eight miles west of Moose City, in the vicinity of today's Red Pass Junction, Mile 29 became the next major and hilarious camp, and flourished until the contractors finished the bridge which enabled the track to cross to the south side of the valley.

The official names bestowed on both Resplendent, the railway station of construction days, and Red Pass Junction, the modern station, were derived from the multicolored rocks outcropping on the flanks of an interesting mountain.

Like Moose City, Mile 29 had its share of rough characters. One of the few murders recorded along all the hundreds of miles of construction occurred there when, during a gambling dispute. a long-standing feud came to a head. One of the laborers, said to be a giant of a man who had been in the habit of throwing his weight around, had his bluff called by a man named Taft, and he was carted off to the nearby cemetery. According to reports of oldtimers in the area, one of the all-too-frequent epidemics of typhoid swept Mile 29 and a dozen or more of its victims were buried nearby.

From Resplendent west, because the railway grade could not afford to drop as fast as the river did, it had to be dynamited out of the sloping southern hillside. While the GTP was blasting away, ignoring the fact that its rival also had an interest in the mountainside, the CNR, whose steel had not yet crept as far west as Entwistle, intervened. It proposed to build its line alongside the Foley, Welch and Stewart grade but higher up the hill. Claiming that the GTP blasting was undermining its right of way, it tried to get an injunction forbidding further dynamiting. Whatever effect that action had, it did nothing to speed up the GTP's construction. In spite of delay, the grade eventually reached Mount Robson station and created one of the most scenic stretches on any railway in the world.

For there stands Mount Robson (12,972 feet).

For there, across the gorge, two miles above and a mere six miles from the Fraser River, its glacial ice tops the wall of the highest mountain in all the Canadian Rockies and dwarfs other peaks as it rises to its far-flung crest. Fashioned of gray rock, draped with green glaciers and ermined with strips of snow, this vast curtain presents a view embracing nobility, loveliness, and grandeur, And when in autumn the sun burnishes its hem of golden aspens, glows on its icy green crevasses and silhouettes its long line of cornices extended into a pennant of cloud pinned to its peak against the deep blue of a clear sky, Mount Robson, aloof but intimately close, stands majestic in its magnificence.

Spread out at its foot in the angle between the main Fraser River and its Grand Fork, which carries the run-off from the monarch's melting glaciers, lies a precious area of flat land partly used as a public campground. Here, according to the old Iroquois Cheadle had hired at Jasper, the Iroquois pathfinder Tête Jaune had his cache, probably well back in the trees from the junction of the two streams.

A couple of miles down the Fraser from where Tête Jaune's cache was reported to be, the Swiftcurrent River, after passing through a small flat, enters from the north. This flat, which in 1898 was the scene of considerable prospecting but little mining, was where Mrs. McAuley, the half-breed girl, moved the teepee over her unconscious husband when his face had been shattered by his murderous partner's bullet.

A few miles farther down, the Fraser, constricted and writhing, leaps over its spectacular Rearguard Falls, which are said to limit the upward migration of spawning salmon. Not far beyond the falls, through a ledge above the river, Foley, Welch and Stewart's gangs gouged out a tunnel. After passing through it the railway tracks debouched into the Rocky Mountain Trench and right in front of them lay the flat basin surrounding Tête Jaune Cache. At last the GTP had crossed the summit of the Continental Divide and emerged from the Rocky Mountains on to streams filled with salmon and flowing to the Pacific Ocean.

Far behind the Grand Trunk and still out on the prairie its rival, the CNR, came limping along. By September, 1912, its end-of-steel was at Entwistle, and then for twenty miles until it passed Chip Lake it laid its ties within a stone's throw of its competitor's track, even crossing it one place before diverging south a few miles seeking a bridge site on the McLeod River south of Edson. By that time it also needed a divisional point, and towards the end of 1912 proceeded to lay out one at Tollerton, three miles south of that town.

Five miles west of there its engineers also faced the problem of crossing the coulee of Sundance Creek, made doubly difficult by the obstacle of the GTP's tracks and the Big Eddy trestle. After much soul searching they overcame it by a complicated concrete underpass which still stands as a monument to the folly of railway duplication. It led to a wooden trestle long since torn down, with which the tracks, after crossing the GTP, got over Sundance Creek. From there the CNR grade ascended the creek and curved around to serve the recently constructed Marlboro cement plant, which so soon was to find that its far-touted marl deposit was of little use and of limited life.

From Marlboro for more than fifty miles to the north end

of Brulé Lake the CNR track was never more than one mile from its rival's line. West of Hinton, after crossing Prairie Creek at a low elevation, the CNR engineers built a major bridge over the Athabasca and a mile or so farther on laid out its gateway to Jasper National Park, which it called Entrance.

After creeping along the north bank of the Athabasca River for a few miles to the crossing of Solomon Creek, the CNR grade reached the stretch of rich pasture at the end of Brulé Lake, which doughty old Solomon Caraconté's family had considered their home since they had moved there while Jasper Hawse's house was still in operation. There, in 1824, in a spot which he described as "beautifully Wild and romantic," Sir George Simpson had sat thinking up ways to improve the trans-Canada transportation system, and now, ninety years later, two transcontinental railways were tearing away at the terrain in their wild competition to get to the Pacific coast.

From there, following the west bank of the lake, the grade passed through the Brulé mining area. By that time Mackenzie and Mann's mine was ready to ship coal. After reaching the southern tip of the lake and tunneling its way through a spur of the Bedson Ridge, it passed the site of the Jasper Park Collieries' northern mine. Having its problems with rock cuts and creeks, it eventually crossed Snake Indian River near the site of the massacre, passed close to the remains of Colin Fraser's Jasper House, and followed along the west side of Jasper Lake until on Lewis Swift's property it crossed the GTP line to run between it and the Athabasca River.

Ascending Miette River and crossing the Yellowhead summit, it descended to the south shore of Yellowhead Lake. Toward its lower end the CNR built its Lucerne station. On the extensive flat it laid out all the rail facilities needed for a divisional point and provided the nucleus of a town, which, washed by the waters of a charming lake and surrounded by select mountain scenery, had every reason to look forward to a long, serene future.

By the end of 1913 most of the CNR steel had been laid as far as Lucerne. By that time Mackenzie and Mann, anxiously watching the clouds dimming the economic horizon, found their progress slowing up and began to wonder if they could find the money to finish their line. By Herculean efforts they did find it.

In a manner similar to what the GTP had done and always a mere stone's throw from its rival's line, the CNR skirted the shore of Moose Lake and crossed the Fraser at Resplendent. From there west, however, the stone's throw was vertical. The GTP, which was to descend the Fraser, kept its track at as low an elevation as it could, but the CNR, which was on its way to climb Albreda Pass, maintained all the altitude it could. As a result, after leaving Resplendent (the Red Pass Junction of later days), although the two lines snaked around the bends in parallel curves, the CNR grade gradually rose above the other one.

A year or so earlier and before they came to build their own grade, the CNR officials had complained that the GTP blasting was undermining their prospective grade. Apparently the GTP continued to blast away with gay abandon, and as they did so pushed the waste material over the edge, leaving it to fall where it would. Now when the CNR came to build its grade one or two hundred feet higher up the almost vertical mountainside, the GTP complained that its rival's construction crews were casting their spoil over the edge and blocking their tracks. Since that situation could not continue, the CNR was forced to build chutes over the GTP grade so as to throw its material clear of the tracks below.

When the CNR's grade entered the open area of Tête Jaune Cache it made a sharp turn and almost doubled back upon itself to keep from losing altitude by dropping into the valley and started its line off south toward Albreda Pass, the Thompson River, and Kamloops. By the time it made the sharp bend it too had traversed the Rocky Mountains. By that time both railways had reached the vicinity of Tête Jaune Cache.

12

TÊTE JAUNE CACHE

TÊTE Jaune Cache! There's magic in the very name. Like Koolgardi, Kalamazoo, and Kazabazua, it rolls around the memory. But to really ring in the ears it should be pronounced as oldtimers and all the local people say it — Tee John Cache.

Tête Jaune Cache. It was a name everyone knew. Starting with the Overlanders of 1862, it called to two generations of Canadians. Then, as soon as the GTP did reach it and dispelled its mystery and everyone who wished could look out upon its wide valley, it sank back to the obscurity from which even the roar of giant diesel-pulled trains panting up the grade toward the summit cannot arouse it. And yet after its long years of mystery, its two or three years of frantic fame form a treasured memory for its dwindling handful of oldtimers who still remember.

Today, for three or four miles on the flat land west of the point where Highway No. 5 crosses the Fraser, a few houses, a hamlet, and the remains of scattered, rotting buildings are all that mark the once large and lively community of Tête Jaune Cache. But where are the remains of Tête Jaune Cache's main street? There are no remains. The Fraser River, flowing serenely along, covers what in 1912 was its bustling main thoroughfare, and the score or so of wild Canada geese resting on its gravel bar are completely oblivious of its one-time existence.

Tête Jaune Cache is then obviously in a bad way. But just where was it exactly? As shown by the adjacent map, it stretched along the grade and the south bank of the Fraser for some four miles from Mile 49. That was Henningville station, near the bend where the GTP track coming from the east and crossing Highway No. 5 changes direction and sets off northwest towards the bridge over the McLennan River.

Where was the Yellow Head's original cache? All that can be said is that there is little doubt that it was some ten miles upstream at the mouth of the Grand Fork River. For its site there is no better authority than Dr. Cheadle, who, presumably coached by his Iroquois, said it was there. And yet there is a persistent opinion on the part of such oldtimers as Stan Carr, who has been a well-known outfitter in the area for decades, and Ted Abram, that once there was an old shack very close

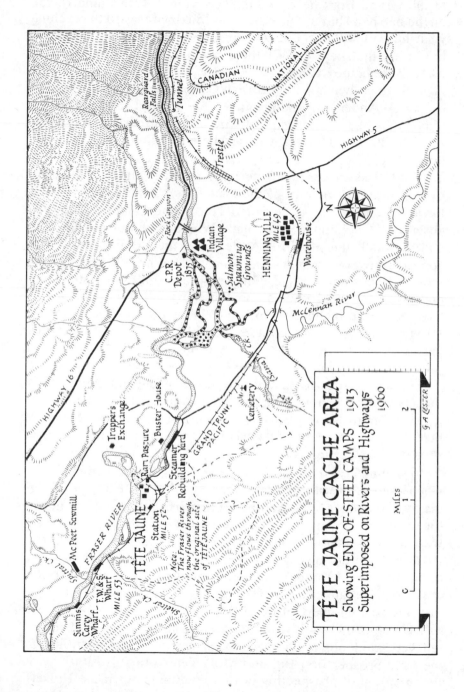

TÊTE JAUNE CACHE AREA
Showing END-OF-STEEL CAMPS 1913
Superimposed on Rivers and Highways 1960

G. A. LESSER

MILES
0   1   2

to the CPR depot of 1872. Even at the time Dr. Cheadle was at the Grand Fork he spoke of the *original* Tête Jaune Cache on the one hand but on the other was looking forward to reaching what he called "The Cache" some ten miles down the river, indicating that before 1863 the name had been transferred to a later Tête Jaune Cache.

On an early map in the British Columbia Archives prepared by A. C. Anderson, he indicated Tête Jaune Cache as on the right bank of the Fraser, with the comment that it was near a "Fall. 20 feet. Head of Canoe Navign. Salmon reach to this point." Anderson, as already noted, traveled through the Yellowhead Pass in 1835 and perhaps at other times. Evidently by that time the vicinity of the little fall and the head of canoe navigation had come to be called Tête Jaune Cache and as such deserved to be shown on a map. Whether or not anyone had built a shack there before Anderson's time is not known. It appears, however, that at some time well before Mary Schäffer's visit of 1908 someone had done so — certainly not Tête Jaune himself. For that Iroquois, on the move all the time, would have had little inclination to waste labor on building a house. His famous cache, of course, would be merely a structure anchored up in two or three trees to keep his goods safe from prowling predators.

It seems strange that if the shack had been there when the Overlanders or Cheadle arrived none of them mentioned it. In order to have been in such a decrepit state when Mary Schäffer was there, it must have been built by some trapper shortly after Cheadle's visit.

Fortunately, there are many oldtimers whose eyes light up when asked to recall the days they spent at Tête Jaune Cache nearly sixty years ago. Amongst them I have been particularly fortunate in enjoying the friendliness of Ted Abram, a man now well into his eighties, who first camped by the Fraser in 1907. As a result of our discussions, correspondence, and his written reminiscences, I too have come to feel like a participant in the drama of Tête Jaune Cache. He has supplied much of the information and related many of the little incidents set out here.

Coming to Canada from Lancashire about 1906, Ted Abram reached Kamloops a year later and fell in with two young frontiersmen and prospectors, Bill and Mort Teare. In July, 1907, with the intention of prospecting in the mountains down the Fraser, those two experienced men, taking Ted the tenderfoot, gathered up some pack horses and set out on the 250-mile trip to Tête Jaune Cache. On their first night in camp Mort Teare initiated Ted into the mysteries of making bannock. As Ted's reminiscences say: "We had no mixing pan and he just scooped a small dent in the flour at the top of the sack, poured in a cupfull of water, baking powder and salt, and worked in the flour with his finger tips until he had a biscuit dough consistency. Lifting it out into a pan, he baked it on the hot coals, the flame above causing it to rise as it browned."

Following the pack trail up the North Thompson, the three prospectors finally crossed Albreda Pass and near there saw a blazed tree on which the words "CPR Survey 1872" was still clearly visible. They completed their month-long trip by reaching the left bank of the Fraser at Tête Jaune Cache, where they found several Indian families camped. Directly across the river they saw a small camp of timber cruisers, headed by Frank Stevens. Not far from Stevens's camp, Frank Reading and Jimmy Moore occupied a small store which they had recently opened with goods they had brought in through the Yellowhead Pass. About that time the packers who were supplying the GTP surveyors arrived at Tête Jaune Cache and to house their perishable goods built a small shack a mile or so west, which came to be known as the Buster House. At the time of Abram's first visit in 1907, those few men and buildings on the north side of the river and the Indian camp on the south made up the entity that was Tête Jaune Cache.

Ted Abram and the Teares camped a night or two and then pushed on west along the pack trail which other prospectors had cut out as far as Horsey Creek. Working out from there, they prospected about a week and then decided to carve a canoe out of a large cottonwood and to descend the Fraser. After they had it hewed roughly into shape, they rigged up a Spanish windlass and drew the half-finished craft over green pole skids till they could put it in the river. In due course, with Mort Teare steering, Bill in the bow, and Ted amidships with his dog between his legs and a cigarette in the corner of his mouth, they pushed their unstable craft into the stream. As the canoe wobbled along, Mort, noticing Ted reaching toward his cigarette, shouted "Ted, for goodness sake, don't switch your cigarette from one side to the other or you'll tip us for sure."

In the vicinity of Holmes River the strata on the hillsides of what is now called Teare Mountain excited their interest.

When they scrambled over it they found an outcropping of good quality quartz, fifteen feet wide. Although in the end their mine disappointed them, the three men worked at it sporadically for two or three years. Several other men prospected or mined in the same general area with similar success.

During those years various parties of surveyors camped at Tête Jaune Cache while they studied a route for the CNR to Kamloops or for the GTP down the Fraser to Fort George. During that time, Foley, Welch and Stewart, looking at the Cache, the head of navigation, decided that when the time came they would make it one of their main warehousing depots. Moreover, both the well-known British Columbia Express Company and the Fort George Lumber and Navigation Company had begun laying plans to provide steamboat navigation on the 315 winding miles of the upper Fraser between Fort George and Tête Jaune Cache, so that once the steel reached that far they could connect with it. By playing a complementary role to the GTP as it built its 183 miles of railway to Fort George, both those companies hoped that the sternwheelers would churn up a handsome profit.

To navigate the river the boats had to be capable of getting through three major obstructions; the Giscome Rapids, some twenty-five miles above Fort George, the Grand Canyon, another seventy-five miles farther up, and finally the rapids near Goat River, about another hundred miles upstream.

As a trial of the possibilities, late in the fall of 1909 Captain J. H. Bonser of the Fort George Lumber and Navigation Company took the little eighty-foot sternwheeler, the *Chilco,* through the Giscome Rapids and the Grand Canyon and ran up as far as the Goat River rapids. In July, 1910, he took the still smaller *Fort Fraser* all the way to Tête Jaune Cache. If others could navigate the upper Fraser, Foley, Welch and Stewart decided to put their own boats on the river, and as a preliminary move set a gang of men to work to improve navigation by blasting a few boulders out of the three sets of rapids.

In October that year Ted Abram and Bill Teare were traveling west through the Yellowhead Pass when they "sighted Harry Carr's wagon in the distance. The team was tied and the tent pitched, . . . this on an open mountain side made us wonder. As we rode in closer Harry's wife came to meet us, and with great anxiety written on her face, told us that Harry had broken his leg. She explained that the grade being so steep, the team was unable to pull the load, so Harry had fastened a block and tackle to a stump to give the horses greater purchase in pulling. While his wife drove the team he was following close to the wagon, ready to put a block behind the wheel when the team should stop. Suddenly, with the heavy strain, the rope broke. Back came the wheel, catching Harry by surprise and breaking his leg. To have this happen in such a place so far from help was a disaster . . .''

Fortunately Foley, Welch and Stewart's doctor at Fitzhugh was only eighteen miles away, so Ted volunteered to get him. His horse, which had already done a day's work, bore up bravely while Ted rode in to Jasper, alerted the doctor and accompanied him back to the stricken man. By that time it was daylight the next morning, and only then was the weary horse turned out to graze. After putting the leg in splints, the doctor recommended that Harry should be sent to hospital in Edmonton, so Bill Teare and Ted accompanied Mrs. Carr on the long wagon trip back to Wolf Creek, where Harry could be loaded on the train for Edmonton. The trip, which took about a week, must have been terrible agony for the patient, when hour after hour the wagon wheels bumped over each of the rounded logs of the miles of corduroy. After spending some weeks in hospital, Harry returned with his wife to Summit City.

In September, 1911, about the time when the tote road was nearly finished as far as Tête Jaune Cache, two young American adventurers, A. C. Jennison and D. C. Adams, prevailed upon a freighter to take their canoe through the Yellowhead Pass and unload it at the log bridge near Resplendent. There they embarked and seem to have made out all right whirling down the Fraser until they came to the box canyon above Tête Jaune Cache. There, however, where a big rock sent the rushing water swirling to one side, they were caught in the eddy and drowned. Weeks later their bodies were found, one of them at the point of an island a few miles below Tête Jaune Cache, which ever since has borne the name of Dead Man's Island.

About that time Ted had an experience on a pack trip which illustrates the kind of accident to which pack horses were prone. As Ted was herding the horses along, Buster, the laggard of the bunch, "decided to jump over a leaning pole. He made an unsuccessful leap, landing on a sharp three-inch limb which pierced his stomach, and with his continued efforts to get over, he cut a gash about four inches long." As Ted chopped off the pole, Buster's intestines started protruding in a bulge the size of a man's head. Abram and his partner Jake "threw him on his back by means of a lash rope fastened around his neck and caught under the hind leg above the hoof, and with a side push, over he went. Since he was a quiet horse, also a pet, I had no difficulty in holding him down whilst Jake went to his dunnage bag to get a needle and silk fish line. Pushing everything back, hair, etc., we sewed him up with four large stitches, and hoped for the best. We stood him on his feet again, and wrapped a canvas very tight around his body, the pack saddle cinches holding it firmly, and Buster recovered." Pack trails were hard on horses.

At times they were also hard on dogs. One night when Abram and his friends were camping on one of their prospecting trips, Ted's young dog Nigger learned a lesson. The men "had a three loaf batch of sourdough bread raising in the oven reflector near the fire. Between the gentle heat from the fire and the sun it was coming along nicely. 'Soon be ready to bake,' said Bob, as he lay down to rest in the tent. Next time he went to see about putting it closer to the fire, the pan, to his surprise, was empty! It was not too long before Nigger showed signs of being terribly uncomfortable. He began to swell up! Now we knew where the bread had gone! Poor Nigger came close to passing out! Between the pain he was in and the chastisement the boys gave him, he learned a sad lesson. He never stole anything again from a pan, no matter how hungry he was."

Even by the fall of 1911 there was little about Tête Jaune Cache to indicate that a year later it would be a bustling town, or indeed a series of towns. Captain D. A. Foster, in charge of the Fort George Lumber and Navigation Company's *Chilcotin,* made a few trips up the river as far as the Grand Canyon, but business did not warrant any steamer ascending as far as Tête Jaune Cache.

The state of affairs, however, was soon to change. At the same time that the GTP had been building its railway west from Edmonton, it had also been building east from Prince Rupert, and on the Pacific end Foley, Welch and Stewart had used sternwheelers on the Skeena River. In 1909, to service the construction crews on that river, that company had two sternwheelers, the *Operator* and the *Conveyor,* built in Victoria. Almost identical and each 142 feet long with a 35-foot beam, they ran up and down the Skeena for a couple of years until Foley, Welch and Stewart decided to ship them to the interior for use on the Fraser above Fort George. That decision set in motion a chain of events which put scores of men to work and built Tête Jaune Cache into a significant town.

During the fall of 1911 both boats were dismantled at Victoria, loaded into ten railway cars and shipped by way of Calgary and Edmonton to the end of steel at Resplendent. From there freighters hauled them to Tête Jaune Cache. While dozens of teams of horses and mules took care of the miscellaneous material that had to be moved to Tête Jaune Cache, one set of six teams working in unison spent nearly a month in all taking first one boiler to its destination and then returning for the other.

The two boilers, each weighing about twenty-five tons, taxed the freighters' ingenuity, but by the beginning of January, 1912, they had taken them in hand. The late Rod McCrimmon, then a young daredevil of a man, was one of those freighters. Straining his father's special six-hundred-dollar team of tall, white Missouri mules to the limit to pull the boilers up the steep hills and hold them back when dropping down the other side, Rod enjoyed a few thrilling weeks.

Like all other freight, the boilers were hauled the twenty-five miles on heavy logging sleighs. For much of the distance the teamsters could follow the finished grade, and since the weather was cold, the ground frozen hard and covered with ample snow, hauling was relatively easy. But because some small trestles and a few bridges over creeks had not then been built, the teamsters had to let their load down to the creek bed and then winch it up the other side, or in places, set up a donkey engine to drag it. Toward the end of the journey they had to resort to the tote road. At the steep descents they cut down trees a foot or more in diameter and anchored their restraining cables to the stumps. Although the whole operation was a hard and dangerous job, only one man was reported killed, and he got caught in a coiling cable.

So, tended with more pulleys and tackle, more winches and snatch blocks than they had seen during their two years afloat, and assailed by teamsters' language, more abusive and filled with more epithets than any seaman could muster, the boilers landed at Tête Jaune Cache. Their arrival, along with carloads of miscellaneous material, marked the real beginning of Tête Jaune Cache's frenetic but short career.

The boat rebuilders, searching for a spot suitable for their assembly work, chose one on the gently sloping south bank of the river at Mile 49. Setting up machine shops and other buildings and cutting timbers for the slips and skidways, they set to work on both ships simultaneously. Because the river was narrow, they had to rebuild the boats end to end and parallel to the stream. By May 12, 1912, when the hulls had been reassembled, open and rising water in the Fraser permitted them to be slid sideways off the slips, and once more the *Operator* and the *Conveyor* were water-borne.

The slaps of their flat bottoms hitting the water were the signals that called hundreds of people to Tête Jaune Cache; butchers and bakers and Bible punchers; scow men, hash slingers, and cheque scalpers; pimps and prostitutes. Ted Abram, who with his team helped this one by hauling his goods from here to there and obliged that one by taking his effects from there to here, found himself serving a three-year stretch as drayman in a town where everything and everybody was in transit.

All at once, in little groups of buildings, Tête Jaune Cache sprang into being: Mile 49, Henningville, where later on the CNR contractor, Palmer Brothers and Henning, had a side track; Mile 51, the boat-building yard, and nearby, the red light district; Mile 52, where the railway station was built in 1912 and where the railway "Y" heading north ended at Tête Jaune town, which was sprawled across the narrow neck of the marshy horseshoe bend with the river's waters lapping at its eastern and western edges; and Mile 53, Foley, Welch and Stewart's warehouse and wharf area. Hard by, a bit east of the town and close to the river, stood the Ram Pasture. Directly across the stream from the boat-building yard, the Buster House peered through the pines, and a mile below it was the "Trappers' Exchange," a log shack sixteen feet by twenty which Ted and Bill Teare had built during the spring of 1911.

With its shacks built of logs and roofed with canvas and in the main facing onto an open stretch of irregular width which some dignified by calling it "the street," Tête Jaune was a busy town. George Crummy and Company had the largest store, but there were a score of others; a photo studio, a drug store, several pool halls, and a shooting gallery; flop-joints, good stopping places, Fat's Restaurant and Dad's Restaurant, and the Dew Drop Inn, and many others, including an emporium where a line of assorted goods acted as a front for a cheque slasher. As well as those, a number of Fort George merchants strung their warehouses along the river bank on each side of that temporary town with its jumble of crudely constructed shacks.

One of those was the Ram Pasture which Ted Abram's friends Slim Niven (6' 3'') and Shorty Allgierer (5' 3''), along with Shorty Swanson, Scotty McCrae, Tom Wilson, and others, built, and in which Ted passed many a jolly evening. They picked a spot amidst several cottonwood trees, and when they laid the first course of logs it turned out that one of the stumps was within the rectangle. Instead of grubbing it out, they sawed its top off evenly and fitted the floor around it. "It'll do for a seat," they declared. As their cabin progressed and they needed a table, they nailed two twelve-inch planks together, extending the full length of the end wall which held their sole window. The table, a tin stove, some bunks, and a few blocks of wood for stools, comprised its furniture.

On many an occasion when some stranger had been maneuvered into sitting on the stump stool, the cook of the day would put supper on the table. As the regular crew rolled their blocks to the plank table, the stranger would hang back waiting for the invitation he knew would come. It invariably came in much the following manner. "Come on, bring up your block and sit in." As he wrestled with his immovable stump, the cabin resounded to a round of hearty laughter.

As it turned out, the location of the Ram Pasture proved to have some advantages and some drawbacks. Before long, Constable Bates of the British Columbia provincial police built his detachment nearby. Seriously understaffed, having less than a dozen men to keep an eye on some five or six thousand workers of all sorts scattered over the large area extending from the British Columbia boundary to Fort George, the wonder is not that considerable crime was committed in the area but that those few men kept it from getting out of hand. In any event, the Tête Jaune Cache detachment never lacked for prisoners, and since most of them were put to work on the woodpile, neither the police nor the boys in the Ram Pasture ever lacked for firewood.

Just as the location of the police detachment solved the firewood problem, Pat Burns and Company's slaughterhouse solved the fresh meat problem. During the main railway construction era in western Canada, Pat Burns, the favorably known meat purveyor, made his fortune by taking contracts to supply meat to most of the construction camps. On the GTP he shipped cattle into a few points such as Fort George and Tête Jaune Cache, slaughtered them there and delivered the meat to the camps. In spite of protests from the boys of the Ram Pasture, George Milne, Burns's superintendent, seeking a site for a slaughterhouse and landing wharf, picked on a vacant area near them. The boys complained bitterly, but were mollified by the offer to provide them with all the meat they needed free of charge.

While along the upper Fraser the Indian population had always been sparse, Tête Jaune Cache, where salmon provided a good part of their food, had always been a favorite camping ground. When the town flared into its sudden prominence, many of the natives decided to camp on its environs continuously and to pick up such work or such favors as the white man's rough civilization cast their way. Those Indians, excellent pilots, found congenial employment amongst the numerous craft afloat on the river. Their wives, however, camped at the Cache were often hard-pressed to find enough food for their families. To them Burns's slaughterhouse was a boon.

The construction camp needed beef — halves and quarters sewn in cheesecloth or canvas; they had no time to fiddle with anything less than those. So, at the slaughterhouse the offal and all the lesser parts and the heads were waste products and caused a disposal problem. The Indian women quickly caught on to the situation and solved George Milne's problem.

Ted Abram, making daily rounds with his team, got to know nearly every man in the town. One of them was a character who kept a small stock of goods but became rich by levying a 5 per cent discount when cashing the laborers' cheques. From him, Ted, handling express packages, regularly picked up bundles of cheques which the man sent to his bank in Edmonton.

Five per cent discount, however, was thought to be a modest charge, and considering the convenience afforded the laborer and the risk taken by the cashier, was probably a reasonable charge. Railway operating crews also found cheque scalping a lucrative business and often charged as much as 10 per cent for the service. Many another institution charged considerably more — in fact, all the traffic would bear. And when a man fresh from laboring in mud and muskeg for weeks came in clutching a pay cheque and parched by a terrible thirst or nursing another primitive need, he cared little about what part of his cheque the bootlegger or madam recorded as discount and what part they took for services rendered.

Most, but definitely not all, of the bootleg liquor found a ready market in the gambling joints, the dance hall, and the bawdy houses in the red light district. The bootleggers tried all the usual tricks, hiding bottles in bales of hay, sacks of oats, or sugar, but two unusual methods provided excitement at Tête Jaune Cache.

One day the police spotted a man getting off the train from Edmonton, clad in a bulky overcoat. Its bulkiness combined with his awkward gait lured the policeman to draw him into conversation. When to hold the man's attention the constable tapped the coat with his knucklers, it gave off a metallic murmur. After he had urged the man into the detachment and divested him of his coat, the constable found him corseted in an aluminum contrivance made up of cells which in total held a couple of gallons of whisky. In the end, unfortunately long after it had been drained, that rig found its way to the Ram Pasture where for months it stood as a fireguard shielding the wall from the airtight heater.

But for sheer ingenuity, few attempts at concealing liquor can have ever rated so high as a consignment of seven frozen, dressed pigs all cleanly covered with sacking. When the police, poking around, turned the burlap back, they discovered that strangely enough the abdominal cavities were packed full of white lard. Further probing revealed that the lard concealed bottles of whisky — well over a dozen in all. Although the story of the dressed pigs has been told of each of the GTP construction camps, it really occurred at Tête Jaune Cache, where Ted Abram's dray took the seven pigs of mournful memory over to the photographer's to be immortalized in film.

Ted's dray team also delivered another interesting item with which one of his friends, hoping to make a bit of money, planned to add to the amenities of Tête Jaune Cache. It was the Galloping Bath Tub. He mounted the tub on wheels, and as Ted says, "patrons paid the dues, $2.00 a time, pushed the contrivance to a quiet, sheltered spot near the river, filled it, lit a fire underneath and in due time had a real comfy bath (all right too, when the mosquitoes were not so bad) two chums taking turns, one on the lookout for peeping toms."

Although many a minor crime occurred in Tête Jaune

Cache's gambling district, only one murder darkened its record and that happened during the fall of 1912. The details of the case are far less interesting than the experience of a lawyer, who, coming on the defendant's behalf, stepped off the early morning train from Edmonton before most of the townspeople of Tête Jaune Cache were awake. Wandering around waiting for a cafe to open, he found the door to the tidy little "Lady Barbers" shop open for business. Deciding that a shave would be an ideal way to start the day, he stepped into the bright, well-scrubbed shop. His pleasure at its sanitary appearance was heightened when a beautiful, bosomy young woman greeted him.

Once she had begun her ministrations, he noticed that in spite of her smile and spic and span appearance, her face and eyes were red from crying. Accustomed to relieving his clients' anxieties, he asked what was bothering her. Then, waving the razor with which she had already shaved half his face, she again broke into tears. When she could talk again, she sobbed out her story. She had been lonely and miserable and extremely worried, she said, ever since the previous afternoon when the GTP medical officer and the provincial policeman had arrested her sick partner.

"Well," said the lawyer, "what did she do? Why did they arrest her?"

"She hadn't done nothin'," replied the lady barber. "She hadn't done nothin'—she was just sick and I could of looked after her. And then the policeman poked his nose in the door and spoke to her—and then he went and got the doctor and he came snooping in and then they took her away. The doctor said the redness of her face was smallpox."

In one continuous and rapid motion the lawyer leaped from the chair, snatched up a towel, wiped the lather off his face, flung a dollar bill on the chair and dashed out the door. Nor did he stop until he had put the length of Tête Jaune Cache's street between himself and the red-faced lady barber and went in to the Dew Drop Inn for breakfast.

Before the scows and steamboats started running in the early spring of 1912, while the water was still low after the ice had gone out, some of Ted Abram's friends, "who were also river men, undertook to deliver supplies by means of long narrow 'pointer boats,' that could carry up to a ton. It was an easy job going down stream, just paddle enough to keep straight. But the return journey was, as the Frenchman said 'a difference ting.' Poling up against the strong current with 12 foot spruce poles, 'pushing the bottom out of the river', as they often remarked, they had no outboard motor and gasoline, so had to depend on 'muscleine.' ''

While at Mile 49 one gang of employees was putting the finishing touches to the boat-building yard, another large gang had been moved to Mile 53 to lay out Foley, Welch and Stewart's camp, warehouse area, and temporary harbor. At that point the Fraser was wide enough that by exercising great care sternwheelers could turn around and dock at the long, newly erected wharf. Parallel to it and stretching two or three hundred yards, the recently constructed log warehouse with its white canvas roof had begun to fill with goods carried in from the boxcars lined up along the newly laid rails—sacks of flour, potatoes, vegetables, sugar, great buckets of lard and jam, rice, cases of dried fruits, kegs of nails, rolls of wire, and tons of material of all sorts. Down its middle for the whole distance a narrow gangway gave access to the shelves and bins lining the side walls. Along it scores of hurrying clerks tallied the merchandise coming in off the boxcars or made up lots to be pushed out to the wharf and loaded on sternwheelers or scows for the trip to any of the dozens of construction camps spotted along the next 183 miles of grade to Fort George.

Fortunately, during 1912-13, Dr. Walter Morrish, still a prominent practicing physician in Edmonton, was one of the scurrying clerks. A young man then, well educated, of a tolerant, observing and humorous turn of mind, he had secured a job with Foley, Welch and Stewart, and on the side, served as a representative of the Reading Camp Association, which he explains in his memoirs: "The deal was transportation to, in my case, the end of steel, procure work for yourself, erect a marquee and teach school in your off-work hours. The association would pay you an extra $100.00 for the season." From his sparkling tales I have gained some insight into the life at the head of navigation on the Fraser—into life in that long-lost, legendary Tête Jaune Cache. Through his eyes I have seen scows by the score set out on their one-way trip down the river and watched the *Operator* and the *Conveyor* thrash away from the dock laden with men and 130 tons of material, steam shovels and locomotives and other heavy equipment for the vast construction project downstream and return empty and hungry for more lading.

Low water in 1912 made it difficult for the *Operator* and *Conveyor* to get away from the yard at Mile 51 where they had been launched. A mile or so downstream, near the Trappers' Exchange, the river made a hairpin bend so sharp and narrow that the sternwheelers had to wait for a freshet to broaden the river enough to allow them to get around. Even then, with bow and stern touching the bank at each end and a gravel bar on the point cramping them in, their captains had to maneuver delicately to get them to creep around it and headed toward the wharf at Mile 53.

On their first trips downstream, both Captain Con Myers of the *Operator* and Captain Jack Shannon of the *Conveyor* were proud of the performance of their reassembled craft. Although each boat was fully equipped with large stateroom capacity and could accommodate 200 passengers, their main mission was carrying freight. On a subsequent trip they loaded up with 300 tons of material and, as well, each pushed a scow laden with nearly 100 additional tons. To navigate on such a river and with such lading, the captain had to be a rare judge of the channels and bars of the shifting stream bed, and each of those men was.

Both of Foley, Welch and Stewart's sternwheelers made as many trips as they could, but in July the *Operator* ran on some rocks in the Goat River rapids and pierced her hull and Captain Myers had to jettison a hundred tons of cargo to lighten his ship enough to allow her to be pulled free. As rapidly as possible he took her to the shipyard at Mile 51 and ten days later she was back in business again.

When many of the light goods which had been thrown overboard went floating and rolling and came to rest in an eddy, they became the first of a long series of goods lost by scow or steamer and cast like bread on the waters to turn up as manna for hands which later on began anticipating, and even arranging, such events. Before long, salvaging such goods cast overboard by necessity or by deliberate design developed into a business of notable proportions and one carried on with unscrupulous abandon.

When the *Operator's* goods went bobbing down with the current, a few men camped temporarily beside the Goat River rapids looked on them as a gift straight from the gods and set to with vigor salvaging and carrying them back to hiding places in the willows. Early next morning, however, Slim Niven and a partner, who were coming upstream in P. Burns and Company's powerful launch, took the scavengers by surprise. As Ted Abram said: "Coming around a bend in the river, through a little fog on the water, they were able to approach without being seen, and they came suddenly into view of the squatters, who thought they were from the Foley camp come to salvage their property, so they scattered. Slim quickly sized up the situation and pulled in ashore. Loading his boat he remarked that it was not every day they could pick up canned tomatoes, corn and peas, peaches and plums in the bushes, in all about twelve cases . . ." By nightfall Slim had the goods safely cached in the Ram Pasture.

But even the flat-bottom sternwheelers could only run during the short season of high water. By September, 1912, near modern Dome Creek, Mile 142, the construction town created by the building of the first bridge over the Fraser below Tête Jaune Cache, the *Operator* and the *Conveyor* were pulled out for the winter.

Meanwhile, Foley, Welch and Stewart's rivals, the British Columbia Express Company, had been getting ready to provide competition for the new lucrative shipping business on the upper Fraser. For his company, Captain J. P. Bucey watched the building of the *B.C. Express* at Soda Creek and launched her in June, 1912. She was 128 feet long with a beam of 29 feet, and because she was intended for work on the upper Fraser, where most of the freight had to be brought downstream, her hull was deliberately designed with downstream haul in mind. Aware that she had cost $65,025, Captain Bucey wangled her through the canyons up to Fort George with care, and after maneuvering her part way up the Grand Canyon in July to pick up a load of rails for delivery up the Nechako River, expressed enthusiasm for her ability. It was not until the next year, however, that he piloted her all the way to Tête Jaune Cache.

So, except for an occasional scow, during 1912 Foley, Welch and Stewart had a monopoly on freight out of Tête Jaune Cache — as indeed might be expected since nearly all the goods and materials moved were their own. After the *Operator* and the *Conveyor* were hauled out for the winter, a great deal of freight went downstream without them. For after all, scows carried the bulk of the goods.

During 1912-13 the Fraser crawled with scows hustling downstream on their one-way trip or hurtling to destruction in the canyons. For those two years scowing on the Fraser was the sole summer avocation of hundreds of men — an avocation demanding strength, agility, and above all, courage. It was, too, an avocation risky and sometimes deadly, but one which at all times challenged all young men whose search for adventure impelled them to seek a life on the frontier. At Mile 51 and at Mile 53 during those years, dozens of men worked all summer making scows, and as fast as they were finished (three or four every day) in crews of four at a time, hundreds of men climbed aboard them. At the height of the 1913 season some 1,500 courageous scowmen, either aboard or hastening back up the river to board yet another scow, lent an atmosphere to the Fraser rarely if ever equaled on any other rapid-studded river.

Twenty feet broad, thirty or forty feet long, flared at both bow and stern, made of two-inch planks, as fast as those scows were put together at Tête Jaune Cache, they were dismantled but a few days later and farther down the river for lumber—if they were not amongst the 10 per cent which the Grand Canyon had dismantled en route. After seeing to their loading with twenty or thirty tons, the four-man crew climbed aboard. Two went to the bow and two to the stern and took over the fifteen-foot sweeps which were set in a framework thirty inches high, so that the men could stand on deck and have lots of purchase to try to prevent their craft from nosing into the numerous sandbars. For that service the men were paid five to ten dollars a day, good pay, which depended upon their experience.

When things went well, as on the one-hundred-mile run before reaching the Goat Rapids, and when it did not rain, theirs were halcyon days floating down the winding, forest-locked river, which by its frequent windings presented a new scene every few minutes. And every view was different as each of the great pine-clad mountain slopes to the right or to the left swung into the line of view. For mile after mile the Fraser was a very lamb of a river, murmuring away and speeding the scow onward. It was, nevertheless, a lamb swarming with mosquitoes, sandflies, and no-see-ums, and moreover, its gentle guile hid many a deceiving sandbar.

As on any river, vigilance was the price of safety, and greenhorns, lulled by a sense of ease, often picking the wrong channel, ended up stuck on a bar. Then they had to wade ashore and camp till the rise in the river level allowed them to get their scow off. If with luck they steered clear of sandbars and got through the rapids and canyons safely, a few days would take them to their destination. There, after turning both load and scow over to the consignee and carrying off their little bundle of belongings, they waited for the next upbound sternwheeler. Or if the steamers were not running, they walked back or poled a pointer to Tête Jaune Cache to repeat the trip with another scow.

The Grand Canyon, however, the scene of dozens of drownings, was a far cry from the generally languid river. As Ted Abram says: "The most dangerous place was the Grand Canyon, not far from the present station of Longworth. The deep, swift river channel rushed madly against an obstacle, 'Green Rocks,' and the only feasible way to get by this rock, was by strenuously working the sweeps, fore and aft, to endeavor to keep clear and make sure the craft was broadside on, to slide by; the throw off, as the water struck the rock, hit the broadside, thus saving it as it swept by.

"A friend of mine, Alvin St. John, was on a loaded scow going through the Canyon. He and his partners, experienced men, were approaching Green Rocks and working hard, when one sweep snapped. Losing steering way, the scow crashed corner on, into the Rock, and sinking quickly, poor Alvin was drowned. I think some of the others managed to get into a small boat they were carrying.

"During the busy season, with so many company scows passing through, an extra four man crew was stationed at the head of the canyon. Being able, experienced men, they went aboard the company scows and helped the others to take them through, thus insuring safety to all concerned."

Since a number of Fort George merchants had warehouses for their own goods at Tête Jaune Cache, there were always a few individually owned scows making their way down the river, and once more quoting Ted Abram:

"Any time a private scow came along, the canyon crew would offer to see them through for the sum of $20.00 or so. Slim Niven was the head man in charge of the crew. He also kept a lookout man at a point on a high rocky bank above Green Rocks who had to alert two men who had a boat below, stationed in an eddy, in case anything happened and the men needed help.

"Well, one day, along came a well loaded scow, with a top load of baled hay. This was scattered to all sides of the scow and covered with a heavy waterproofed canvas, which was not tied down. This party was not willing to pay the price to be seen safely through. The leader, a Swede, remarked 'Oh I tank we make it,' even after being advised of the risk. Slim and his crew watched as they shoved off into the river. The party thought they could make it, but the rock proved them wrong, as the scow shot corner on, and crashed. The crew knew they were sinking and all four jumped onto the tarp at different spots, to hold it down over the hay as it floated away. Slim told me that if it hadn't been so tragic it would have been amusing to see the four men jumping from one place to another on the baled hay, as they strove to keep it from escaping from under the tarp. Happily, the boat crew were alerted, and swung their boat into the river, rescuing them all. They had saved $20.00 and lost the scow and their reputation as good river men.''

The boat to which Mr. Abram referred also served as a ferry for crossing the river. At the canyon most of the scows took on a pilot and he would signal the boat to move out into the stream so as to be in the best possible position to pick up any of the scowmen in case of disaster. Willis J. West, writing in the *British Columbia Historical Quarterly* in 1949, told of a case which happened during 1913 when a scow with a pilot struck a rock. Of all the men, the boat was able to rescue only the pilot. The rest of the men were never seen again, but he, plucky man, no sooner stepped out of the emergency boat than he nonchalantly strode off along the path bordering the canyon and in a hour or so guided another scow through the maelstrom. As early in the season as June, 1913, twenty men were said to have drowned in the canyon and for the two seasons fifty such deaths were reported, and there is no reason to doubt the accuracy of the report.

Some scowmen, however, could not face going through the canyon, and one of those of whom Ted Abram tells was a husky, athletic Scot who was the champion wrestler of Tête Jaune Cache. "He was very proud of his physique. The story goes that when loading the tons of supplies onto the scow, he would pick up two one hundred pound sacks of flour, one under each arm, and proudly carry them, whilst the other men were kept busy and quite satisfied to carry one sack at a time." On one trip when his scow tied up at the canyon to await a pilot, the Scot "was a little apprehensive of the situation, or perhaps during the waiting period his courage failed, and when they pushed the gang plank out for the canyon crew to come on board and before it was drawn in again, he walked ashore. His men looked at each other, then called to him: 'Where are you going?' He replied: 'I'm going to walk arroound.' 'Oh well,' they said, 'we'll walk arroound too', and they all deserted the ship and left the canyon crew to paddle their own canoe! as it were.'' Thenceforth he was nicknamed ''Old Walk Arroound.''

A great deal had to be learned about scowing down the Fraser, and early in the 1912 season Foley, Welch and Stewart learned some of it the hard way. Dr. Morrish chuckles as he tells of it. At the warehouse at Mile 53 one day he carefully tallied out all the lading of three or four of the early scows, of one of which he said: ''We put on dozens of caddies of tobacco, several cases of Old Chum and snoose but the significant part of the load was cases and cases of liquor — legitimate liquor owned by Foley, Welch and Stewart and consigned to some of their camps—whisky, brandy, beer and even some cases of champagne. Curiously enough, of them all only the scow with the liquor was wrecked. It simply disappeared. After that the boss said 'We'll send no more liquor down in scows, we'll ship it on the steamers.'

''For years,'' says Dr. Morrish, ''I wondered what had happened to that scow and then one day over twenty years later a patient came to my Edmonton office — a man from Waskatenau — and after I had treated him we sat and talked, and I found that he too had worked at Mile 53 and had been a scowman. We talked away and I mentioned that scow load of booze, and by the long arm of coincidence this man had been a crewman on it.

'' 'What happened to it?' I said. 'Did it hit a rock?'

'' 'Hell no! — hit a rock!' he said. 'It hit the same snag many another scow with valuable food and drink aboard did.'

'' 'What kind of a snag?'

'' 'We beached her at a much used spot around the bend above the canyon so that the observers on watch there could not see us and unloaded all the booze and hid it in the bushes. Then we set a charge of dynamite on her with a long fuse and pushed her off. A coupla hundred yards downstream she struck a rock all right — blew all to smithereens. Lots of scows went that way.' ''

Once navigation ceased for the winter, construction crews spread along a hundred miles of grade downstream from Tête Jaune Cache had to rely on freighters once more. Hauling on the ice was precarious and the dangerous spots were usually known to the rest of the freighters because someone's load of cement had broken through here and another's load of machinery or other gear had broken through there and those following gave those weak spots in the ice a wide berth. At some of those places the teamster would stand on the front of the sleigh runners all ready to disengage the horses if necessary. If he heard the ice beginning to crack, he would grab the ring on the bolt that held the doubletrees, yank out the pin and whip up his horses so that they would spring to safety ahead of the sinking load.

Ted Abram relates how as the last team in a swing he noticed the ice bend as the previous team passed over it. Fortunately he stopped short of the weak ice, unhitched his team and by means of chains hitched them to the end of the sleigh tongue. Whipping his horses up he got them across the bad spot without going through. His load of seventy quarters of beef did not fare so well; it crashed through, leaving only the front of the sleigh sticking out of the hole. But he had saved his horses. With the help of his companions he fished the beef out of the water, carried the seventy quarters to solid ice where he loaded up again and went on.

Early in April, 1913, to mark the opening of navigation for the year, Captain J. P. Bucey of the British Columbia Express Company arrived at Mile 53 on the train from Edmonton. As soon as the run of ice in the Fraser subsided he and a companion canoed downstream to study the river and particularly the Grand Canyon. He was planning to run the *B.C. Express* from Fort George to Tête Jaune Cache. During 1912, while the *Operator* and the *Conveyor* had been running downstream from Mile 53, Foley, Welch and Stewart had not needed their services below the canyon, so they sheered away from trying conclusions with it.

Late in May Captain Bucey set out from Fort George for his first round trip to Mile 53 and after passing up and down through the Grand Canyon returned to Fort George about a week later. Both the *Operator* and the *Conveyor,* equally on their toes, passed down through the canyon shortly after Captain Bucey and tied up at Fort George a day later. From then on during the 1913 navigation season the *B.C. Express* maintained a weekly round-trip schedule from Fort George to Mile 53.

Fortunately, one of Captain Bucey's early passengers was Willis J. West. All anticipation, at Fort George he boarded the *B.C. Express* for the round trip and his experiences justified his anticipation. Late in the afternoon she made her way up the lower canyon nearly to the whirlpool and Captain Bucey tied her up and walked ahead to study the water. West recorded the trip:

"The writer accompanied Captain Bucey on his hike to inspect the whirlpool. The trail along the high rock wall of the canyon was rough, and in places it was necessary to climb ladders made of poles to get to the higher levels of the trail. A point on the high ramparts of rock was soon reached from which the whirlpool could be viewed directly below, and it was an awesome sight to watch the full volume of water in the Fraser pour through a narrow gap from the basin into the raging maelstrom which seemed to be created by the peculiar rock formation of the river-bed. The whirlpool extended about 200 feet from shore to shore and was continually emptying and filling. There did not seem to be a great deal of driftwood coming down from the basin, and Captain Bucey, after studying the scene for a while, decided it would be safe to proceed.

"After making sure that the passengers were all aboard, the captain turned his ship into the stream. Soon the whirlpool was reached, and with a full head of steam the *B.C. Express* was steered into it. When the steamer had reached the strong current running into the narrow channel leading up into the basin, she appeared to hesitate and then started to drift back into the whirlpool. Although Captain Bucey tried several times to steam up through the gap, the ship was unable to make progress against the strong current. The captain then decided it would be necessary to line her through and he started, therefore, to maneuver his ship over to the left side of the canyon. Suddenly a spruce tree about 70 feet in length with a large root appeared on the surface of the whirlpool, and before the steamer could avoid it, it had swept underneath her and lodged against her three main rudders. Held there by the strong current, the spruce tree put the steering-gear out of commission and the captain lost control of his ship. The tree was so lodged against the ship's rudders that when she went ahead she turned sharply towards the left of the canyon and when she steamed astern her stern would likewise swing to the left. Fortunately, the stern-wheel was not obstructed nor damaged in any way, so the captain began to maneuver the ship by means of the wheel. His plan in these maneuvers was to drop the ship down stream to a point where the canyon wall was low enough for him to put a deck hand ashore with a line so that the boat could be tied up and the ship's carpenter and deck crew put to work detaching the rudders in order to dislodge the spruce tree from under the ship.

"Most of the passengers did not appear to be excited or worried by the plight of the stern-wheeler. They were confident that Captain Bucey was capable of meeting the emergency and were curious spectators of his efforts to reach a suitable landing place down the river where the rudders could be freed. The captain would signal to the engine room for slow speed ahead, then when the nose of the ship would reach the wall of the canyon, he would signal for the engines to be stopped so that the ship could drift down stream with the current. She was still in the whirlpool and had just touched the canyon wall with her bow when suddenly a heavy-set male passenger less nonchalant than his travelling companions raced across the forward deck and leaped on to a narrow ledge of rock. He had barely landed on the ledge when the steamer drifted away and he was left clinging to the rock barely 6 feet above the surface of the turbulent whirlpool. There was nothing the captain could do to rescue this frightened passenger at the time, for with the rudders out of order it was impossible to return up stream. As the steamer drifted down the river and round a turn out of sight of the self-marooned man on the ledge, there were few on board that ever expected to see him again. In about half an hour the captain had succeeded in working the *B.C. Express* down stream to a position where he was able to land a deck-hand with a line, as planned, and eventually the steamer was safely tied up and the crew busied themselves with freeing the rudders.

"Meanwhile Captain Bucey turned his thoughts to the rescue of the passenger who had leaped in panic from the ship. He consulted with A. K. Bouchier, the agent of the Express Company at Mile 53 B.C., and asked him to see whether he could locate and possibly rescue the frightened castaway. Bouchier was a tall, powerfully built young man, and as soon as he and the three companions he had selected to assist him could get ashore, they started to work their way up along the side of the canyon to a point overlooking the whirlpool. When they reached the edge of the cliff, to their surprise and delight they saw the passenger still on the rock ledge about 70 feet below. They had taken with them about 200 feet of line from the steamer, and with some of this they lowered the lightest member of their rescue party down the face of the cliff to the ledge, where he secured the rope around the passenger, who was then hauled up to the top of the canyon wall to safety. The occupation of this passenger was peddling diamond rings to the prostitutes and others in the towns and camps along the line of railway construction. For carrying the rings he had two leather jeweller's cases fitted into two large pockets inside his coat. When he reached the top of the cliff, his first move was to clutch at his pockets to assure himself that his rings were safe, then he collapsed on the rocks, and it was some time before he had recovered sufficiently to be assisted down to the ship, where he was put in his berth and given a stiff drink of Scotch.''

Next morning after the tree had been taken out of the ship's rudders the *B.C. Express* started again and ''. . . to the surprise of the passengers who had risen early to watch the second contest with the whirlpool, the ship had no difficulty in steaming up the narrow gap into the basin without making use of the cable. The explanation was that now the whirlpool happened to be full and overflowing, whereas on the previous afternoon it had been emptying when the steamer had made her unsuccessful effort to steam up the gap.

''At the upper end of the basin the passengers were put ashore to walk along the trail to the head of the canyon, and the steamer started up through the turbulent current of the narrow and crooked upper canyon. It was necessary to put out a line three times in succession before arriving at a point where the force of the current had moderated sufficiently for the steamer to proceed for the remainder of the distance to the head of the canyon under her own power.''

After delivering some freight and tying up for the night at the wild construction town of Mile 121, the *B.C. Express* reached Mile 53 at nine o'clock the next morning. When at four o'clock that afternoon she left Têtė Jaune Cache, she had the biggest load of freight and passengers she ever carried, and her gross earnings for the day and a half trip to Fort George were over $12,000.00.

Like all sternwheeler captains, J. P. Bucey not only had an overwhelming vocabulary of picturesque profanity, but also had an iron nerve which enabled him to make the quick decisions so necessary in the emergencies of maneuvering his ships through canyons. Inured to the roughness of frontier areas by his years of experience on many an American river, and hardened by constant exposure to pioneer callousness, he was a man capable of making instant and irrevocable decisions, as he demonstrated to Willis West.

"A few miles below the Grand Canyon he noticed a white flag on the bank, and consequently he turned his ship in and made a landing. Twenty men were waiting to be picked up; they were quickly taken on board and the ship backed out into the river and again headed down stream. The men were railway workers, who, with their pay cheques in their pockets, were on their way to Fort George for whiskey and other ways of parting themselves from their money. As soon as they came aboard, the purser proceeded to solicit their fares, and the first man to whom he spoke refused to pay, even although the purser offered to cash his cheque. The purser realized that if this man succeeded in evading payment, there would be no hope of collecting fares from the other men who had been picked up at the same landing for the 90-mile journey down the river. From the forward deck he called up to Captain Bucey in his pilot house and explained the situation. Without hesitation the captain turned his ship about and made an up stream landing. As soon as the ship was moored, he descended to the forward deck where the purser indicated to him the man who had obstinately refused to pay his fare. The captain repeated the purser's request, and when the man answered emphatically that he had no intention of tendering his fare, Bucey stated that he would permit no one to travel on his ship without paying his way. Summoning two deck hands, he pointed to the man and ordered them to throw him in the river. The deck hands seized the stubborn passenger, rushed him to the edge of the forward deck, and tossed him overboard. It all happened so quickly that the onlookers were astounded, and they rushed to the railside to see what had become of the man who had insisted on a free trip. Meanwhile Captain Bucey returned to the pilot house, called to the crew to let go the line, signalled to the engine room, and backed his ship into the stream and headed down river. He appeared to be completely uninterested in the fate of the man whom he had ordered to be thrown off the ship into the swift and treacherous water. This act had been a very dangerous proceeding, even although the man saved his life by turning out to be a powerful swimmer, for, favoured by a strong current setting towards the shore at that particular point along the river, he had floated down with the current past the ship and was able to grasp some bushes growing along the bank and pull himself ashore. The purser had no further trouble collecting the fares from the other railway employees, who were quite subdued by the treatment meted out to their companion.''

The *B.C. Express* continued to provide a weekly service between Fort George and Tête Jaune Cache. On each round trip she cleared a profit of at least $5,000; so that during the twelve weeks of her service on this run she repaid her entire cost. At that point, however, the GTP, or Foley, Welch and Stewart, or both, came up with a trick that cut short her career of running up to Tête Jaune Cache and one which illustrates how government rules and regulations and even the law itself could be manipulated sixty years ago.

One of the laws which was fundamental to all steamboat traffic was that no one could place any barrier across a navigable stream, or if he did, he must insure that it could be opened to permit a ship to pass through. Of more importance in those days than now, this law which provided for unobstructed water transport was usually enforced by the Federal Water Resources Authority. When, therefore, in August, 1913, Captain Bucey on his way up the Fraser encountered a cable strung across the river at the site of the proposed GTP bridge at Mile 141, his first reaction was to send one of the crew for his shotgun. Wiser counsels prevailed, however, and with difficulty he was restrained from shooting some of the bridge contractor's men.

Obstructing a navigable stream was an unheard-of affront. The British Columbia Express Company immediately took the case to court, and the magnitude of the crime, combined with irrefutable evidence, should have won the case for the company and should have resulted in the offending cable being torn down. But, incredibly, the British Columbia Express Company lost the case at the provincial level, and more incredibly still, on carrying it to the Supreme Court of Canada lost again.

At that time, however, except as an example of how the law could be manipulated, it mattered little because navigation on the upper Fraser was over. With its passing, troublous times hit Tête Jaune Cache and it crumpled up like a wet sock. By that time regular trains were operating to McBride and steel had been laid many miles below that. During the last half of 1913 the gangs spiked down 180 miles of steel. When in August, 1913, Collingwood Schreiber inspected the line, he found Foley, Welch and Stewart rushing the job to completion and reported that some 3,500 men were working on the grade along the Fraser and that at their disposal they had thirty-two construction locomotives, twenty-three large steam shovels, and plenty of other equipment. Finally, on January 27, 1914, the track layer pushed its way over the last crossing of the Fraser into Fort George, which by that time had been renamed Prince George. During that winter the *Operator* and the *Conveyor* were tied up at Prince George and were not used upstream again.

Everyone, of course, knew that when the GTP steel passed on west the town of Tête Jaune Cache would disintegrate, but no one realized that it would literally disappear. During the winter and on into the spring of 1913 it put up a brave front. Ted Abram continued with his draying, Mrs. Middough kept on teaching at the school, the Galloping Bath Tub was trundled back and forth to the river bank, and Dad Renshaw's restaurant remained open.

After the ice went out of the Fraser and the melting snows from a thousand creeks began to pour into the river, it overflowed its low banks and Ted Abram had to urge his dray horses through three feet of water along the main street. During the height of the flood the residents moved about in rowboats and in hip waders. When, after a few days, it subsided, it stranded trees and other driftwood here and there along Tête Jaune Cache's drenched and sodden thoroughfare. But as well as debris, the flood left another legacy — typhoid. The dread disease, following the construction camps from Edmonton, hit Tête Jaune Cache as a minor epidemic. If any died at the time, their deaths have not been recorded.

While one by one Tête Jaune Cache's remaining residents dribbled away, the CNR, coming in from the east and avoiding Tête Jaune Cache itself, graded its lines around the elbow and headed off to the southeast, toward Starvation Flats, the Albreda Pass, and ultimately to Kamloops. As a convenient jumping-off point for servicing their camps up Canoe River way, the CNR obtained a siding on the GTP, a couple of miles beyond Tête Jaune Cache, and called it Henningville. It grew into a small hamlet with a CNR warehouse and perhaps a dozen buildings, including Austen Brothers store, Cox's post office, a pool hall, and other amenities. In October, 1913, Mr. Renshaw, abandoning his restaurant, put up a frame building to house his hay and feed business at Henningville.

Meanwhile, the erosion the spring flood had started at Tête

Jaune town continued. Shortly after Renshaw moved the last of his goods out of his former restaurant it toppled over and went drifting down the river. By that time only a few diehards remained in what had been such a busy town.

Farther to the west, near Fort Fraser, on April 6, 1914, the last GTP spike was driven and thenceforth regular transcontinental trains to Prince Rupert passed through Tête Jaune's pass and roared past the vestiges of what so recently had been Tête Jaune town. Shortly after, in October, 1915, the CNR transcontinental line was completed to Vancouver. At last the Jasper valley and Tête Jaune's pass, emerging into the twentieth century, began fulfilling their destinies as corridors resounding to the roar of railway cars rolling goods across Canada to Cathay.

But before the first transcontinental rolled over the McLennan River bridge the buildings and the main street of Tête Jaune town had also set off west to end their days alongside the remnants of many a broken scow in the driftpiles down the Fraser. The high water of 1914 cut through the neck of land, and where the busy town had once stood, where the lawyer had leapt from the lady barber's chair, where the whisky-packed pigs had gone to the photographer's, the inscrutable Fraser flowed calmly along. Tête Jaune town had come to the end of its road.

At Mile 51 where the girls had gamboled and then had gone on west with the grade, nature strewed the flats with a clean, resinous growth of young pines. Eventually the wharves at Mile 53 buckled and yielded to the river, and on the log warehouse time exacted its toll. Even by the winter of 1920-21, when by a curious chance the once elegant *B.C. Express* revisited the scene of her prima donna days, she found it in ruins.

At the time she too was in a sorry state, for her owners had dismantled her, lashed her boilers, ironwork, and furnishings to railway cars and sent them rolling east over the very rails she had brought to the grade. Allowing her little time for a wistful glance at Mile 53 and a last look at the Fraser, they hurtled her through the Yellowhead Pass. Hustling her on through Jasper, giving her introductory peeks at the gathering waters of the Athabasca, hauling her east to Edmonton and Fort McMurray, they reassembled her and set her afloat on the Athabasca. There, for several years, she gave valiant service.

But unfortunately, for the next half century at least, the flats at Tête Jaune Cache were to see little service. For Tête

Jaune Cache was merely a memory. And yet, so long as Canadians remember the stalwart men who built railways with shovels, the horses who broke their hearts and their bones in the windfall of the pack trails, and the stout-hearted scowmen who ran the canyons, the memory of Tête Jaune Cache will live on.

13

ONE RAILWAY TORN UP

IN THE same way as fate dealt harshly with Tête Jaune Cache, the long-suffering laws of economics, never gentle with politicians who try to flout them, clamped down on the CNR and the GTP. The wasteful duplication of twin railway grades from Entwistle to Red Pass Junction had been too glaring to escape retribution.

The GTP had completed its transcontinental to Prince George by April, 1914. The CNR, held up by delays over its bridges across the Pembina and McLeod rivers, was not completed to Vancouver until October, 1915. By that time Canada was up to its ears fighting World War I, and even the politicians began to look around for ways to economize. One obvious move was to consolidate the parallel grades west from Edmonton and to run both companies' trains over one set of tracks. Steel rails were needed for military railways to support the troops in France and Flanders, so in July, 1917, Fred Driscoll supervised tearing up eighty miles of CNR steel from Chip Lake to Obed and shipping it to France. Shortly after that, some twenty-five miles of CNR track between the Snaring River and Geikie were abandoned.

Those were but the first moves in a process which, by abandoning most of the CNR grade, retaining most of the GTP grade, and making minor changes here and there, ended up leaving only one operating railroad from Edmonton to Jasper. Abandonment cut off main line service to the thriving little town of Pocahontas and its busy mine. Thenceforth it was served by using only the portion of the old line which ran south to Snaring Junction.

By December, 1918, the Dominion Government, which had felt called upon to rescue other railways from the certain bankruptcy into which a combination of its policy and their managements' indiscretions had plunged them, also took over the insolvent CNR. Though the GTP was in much the same financial mess, it fought off the government ax until July, 1920, when it too was beheaded and thrown into the bag of remnants of railroads then unofficially called the Canadian National Railways. It was not until October, 1922, when Henry Thornton took over the responsibilities of that widespread but nondescript assortment of railways, that the government corporation became officially known as the Canadian National Railways.

Back in the days when the great Sir Wilfrid Laurier was at the height of his power and when he should have prevented the sorry duplication of so many railway lines, and particularly of those two transcontinentals, great dreams beclouded even his vision. In those days of unsound speculation and political corruption even he had been swept into the unreal world of insane railway competition. But politicians were no more responsible than the public at large. Bankers, manufacturers, merchants, western farmers, investors, and speculators from end to end of the country shared the same fever. All of them, from the humblest voter to the most embroiled politician, shut their minds to the risk of the great gamble and with hands spread wide for any passing graft, turned their eyes away. The prime minister and the politicians were not alone to blame; they were but the servants of a public which condoned and permitted such practices—provided they stood a chance of getting a cut of the booty.

Nevertheless, the great era of speculative railway building left the Yellowhead Pass with all it needed—one transcontinental railway where giant locomotives panted as, with easy grace, on any one trip they pulled far more freight through the pass than all the voyageurs and all the pack horses had done in all previous time. At last the easy grade of the Yellowhead Pass had been recognized and finally had come into its inheritance.

Under the new Canadian National Railways management the Canadian Northern's divisional point at Tollerton was abandoned, leaving Edson, its rival, free to expand. Deciding whether to retain Lucerne on beautiful Yellowhead Lake or Jasper as the next westerly divisional point was a more difficult problem. Each town had been established for nearly ten years, each had a choice location, and each had a population approaching three hundred. The final decision appears to have been taken in 1923, and the order which was to extinguish the pleasant townsite on the south side of Yellowhead Lake was issued. By the end of 1924 everyone, including Dr. Thomas O'Hagan and Tom Young, the locomotive foreman, had moved to Jasper, the rails of the one-time yard had been taken up, and although the CNR retained the name for a whistle stop on the north shore of the beautiful lake, Lucerne the divisional point ceased to exist.

When Lucerne disappeared and the CNR steel had been taken up west from Geikie station, Resplendent blossomed out as Red Pass Junction, the point where the taking up of the steel had stopped and where the two railways diverged. West from it, what had been the GTP line continued to Tête Jaune Cache and Prince Rupert and the coast, and what had been the CNR started its long climb toward the summit of Albreda Pass and thence to Vancouver. From then on along the newly revised right of way, long, sleek railway trains, powered with their own snorting pack horses, the panting steam locomotives, sped passengers and goods to tidewater.

A new race of hardy, courageous men—Scotsmen and Bluenoses, Yankees and Italians—had come to replace the one-time Iroquois or French, a new race calling themselves not voyageurs but railwaymen. Past the echoing rocks, across the boiling streams, and along the cliffs to which pack horses had clung while carrying leather to New Caledonia and otter skins bound to Russia and returning with packs of other furs, this new breed sped. Shoveling coal, watching for slides, and whistling for tunnels they carried prairie wheat and coal west to the seaboard and returned laden with merchandise and with silks from Japan. Where in 1863 Dr. Cheadle had given free passage to the rogue O'Byrne and where, across the Fraser on the shale cliff, he had to pry a boulder off the path, cautious railwaymen stopped their locomotives to climb down and roll rocks off the track. Along the shore of Yellowhead Lake, where in 1862 Catherine Schubert's husband had killed a horse to feed her whimpering children, and farther along where A. L. Fortune's stomach had rejoiced as he roasted a skunk—here, in dining cars, surrounded by crisp linen and shining cutlery and looking languidly across Yellowhead Lake to the heights of the Seven Sisters, ladies clad in silks sat nibbling imported delicacies and grumbling because they were too highly or too lightly seasoned. Now, travel through the pass was effortless, nay, luxurious, and it all seemed so simple. It could be taken for granted.

But to a train crew everything had to be watched, nothing could be taken for granted. At a divisional point such as Edson, where the crew climbed aboard, the hogger (engineer) with his goggles, a long-peaked denim cap, his polka dot handkerchief, and his timetable, and the tallow-pot (fireman) with his wad of waste and his battered black bag, followed by the brakeman and the conductor—they knew that nothing could be taken for granted. On a summer afternoon where the tracks unrolled before them down the narrow, curving lane, walled in by an unending fifty-foot high hedge of pine trees, and the sun flashed back from pond or rill or river, not even then could they relax for a minute. For constant watchfulness was the price of safety for themselves and their hundreds of passengers, and watchful they were.

And yet it was an exhilarating trip, easing out of the muskeg of the Edson yards, slowing to creep around the curve of the Big Eddy trestle, then pitching more coal and letting the engine get her teeth into the rails to take the climb up the Obed ridge. Clacking over the joints, listening to the bumping of the couplings as they swayed around curves and flashed past the switch lights and station semaphores, passing Marlboro, Bickerdike, and Medicine Lodge, merely wider spots cleared out of the pines, the crew returned the waves of the section men and the handful of people at those stations.

On a fall day when the lakes were blue and the hillsides gold and the locomotive puffed up the defile of the Athabasca past old Entrance and Brulé Lake and the Bedson tunnel, and roared along the open valley, they knew that no scenery on earth could surpass it, but they had other things to watch for. Coasting into Jasper station after dark, watching the switch lights turn from red to green and the brakeman's lantern bobbing up and down, was always a pleasing relief. Leaving there with the full moon drawing long streaks on the water courses and lakes or burnishing the face of cut or cliff, and with the full-voiced steam whistle roaring defiance at the mountains and carrying miles to assure lonesome ears that the train was on time and that all was well with the world, the crew was ever alert. Rolling down from the summit, coasting most of the way past Yellowhead and Moose lakes and along the tracks clinging to the wall of the Selwyn Range, the crew could look across the river to ascertain Mount Robson's mood. Then turning the elbow near long-gone Henningville, passing Cranberry Lake and the Albreda summit, and eventually pulling into Blue River to leave the locomotive smelling of coal smoke and humming with achievement and contentment—all along there were many things to attend to and many things to watch for. To the passengers and to the waving well-wishers at each tiny station deep in the valleys and forests it was all romantic and wonderful.

But most romantic of all were the silk trains, now only a memory though in their day taking precedence over all other traffic. The last of them on the CNR roared east out of the pass in the early thirties at a time when synthetic fabrics were pushing silks aside. In their day it was vital to the industry that the bales of raw silk unloaded at the Vancouver docks be rushed at express speed to New York. The Yellowhead Pass saw about a dozen a year—a dozen long train-loads of raw silk roaring down the valley. In 1927 the CNR swept the largest Canadian silk train east. Behind the steaming locomotive twenty-one cars flung themselves around the curves above Tête Jaune's flat, carrying 7,200 bales worth seven million dollars, and crossed from the Pacific to the Atlantic at New York in eighty hours, three-quarters of the time taken by the fastest passenger trains. For time, as the lawyers say, was of the essence. As the silk trains approached from the west and flashed past gawking bystanders at each station, all other trains were cleared into side tracks. At divisional points, such as Jasper, alert crews stood beside a fresh locomotive with its safety valve on the verge of popping, ready to uncouple the perspiring incoming engine and hitch on their eagerly panting steamer, so that within two or three minutes her majesty, the silk train, could hiss off east.

But to the crew of any train there was little romance when winter's grip—thirty to forty below—sifted snow across the station platform and wrapped the engine in a white ghostly fog, and when hose connections broke with frost or couplings cracked, and brakemen clinging to icy grab-irons went about their dangerous duties. For winter, when a fog of steam blocked the view from one side and then, as the locomotive took the next curve, blocked the other side, and hogger and fireman peered ahead from cab windows—winter was the test of a railwayman's courage. Winter with its blizzards and drifts, and spring with its snow and mud slides and washouts, these were the dangerous days and nights.

To hear about the pleasures of railroading, however, as well as the stories of the grim phases, one must talk to some of the retired railwaymen of Jasper. It has been my good fortune to listen to a few of them; Charlie Whitten, who worked for the GTP in 1912; Mel Peterson, one-time conductor, relaxing after his forty-four years' service; Tommy Ross from Dornoch, Scotland, who worked on the track layer on construction and fired locomotive No. 112 for the first through GTP train which arrived in Prince Rupert on April 9, 1914. And talking to others, too, including Ross McKee, over ninety now, whose mind, ticking like his railwayman's watch, slowly maybe but precisely, recalls his first trip to Jasper in April, 1912.

Although Ross McKee retired in 1944, he can cast his mind back to the days of nearly sixty years ago when as hogger on a freight creeping west, he nosed his engine into the snowshed just west of Robson station and was confronted suddenly with a great gush of water. He stopped immediately and waited, holding his breath, knowing something was going to happen. It did—a small slide oozed down past the east end of the shed and a large rock knocked the second car from the engine off the track, but "nobody was hurt," says Ross McKee. Another time on the side hill facing Mount Robson, as the engineer eased his locomotive cautiously along, he saw a large rock smack in the middle of the track. While a few other rocks continued to dribble down the mountainside, McKee and the brakeman got out, and as the hogger inched the engine forward, held a tie ahead of the cow-catcher till it pushed the rock over the side. All the while, here and there, an odd football-sized rock came crashing down, "zip, zip. I had horseshoes in my pocket that time!"

McKee's most poignant memory, however, is of a snowslide in the same general area, which, extending past the end of the snowshed, covered the track yards deep in snow and ice. " 'Twas in twenty-two, I think—yes, in twenty-two." They called him in Jasper at 9 p.m. to drive the extra engine coupled on behind the rotary plow. Shortly after he and the others went to work on the slide, a bearing on the rotary engine heated and threatened to seize up. Paddy Bateman, the rotary engineer, signaled McKee that they would back out of the cut they had made till the engineer decided they were clear of the danger area and could stop to examine the bearing. When they stopped, McKee, looking out his cab window in the dark, could just make out the CNR grade above them on the mountainside, while looking out the other he could see how the ends of the ties nearly overhung the Fraser River a couple of hundred feet below.

For a minute or so all was silent except for the rumbling of the boilers, and then he heard Bateman and the roadmaster climb out on the mountain side of their cab and start to examine the bearing. Then without an instant's warning, another slide slammed down, burying the rotary and covering the boiler of McKee's locomotive. He and his fireman and Harry King, the section foreman from Jasper, jumped out on the river side of his cab and with great difficulty shoveled their way forward through the two or three feet of snow and reached the rotary. They knew that Bateman and the roadmaster, crushed by fifteen feet of snow and rocks and jammed against the rotary, would in all probability be dead, but hoped to help Tommy Wharton, the brakeman, and Berry, the fireman.

When after a struggle they reached the forward cab, they found that its roof had been smashed in and had pinned Wharton under it. Although his leg was broken, he was still alive. Of Berry the fireman there was no trace. Wharton concluded that the impact had thrown him out of the cab and had probably catapulted him down to the river, but in the dark they could see no sign of him.

It took them an hour, working feverishly, to free Wharton and doing so entailed several trips back along the river side of the track to get extra bars and jacks, and each time they floundered in snow well above their knees. Finally they carried the disabled brakeman back to McKee's cab and started shoveling snow over the bank. In a few minutes Harry King's shovel touched Berry, who had fallen on the end of the ties and had been buried under the snow and rocks over which the other men had tramped back and forth. When they uncovered him he raised his arms toward them, groaned once, and died.

"If we'd only a known," said McKee, his voice breaking as he recalled the scene stamped on his memory half a century ago, "if we'd only a known as we tramped back and forth over Berry's face—if we'd only a known we could have dug him out and saved him. Three good men were killed in that slide."

As with voyageurs, so with the train crews, death might lurk around any corner.

But silk trains and snowslides and an abandoned railway grade, are years ahead of this story. Other men, venturesome as voyageurs and intrepid as the men of the running trades, continued to take up the challenge of the lofty peaks of the Yellowhead Pass.

Before the blasting explosions of the railway builders or the clanging of the track layer had entered the pass, several mountaineers, by pressing on to their objectives over two hundred miles of pack trails, had matched wits with Mount Robson and failed. Coleman and Collie, Amery and Mumm had all done so. Even Rev. George Kinney, who in 1909, after one of the pluckiest climbs on record, thought he had stood on Mount Robson's crown, had spent weeks with pack horses before he came in sight of his majestic challenger. With the coming of the railroad, however, Mount Robson and its lofty neighbors of the pass found themselves open to direct assault from base camps within sound of locomotive whistles echoing from the valley below.

The first attacking party to approach by the new railroad and to which was extended official credit for conquering Mount Robson came in 1913, bearing the banner of the Alpine Club of Canada. During the four years since Kinney's magnificent climb a doubt had disturbed all of Canada's mountain climbers —had Kinney really reached Robson's top? In case it should be true, A. O. Wheeler of the Alpine Club got together another team, Albert MacCarthy and William Foster, and put them under Conrad Kain's capable direction.

Eight hours of strenuous climbing carried them to success. Mount Robson, the mightiest all-Canadian peak, had been conquered!

Standing on its very summit, bracing against the harsh wind and treading gingerly on the treacherous ice, they congratulated each other. Looking down far below — almost vertically down —they saw the Fraser River valley and the Grand Forks, where, nearly a century earlier, their fellow pioneer, Tête Jaune, had made his cache. Far below, coiled beside the green streak of the river, snaked the railway, a mere scratch on the hillside.

They confirmed the truth of what Curly Phillips had confided to Kain—that in their climb four years earlier he and Kinney had reached the edge of the highest ice dome of all, which rose yet another fifty feet but which in the uncertain light, with great curtains of mist and fog rising and falling and swirling around them, they dared not climb. Foster and MacCarthy, experienced climbers, assisted by Kain, one of the world's best guides, had reached the summit which Kinney, a distinguished climber, aided only by his raw amateur friend Curly Phillips had assailed. Well might Kain say "They deserve more credit than we."

Although in 1909 Curly Phillips had been a novice in mountain climbing, he had always been a resourceful packer and guide. This he demonstrated once more in 1913 when serving some of the Mount Robson party. On that occasion a climber by the name of Haskett-Smith was not only disabled but got infection in a cut inflicted by a falling stone. He became so ill that a doctor in the party said his only hope lay in getting him to a hospital, and asked if Phillips could get him there. Curly rigged up a canvas stretcher and then with a number of men set out. By changing bearers every ten minutes, the party covered the nineteen miles to the railway in time to load their patient on the evening train for Edmonton.

That summer, assisted by the railway, other climbers set their hopes on other Yellowhead Pass peaks. That summer, stepping down from the train came two other famous climbers fired with ambition—Arnold Mumm and Geoffrey Howard. As far as Fitzhugh they came as separate expeditions; Mumm with his well-known packer, John Yates of Lac Ste. Anne, and Howard with an equally capable Fred Stephens.

In 1913 Mumm decided to climb Mount Geikie, which three years earlier, when on Yellowhead Mountain, he had made out rising far above its fellows some twenty miles south of his vantage point. This was the peak (10,854 feet) which in 1898 J. E. McEvoy, the geologist, had named after the famous Scottish scientist. When talking over his projected climb with various local people, including Lewis Swift, Mumm heard conflicting opinions about the best way to approach the great mountain. Some of them felt that the mountain McEvoy had named was really the voyageurs' Montagne de la Traverse (Edith Cavell 11,033 feet), which, as is known, is some sixteen miles east of Geikie. In the end he approached Mount Edith Cavell up the Whirlpool but was turned back by a storm.

It took some years to straighten out the confusion between Mount Edith Cavell and Mount Geikie. Although Mumm had confused the two, A. O. Wheeler, writing in Volume IV of the *Canadian Alpine Journal (1912)*, did not share that opinion. He had approached the divisional point of Fitzhugh from the north and looking directly south on Mount Cavell wrote: "One fine wedge-shape peak rises supreme. It was named Mt. Fitzhugh, as it is in full view from what will some day be a city of that name. Mt. Fitzhugh is snowclad the year round and has an altitude of 11,188 feet. Around its base can be seen a snowfield supplying a fine glacier, which at our low altitude was hidden from view. There seems to be an impression in the locality that this is the Mt. Geikie of McEvoy's map. Such, however, is not the case, for Mt. Geikie lies further west and is either a peak of the Great Divide or very close to it. The Altitude is placed at 11,016 feet . . ."

In 1915 E. W. D. Holway and Dr. A. J. Gilmour made the first ascent of Mount Edith Cavell. Later, when Holway described the climb, he wrote that on July 31 they started "for Mt. Cavell, then known locally as Mt. Geikie." Three days later, without undue effort, they reached its summit. Curiously enough one of the photographs he took to illustrate his article was entitled "The Summit of Mt. Edith Cavell (formerly Mt. Fitzhugh)." At the time of the climb Nurse Edith Cavell was still alive. She was shot by the Germans in October, 1915, and her death aroused so much sentiment that among other memorials her name was bestowed on this beautiful mountain. When Holway wrote the article some time in 1916, that had been done.

It is interesting to note that in the decisions of the Geographical Board of Canada as recorded on page 3132 of the *Canada Gazette* of March 25, 1916, the official name is given as Mount Cavell, not Mount Edith Cavell. In that decision it is evident that up till that time the mountain had no official name, because the *Gazette* does not mention any change of name. It would be an interesting study to try to determine whether regardless of all modern maps the official name is still the courageous nurse's surname only or if another subsequent ruling yielding to popular sentiment changed the name to that shown on maps.

Just as the unofficial Mount Fitzhugh had its name changed, so did Fitzhugh the village. When a name had to be found for the divisional point at Mile 112 in the mountains, it was called Fitzhugh, after Earl Hopkins Fitzhugh, an American who at the time was First Vice-President of the company.

As Fitzhugh it was known for two or three years, while in 1911 the GTP laid out its yard and built a twelve-stall roundhouse and a station and the National Park Authorities began consolidating their position. Although the park had been set aside in the fall of 1907, it was some time before it was given an official name. Two logical choices faced the authorities: Athabasca Park or Jasper Park, but since the latter was the name by which everyone had known the area since the days of Jasper Hawse, they settled on it. In 1912 they laid out and cleared their new townsite and on June 1, 1913, Fitzhugh officially became Jasper. The railway company, which most of the time had been extremely highhanded with local people, and, for instance, had forced the name Edson on the area which formerly had been called Heatherwood, considered it good business to fall in line with the park authorities and renamed their station Jasper.

The town progressed slowly. In 1913 Geoffrey Howard the

mountain climber described it as being a "huddle of log shacks and bales of hay" prominent in which were a pool room and Stevenson's one-story wooden hotel. At that time the whole valley was recovering from the effect of the bad fires which had swept the area about 1891 and it was covered with a new growth of head-high pine.

By 1913 several men who were to loom large in Jasper's history had moved to the town. Among these was Willard Jeffery, who, after following the GTP construction with stores, set up in business in the hamlet. Curly Phillips, too, the guide and packer who, as a relatively inexperienced man, had climbed Mount Robson with Rev. Mr. Kinney and for a few subsequent years had worked in tie camps, moved to Jasper in 1912 and built his corrals. Fred Stephens, the outfitter, and Alex Wylie, one of the area's outstanding packers, also began to consider Jasper as home.

About the same time, Fred Brewster, who had been packing out of Prairie Creek in association with his brother Jack and a man named Moore, moved into Jasper. As well as packing for various mountaineering parties, the two brothers, and especially Fred, became associated with the National Parks Department in the many ventures it had to undertake to provide preliminary facilities.

Fred Archibald Brewster, who for nearly sixty years was to become Jasper's pre-eminent citizen, was born in Kildonan, Manitoba, in 1884, but at the age of four his parents moved to Banff and into the same mountain environment which Fred later found at Jasper and which brought him fulfillment for the long decades of his adventurous and contented life. He completed his formal education by graduating from Queen's University in engineering in 1909, and two years later arrived in Jasper. From then on, pioneering roads, cutting them out, establishing camps, and packing for tourists, filled his busy years. His first tourist venture occurred in 1911 when he provided pack trips for those who wished to visit Maligne Lake.

That same year, not long after one of the native children had been interred, Fred helped to dig the first white man's grave in Jasper's cemetery for his friend Dave Gallacher. His death was the result of one of the practices of the time amongst a gang of men who operated in Edmonton. Ever on the alert for someone incautious enough to allow them to suspect that he carried a considerable sum of money, they followed their victim when he stepped into a bar for a drink. Sometimes, in collusion with a barman, they saw to it that his drink was doped and, as soon as he became insensible, they stole his money—"rolled him"—and left him to regain consciousness to find his wallet missing. At other times they involved him in a brawl, beat him up and took his money. The details of Gallacher's case are not clear. He was a fine type of man, moderate and careful, but he made the mistake of carrying fourteen hundred dollars when he went to Edmonton. There he was mauled so badly that a few weeks after he returned to Jasper he died from his injuries. Six of his friends, Fred, George and Jack Brewster, Press Berry, Harry Miller, and Dick Langford, buried him.

One of Fred Brewster's most interesting projects started in 1915 when he and his brother Jack, in collaboration with the Edmonton Tent and Awning Company and the CNR, built the tourist attraction which for a while was known as Tent City. They spotted it amidst the Douglas firs on the north shore of what was then called Horseshoe Lake. It consisted of ten tents with wooden floors and was the forerunner of Jasper Park Lodge on the lake now known by the more fanciful name of Lac Beauvert.

Having set that project in motion, Fred Brewster went to war. He ended up as a major in an engineering battalion, and after a distinguished record, came home to Jasper in July, 1919, with a Military Cross and Bar.

All the while, although the town of Jasper grew slowly, many interesting people congregated there. One whose brief but delightful memoirs give us a look into life in the town during the early days was Mrs. B. R. Arends. Soon after her arrival in December, 1915, Dr. Gow, Jasper's first physician other than those who had been employed by the construction contractors, asked her if she would help by nursing some of his patients. As Mrs. Arends says proudly, ". . . we never lost a patient. Many babies were born that year, all at home under the most primitive circumstances—no running water, no electric lights, no plumbing—just prayers and hard work."

One day a young woman from another town along the GTP line came to her explaining that she was pregnant and did not want to disgrace her people by remaining at home. She asked if Mrs. Arends would keep her "until it was all over. She had not told the baby's father. I took her in, and then proceeded to find that father. Time was passing and her time was very near. Finally I found him, sent him a wire and he came, after a few days. They talked it over and decided to marry—but—he had to go to Edson for the license and the trains only ran every third day—which meant waiting for the train to go east, and then a wait for the return trip. Besides that, the preacher came only once in two weeks. Oh! those days of anxious waiting! Finally on Christmas eve the preacher came. Her pains started! We couldn't find the doctor! However the preacher started the wedding ceremony with them using my wedding ring which was big enough to fit two of her fingers! The pains were real by this time, and the bridegroom was kneeling beside the bed saying his 'I do's'. The baby was born just as the doctor walked in and the preacher and the bridegroom were going out the door. We didn't have nerves in those days and in an hour's time the house had quieted and we were all fast asleep.''

Mrs. Arends has fond memories of what she called the Bed-Bug Flyer, the small train which operated between Jasper and Pocahontas. After Dr. Gow left Jasper, Dr. Grey was still practicing in the coal mining town, so "as we had no doctor in Jasper, it was necessary to journey to Pocahontas to see Dr. Grey. At that time we had to get a permit from a medical man to buy a bottle of liquor. Needless to say, every pay day the Bed-Bug Flyer had a carload of passengers all to see Dr. Grey and get their permit.''

Illustrative of some of the wholesome pleasures the people of Jasper enjoyed, Mrs. Arends's memoirs recall their blueberry-picking excursions: "We, of course, knew all the railroad men. We were a very small town then, and naturally, all close neighbours. So a bunch of us would make arrangements with a crew leaving Jasper for McBride to take us as far as Rainbow or Red Pass in a caboose. These freight trains left Jasper anywhere from one a.m. to four, but whatever the time, you could depend we were always on time and packed in that caboose with our berry pails and lunch buckets. Actually I don't think the boys liked the idea very much, as we must have been a great nuisance to them. However, they made and served us coffee, and on leaving us in a desolate place along the railroad track, would kindly give us a few fusees to light up until we could gather wood, which, thank heaven, was very plentiful. Then we would light a big bonfire and sit around the fire and talk until daybreak. The boys made arrangements with the engineer to start blowing the whistle several miles from the berry-patch on their return trip — usually the evening of the same day —so that we could all be lined up along the track ready to hop on with our loads of berries. We usually had a lot of funny experiences to relate, and the return trip was sometimes quite a lively party. We made this trip several times during the berry season and I'm sure the railroad boys, though very noble during the sessions, were truly glad when it was all over. We usually managed to have the wife of one of the crew with us and that helped a lot.''

Mrs. Arends's memoirs also recall the time in 1921 when scarlet fever raged in Jasper. By that time Dr. Thomas O'Hagan had come to practice in Lucerne and in time of need he came to Jasper, for Pocahontas had folded up and Dr. Grey had sought other pastures. In its ten-year life Pocahontas had shipped nearly a million tons of coal, but by 1921 the best of the seam had been mined. Mining processes had fractured much of the coal and continued operation of the mine had become uneconomical. Even the company's mine near the Bedson Ridge across the river on the CNR had proved unsatisfactory.

So in May, 1921, Pocahontas, the town which at times had housed over a hundred miners, closed up and the railway grade west to Snaring Junction was abandoned. Today at Pocahontas the observant tourist can still see the dump where the waste coal was discarded. He has more difficulty seeing the little cemetery where lie the victims of life's ordinary wear and tear and of the Spanish 'flu of 1918 and the casualties of the miners' hazardous occupation. In 1915 alone, falling rock or coal had taken three lives and claimed another victim the next year. During 1917 the mine changed its tactics and on separate occasions asphyxiated four men. Though mining had its own fascination, it exacted a heavy toll.

With Pocahontas shut down and Dr. Grey gone, Dr. O'Hagan at Lucerne was the only physician in the valley. When by 1924 Jasper had won its battle for supremacy over Lucerne and the latter ceased to exist, Dr. O'Hagan, already famous for his skill, sense of duty, and kindliness, went to Jasper, where over the decades his acclaim grew.

Gradually Jasper began to find itself the sole town in the Athabasca valley, a destiny it assumed with relish. A decade earlier, on Lewis Swift's farm almost at Jasper's back door, Swiftholme, the townsite which the rugged pioneer had planned and plotted and which had threatened to become a rival, had died aborning. Then in their turn, Pocahontas in 1921 and Lucerne in 1924 had folded up, leaving the town of Brulé with its mine and its population of some five hundred souls as Jasper's only rival.

For a few years longer Brulé's Blue Diamond Mine, the successor to Mackenzie and Mann's original venture, continued to operate. Finally its seams became dirty and it closed up in July, 1928, leaving Brulé to wither. When that happened, Jasper was left as the only significant town between the divisional points of Edson and Blue River. Marlboro, which at one time had been so full of promise, was already doomed. The Marlboro Cement Company's finances were becoming as shaky as the deposit of white marl beside the railway track was sketchy. Within a few years the plant closed and Marlboro was left with a little store, many unoccupied houses, and a lonesome concrete stack standing as a memorial to an adventure in which Edmonton businessmen lost hundreds of thousands of dollars.

For a decade or so Hinton, which had been dormant since the days of railway construction, stepped in to take its place. While many venturesome men had investigated the nearby coal seams and at times had started mines at Drinnan and Bliss, it was not until 1928 that the Hinton Collieries Ltd. started an operation which for many years appeared to be successful. As a result, Hinton grew into a town of several hundred. When in 1938 five miners were killed in an explosion the property never recovered from the catastrophe and closed down two or three years later. Except for Jasper, which even during the depression continued to grow slowly, and a few sawmills dotted along its right of way, the CNR found little revenue in the local traffic generated along its several hundred miles of roadbed crossing the Continental Divide.

Lying in its chinook-kissed valley, basking in the sun, looking up at Pyramid Mountain, Roche Bonhomme, and Mount Edith Cavell, Jasper, observing the present with impatience, nevertheless faced the future with confidence. The headquarters of what must soon become one of Canada's main recreational areas and the focus of Canada's foremost transportation route, with the busy track of one transcontinental sweeping through its valley and the abandoned grade of another looping along beside it, Jasper's residents began to dream. Of their many dreams, one which soon assumed pressing importance revolved around the abandoned grade. Motor cars had come of age and now there was need for a road which would let all of Canada's automobiles enter Jasper's fabulous playground.

14

ADD A PIPELINE AND HIGHWAYS

SHORTLY after the 1914-1918 War had ended, the war to which Nurse Edith Cavell's life had been sacrificed, the park authorities brought the first car to Jasper. In May, 1920, Jack Brewster freighted in another and soon other citizens acquired those luxuries. But while they could scoot around on the local trails and while between Jasper and Edmonton there were many remnants of the old tote road, and, of course, untold miles of abandoned grade, it was impossible to drive a car from one of those points to the other.

But outsiders also had been looking at the unused railway grade. As early as 1917 Fred Driscoll, the surveyor, had suggested that in the abandoned grade Albertans had a firm foundation for a highway to Jasper. As soon as the war was over, he and others, and particularly an active young lawyer named Charles H. Grant, President of the Edmonton Automobile and Good Roads Association, began to act and agitate toward getting a passable road to Jasper. And to them the idea of a Yellowhead Highway was born. It was first of all to be a road to allow Edmontonians to get to Jasper. But as the idea grew it came to be a dream of a highway which would give all Canadians access to that marvelous scenic park, and ultimately the road was to become a trans-Canada highway following the old fur traders' trail across the prairies and through the mountains to the coast.

As its first step in enlisting popular support, Grant's organization offered a gold medal for the drivers of the first car to travel by way of the Yellowhead Pass and Kamloops from Edmonton, the capital of Alberta, to Victoria, the capital of British Columbia.

With the backing of Lines Motors in Edmonton and using one of their Overland Fours, Charles Neimeyer, the driver, and Frank J. Silverthorne, mechanician, took up the challenge. With a dramatic send-off, involving Charles Grant, Mayor Duggan, and several hundred citizens, the venturesome pair set forth after lunch on June 17, 1922.

By nightfall, traveling the rough graded roads and trails, the car, more or less intact, reached Entwistle, some sixty-five miles away. From there west, heaving and pushing their car out of mudholes and crossing hitherto untrodden muskeg for a couple of miles, they drove it on to the abandoned railway grade. Along it they made good time—faster than they could have walked—except where several of the numerous old trestles had been burned. At these they had to roll the car down the bank, make a bridge over the creek and then get back up the other side and onto the grade again. At Carrot Creek, building their own bridge took them six and a half hours. Finally, they spent the night of June 23, six days out of Edmonton, at J. W. Campbell's home in Jasper. In their own fashion they had traveled what was essentially Moberly's old trail and had done it in about half the time which he and his pack horses had been accustomed to take for the trip. Most important, they had driven the first car to Jasper.

Into one of the old cuts beyond Lucerne a minor slide had dumped a few tons of rock, including one piece about the size of a large table. To move it was hopeless, and to surmount it was impossible, so for seven hours they labored, gouging a way into the bank to let their car squeeze around it.

Before they reached the thriving city of Kamloops on June 30, they found themselves overtaken by unsuspected rivals in the persons of George G. Gordon and J. Sims, driving a Model T Ford and sponsored by the Good Roads and Automobile Association of Alberta. Though the Ford had left Edmonton nearly a week later than the Overland, it had arrived in Jasper only three days behind. Its drivers had benefited by the bridges the first pair had made, and going on west could use the way they had scooped out around the fallen boulder.

By that time the Victoria Automobile and Good Roads Association had announced that it also had gold medals for the winners. For the remainder of the trip from Kamloops to Vancouver the two cars raced over long stretches of fair roads and reached the coastal city on the morning of July 4. Taking different ferries to the island, both pairs of men reached Victoria the same day and both were given medals.

And they deserved them. Neimeyer, the pioneer, had taken seventeen days to get to the coast and Gordon had taken nine, but their Overland and Ford had been the first cars over the Yellowhead road. Grant had achieved his purpose of publicizing the Yellowhead route.

But as the weeks went by rumors began making their way

back to Edmonton, rumors from trainmen which said that in places one or both cars had been loaded on freight trains. A year later when Charles Grant became convinced that they were true, he decided to drive to Jasper to prove that such a feat was possible without resorting to shipping the car.

Thinking it wise to wait until the first week of November when to some extent the fall frosts would have firmed up the ruts, he and Frank Mitchell started west in a Model T Ford in 1923. They paid little attention to the chilly weather until they spent the first night of their trip at Carrot Creek. Then, worrying about the difficulty of cranking up the car and getting the engine to start next morning, they stopped it on top of a hill. Luck was with them at dawn when, after brushing off the hoarfrost, Charlie sat behind the steering wheel while Frank pushed the car down the decline. Halfway to the bottom the engine spluttered and started, and when Frank, running to catch up, climbed in everything was in fine fettle. The rejoicing engine rattled the chassis and shook the men who, wreathed in smiles of accomplishment and anticipation, set their faces toward the mountains still invisible beyond the miles of muskeg ahead. Charlie and his partner spent the second night at Obed and reached the park next day, November 7, having made what Grant called the first trip from Edmonton to Jasper "on our own wheels—but mind you over the bridges that Neimeyer had built."

Along the route which in their way and times David Thompson, J. E. Brazeau, and Henry John Moberly had pioneered, Grant and Frank Mitchell had pioneered in their way and time. Though as a highway the old railway grade left nearly everything to be desired and was yet to experience wearying decades of gradual improvement, nevertheless Grant had shown that a car could be driven to Jasper Park. Even then for a few years the task of recording how many cars from the outside entered the park took little of the staff's time. In fact, till 1926 they did not bother to keep such records. That year, however, six cars crossed west into the park and they were followed by ten the next year, ninety-three in 1930, and by a spate of automobiles in 1931—188.

Meanwhile, considering the times, Jasper Park itself had been progressing rapidly. On the shores of the newly named Lac Beauvert where the tent city had been, the CNR opened its splendid lodge and golf course. As a resort for the rich who came by train it was an immediate success. By 1924 the graveled road to Mount Edith Cavell had been finished and during 1927 the highway from Jasper to the lodge had been surfaced with McMurray tar sands. By 1928, using the abandoned railway grade, the authorities had completed a gravel road from Jasper to the park's east boundary.

Amongst a number of other activities, the park staff imported a carload of elk in 1920 to form the nucleus of the many bands of these regal animals which now thrive in the region. In another successful effort aimed at stocking a stream with speckled trout, Fred Brewster took a hand. No fish had ever been able to overcome the barrier of the Maligne Canyon and as a result none lived in the river or in Medicine or Maligne lakes. Fred, working with the park authorities and biologists from the University of Manitoba, made a survey of the possibility of stocking the stream system and recommended that it be done as an experiment. The results were highly successful.

After his return from the war, Fred had resumed his old niche, acting as father confessor to all worthy causes and continuing to build up his tourist activities. As well as personally taking parties out on exploring or hunting trips, he kept improving his facilities at Maligne Lake and before long built a chalet there. The Tonquin valley with its beautiful lake and magnificent mountain scenery attracted him so much that he built another there and took parties back and forth.

In similar ways, the Otto brothers, who at times had been associated with Fred, did a thriving business catering to well-heeled tourists. So too did Alex Wylie with his long strings of pack horses and his corrals in Jasper. And, of course, Curly Phillips found plenty of parties who enjoyed his rare qualities as an outffitter and guide.

Gradually Jasper grew and more and more tourists came through its east gate to revel in its beauty and to enjoy its invigorating atmosphere. When its merchants at last began to feel that their pioneer days were over and that they could look forward to some well-earned prosperity, the depression struck. The Dirty Thirties were upon them. Even Jasper Park Lodge, accustomed to catering to a world-wide clientele of the rich, felt the pinch.

The depression ruined many of the wealthy, and those whose sources of revenue did not dry up, began to pull in their horns. The flow of rich tourists to Jasper Park Lodge slowed up. The pace of Canadian commerce slackened to a crawl, and fewer and shorter trains swung around the curves of Jasper and Brulé lakes. Within a year or two all silk trains stopped running. The Dirty Thirties, however, fell most heavily on Canada's working men and by 1931 thousands of them were out of work and at their wits' end. At the beginning of the depression they scurried about trying to find work, and when that proved impossible, hundreds began traveling more or less aimlessly back and forth across Canada.

If the passenger trains brought fewer paying customers to admire the Jasper valley, the freight trains made up the lack, and every day all summer they carried scores of unemployed men back and forth through the beautiful valley. In the beginning these transients traveled as tramps had always done—on the rods—but as the depression deepened and hundreds of men were on the move, they traveled in style, with a dozen or so sitting on top of each freight car.

As the heart went out of the economy, all governments, sorely pressed in all directions, tried desperately to help the unemployed, but in most cases had to struggle hopelessly, trying to spread a pittance of resources over a pile of needs. Edmonton, like all other cities, watching the bread lines grow throughout 1930 and into 1931, advocated that those men be set to building highways. High on its list of priorities it placed the upgrading of the road to Jasper. When in due course the Dominion Government got around to doing that sort of thing, it set up relief camps here and there along that road. The superintendents of the Jasper and Banff national parks also had highways to build and welcomed the organization of relief camps along their trails. Starting from both the Lake Louise and the Jasper ends they set the unemployed to work on what they called the Jasper-Banff, or the J-B Highway.

Mickey McGuire, now retired, who worked as a foreman on that road under engineer J. H. Mitchell, has many a droll tale to tell of his experiences during the construction of that first J-B Highway. While his authority extended only to the Icefields at the southern limit of Jasper Park, his stories are of an era which seems very remote from the 1970's. With Canada's present rich economy and with all the huge hauling and road-making machinery now available, it is perhaps hard to grasp the conditions which prevailed during the construction of the J-B Highway.

238 • *Overland by the Yellowhead*

Work started in 1930 from the Jasper end with a conventional tote road, clearing crews out ahead, followed by the grade and bridge builders, and by 1938 the road was open for traffic to the Athabasca glacier. Then, as Mickey said, tourists could drive from Jasper, step out of their cars and with no effort at all stand toe to toe to a glacier. On completion of the "big hill" section in Banff Park, as a good gravel road, in June, 1940, it was opened for travel to Lake Louise. As the work progressed in the early thirties, new relief camps came into being. To those, as Mickey points out, flocked men from all walks of life; university students, men who before the depression had held responsible office jobs, factory hands, farmers, and professional men. They worked eight hours a day for six days a week, and for the first year of the construction at least were paid fifty cents a day. While for their fifty cents they may not have overexerted themselves, nevertheless they gave what in today's world would be regarded as a good day's work. They were men vexed at their inability to find employment and of the frame of mind which abhorred the charity of soup kitchens and relief, and were glad indeed that in those camps they were paying their way. After 1931 they were paid a small but definite hourly wage. Mickey reports that in the camps morale was good and that an excellent camaraderie existed between the foremen and the men. Moreover, the food was copious and wholesome.

The surveyors and foremen drove rattletrap light-delivery trucks. The other internal combustion equipment used on the seventy-odd-mile stretch of most difficult mountain road was one 30 HP farm tractor, which could haul six wagons, for the heavy work, and two 28 HP tractors, which pulled the road-grading machines around. There were remarkably few teams of horses. Instead, the one hundred to one hundred and fifty men at each camp, a total of maybe eight hundred at any one time, wheeled and pushed and heaved the grade into place. The blacksmiths' days were filled with sharpening drill steel, which some men held steady and rotated by hand while other men, swinging sledge hammers, pounded it into the rock to make the holes in which the dynamite charges were to be set off. "And," says Mickey, "on the whole job there was no loss of life—just a few broken legs from falling rock and a few ribs cracked by pick axes or hurtling crowbars."

On one occasion a cook averted an accident by fleeing. As he turned around from his pots he saw a brown bear ambling through the door of his canvas-walled kitchen. Seizing his cleaver, he slit the nearest canvas wall and stepped through to leave the bear in full possession of the premises.

So with crowbars and wheelbarrows, bothersome bears and a bit of home-brew, Mickey McGuire and his men completed their portion of the J-B Highway.

During the years he had been wrestling with it, the province of Alberta, struggling with economic adversity, had made very slow progress on its Edmonton to Jasper highway and of converting the old CNR grade to a graveled road, which in dry weather might be passable. For some years the CNR had been obdurate in refusing to part with those portions of its right of way, about ninety miles all together, which could be used to provide a well-settled base for a motor highway from Entwistle to Obed. By the time Mickey's road was finished, however, the Edmonton-Jasper stretch was in reasonable shape. Then, with both the J-B and the road to Edmonton operating, tourists could come up from Banff, or indeed make the circle tour from Lake Louise to Jasper and Edmonton and back through Calgary and Banff. Unfortunately, almost as soon as its completion began giving Jasper merchants a much-needed shot in the arm, World War II was in full swing, and for five years national parks stagnated.

Shortly before the start of the war in 1939, everyone in Jasper lamented Curly Phillips's death. Late in March, 1938, he and his friends, Reginald and Allan Pugh, had gone on a ski trip to Mount Elysium near the headwaters of the Miette River. They were fully aware that it was a bad time for slides, and although they proceeded cautiously, had to take some risks. At the edge of one of the avalanche slopes, while the others moved forward slowly, Allan Pugh stopped to adjust his ski harness. As he knelt fiddling with the straps, he heard the roar of the rushing slide and looked up to see his brother and Curly overwhelmed and crushed by tons of ice and debris and swept down the mountain.

Curly Phillips, the man known to alpinists everywhere, the careful guide who rarely took chances and who for over thirty-five years had taken parties through all the passes, had been killed on the mountains he loved, with his boots on. While he was only fifty-four years old, he was one of the thinning ranks of Jasper's oldtimers.

Two years later, in March, 1940, Jasper's patriarch, Lewis J. Swift, the first white man who had settled in the valley, forty-seven years previously, died. For some forty years before moving into town to retire he had watched the whole remarkable progress of the valley. As mountain climbers and surveyors came and went he had welcomed them to his hospitable home, glad to see visitors from outside and secure in the knowledge that on his little farm he had all the material and spiritual requirements he needed.

Eventually, while he had co-operated with the park authorities and at times had acted for them in such capacities as game guardian, he and his land had become a bone of contention stuck crosswise in their throats—the only piece of freehold land in the park. When the GTP and the CNR came through, he had sold strips of his quarter section for their rights of way. He had even dreamed that one or other of them would use his land for a divisional point. When neither did, he had gone to the length of subdividing it himself and had tried to sell lots in his townsite of Swiftholme.

In 1926 the park authorities had offered to buy him out for six thousand dollars. Times had been good and Lewis Swift had been contented, and had refused their offer. But during the depression, after another decade had passed over his head, the softer life of retiring to Jasper town began to appeal and he agreed to accept the six-thousand-dollar offer. By that time the depression had tightened the government's purse strings, and feeling that Swift was now at their mercy and that time would tumble his land into their hands at their own price, the authorities decided to out-wait the old pioneer.

But he outwitted them and sold his land for eight thousand dollars to A. C. Wilby, formerly of England. Wilby, who became a thorn in the park authorities' side, spent money freely and developed a costly set of buildings along "dude ranch" lines. When two or three years after he died in 1947 the land and buildings were offered to the park authorities for seventy thousand, the department in Ottawa procrastinated, and in 1951 Gordon F. Bried bought the property. Finally, in May, 1962, tired of shilly-shallying any longer, the park authorities bought it for $277,850. At last Swift's old ranch became park property and the last vestige of freehold land in the park disappeared.

A year after Lewis Swift's death, his widow, Suzette, received a visit from an old man returning to the scenes of his vigorous days. Out of a limousine driven by his Florida chauffeur stepped Jack Gregg, aged 101. Some thirty years previously he had sold his interests in the Coal Branch area and returned to his native land. In short order he got involved in Florida real estate and soon became wealthy. As he and Suzette sat talking of the old days when Lewis Swift and he had urged their horses over the pack trail to Edmonton, he also talked of his childhood. He had been born in Iowa in 1840. When he was six, giving him his first taste of the adventurous life ahead of him, his family set out for the Pacific Coast along the Oregon Trail. Of all his memories, that trip was graven deepest in his heart, for somewhere in Wyoming as the wagons halted during the confusion of an Indian attack, he stood and screamed when an arrow pierced his mother's breast, and even as he held tightly to her skirt she crumpled upon him, dead.

For a long time Suzette and Jack Gregg sat reminiscing, and then a few weeks later she heard of his death in Florida. Her own death took place late in 1946. Nearly fifty years earlier, as Suzette Chalifoux, the white-skinned half-breed girl, she had married Lewis Swift and gone to share his lot in the valley of the Athabasca. Over all those years she had welcomed visitors and extended untold kindnesses to them. During her last years in Jasper town even the most recent newcomer came to know this fine old lady, who in her graciousness was representative of all the many virtues of the Métis race as they were at the turn of the century. As she had lived, so she was carried to her grave, respected by all.

Suzette had lived long enough to see the allied armies victorious in World War II and long enough to see Jasper through the doldrums as a tourist mecca during wartime. She also witnessed the marked increase in the amount of freight which the exigencies of war had brought to Jasper's great transcontinental railway. She probably did not see the German soldiers in the prisoner-of-war camp at Brulé nor the Japanese internment camp at the summit of Tête Jaune's pass. In it a number of Japanese, ignominiously yanked from their peaceful enterprises at the Coast, spent a year or so. As a diversion from their other activities, they built a tea house in that camp and for several years it remained as a curiosity shown off by the few local people. Their main occupation, however, was forced labor clearing a new right of way on sections of the Yellowhead highway. In different groups they cut the timber off much of the road toward Tête Jaune Cache and along the river toward McBride on the one hand and toward Blue River on the other. It was necessary to keep them busy, and the British Columbia Government, looking to the day when the war would end, also looked to the day when a new trans-Canada highway would sweep transport of all sorts through Tête Jaune's pass.

And, indeed, when the load of the war was lifted from Canadians' shoulders and they realized that the depression of the Dirty Thirties had gone, they began to earn and spend money as they had never been able to do before. Canada had grown up, and Canadians were wealthy. Of the hundreds of projects they undertook, highways were high on the list. While no government could spend as much money on regional projects as local people thought it should, Jasper National Park and various highways leading to it came in for their share.

Highway No. 16 from Edmonton to Jasper (a part of today's Yellowhead Highway) was hard-surfaced by 1951, and during the next few years sections of it continued to be widened and improved until from the metropolis to the heart of the park a splendid ribbon of asphalt, using much of the old railway grades, followed Brazeau's trail of a century before. In time, too, the Jasper-Banff highway was realigned and built up to a new high standard and paved. This time the work was done by giant bulldozers, lowboys, and huge Le Tourneaus. So rapid had been the changes witnessed within a few years that Mickey McGuire's pitiful shovels, wheelbarrows, and crowbars were merely a fading memory, and some said an unreliable memory at that. His tales, true to the last comma, came to be thought of as too naive to believe.

And when all those highways had received their just share of financial help, governments and engineers began looking at the idea of a Yellowhead highway. Urging them on was Charlie Grant, who back in 1922 had taken the steps that had sent the first two cars over it from Edmonton to Vancouver. But progress was very slow and disappointing, because when an official Trans-Canada Highway was constructed, it, like the first transcontinental railway, was built west from Calgary through the Kicking Horse and Rogers passes and once more Tête Jaune's pass was sidetracked.

Although the governments appeared tardy in building a good highway through the pass and down the Thompson River, another form of transport, financed by private enterprise, looked the route over. Once more the Jasper valley and Tête Jaune's pass proved to be a natural corridor from the prairies to the

Pacific when early in 1952 Trans Mountain Oil Pipe Line Company started building its twenty-four-inch line through the famous pass. Originating in Edmonton, where it collected the increasing output of Alberta's burgeoning oilfields, that twenty-four-inch-diameter line, 711 miles long, which was to carry two hundred thousand barrels of oil per day, made its way through the pass and down the Thompson River to Kamloops and on to Vancouver.

Paralleling the CNR and Highway No. 16 west to Tête Jaune Cache, the contractors bulldozed a right of way where the old tote road had been, and completed the line in eighteen months. But what a difference the project exhibited from the days when the railway had been built or even when the crews had worked out of relief camps a mere twenty years earlier. The famous contractors, Canadian Bechtel Limited, took over the work and sublet various stretches to other organizations such as Comstock Mid-Western, which laid most of the line as far west as Red Pass Junction. And on the work they brought to bear the latest equipment that an expanding technology could devise—roaring diesel-driven shovels and back-hoes, lowboys, the latest in welding equipment. Even the surveying was done by methods undreamed-of in the days when the railway lines had been built. That pipe line was the first ever to use a helicopter as part of the construction equipment. Airplanes and cameras surveyed the line, flying and photographing a route, and then on the pictures draftsmen marked the center line of that new method of transport through the old pass.

No tent-roofed log shacks arose beside that line, no canvas-sided cook shacks allowed an easy exit for a bear-besieged cook. The construction camps, holding some two hundred and fifty men, consisted of the latest in electrified, propane-heated trailers, which were moved along as the work progressed. When the engineers and foremen and men working out from them, all well versed in burying pipe lines, came to size up and to perform the job of laying a line up one side of a steep hill and lowering it down the other, or of bending it sharply around a spur of rock, they shook their heads. Not that they could not do it, but while all of them had laid similar "big inch" pipes over higher summits or pushed them over whiter torrents, none of them had seen 711 miles of continuous line through such terrain. As a result, recalling the one-time collector of curious facts, they dubbed it the "RIPLEY" line, which they said meant "roughest inch pipe line ever yet."

It, too, needed divisional points, for though mighty pumps at Edmonton forced the oil up and down over hill and valley, even they could pump it only a hundred miles or so before the friction in the pipe slowed the oil to a crawl. Then fresh pumps took over at Bickerdike, Jasper, and Kamloops. As it had done so often in the past, Swift's old ranch played its part in the new project. The construction company rented all of the dude-ranch buildings from Gordon Bried, and used them for one of its main headquarters. Moreover, Trans Mountain Oil, needing a site for its Jasper pumping station, found it on Swift's old freehold land.

Finally, on October 15, 1953, the line was finished and the pumps at Edmonton started churning away day and night to fill it. Days later, when they had jammed millions of gallons into the line, the first blob gushed into tanks at Vancouver. The first of the oil which had coursed silently through its 700-mile cavern had made its unobtrusive way over Tête Jaune's pass. Ever since, flowing silently, unheeded by tourists traveling by car, bus, or train, it has continued to add its share of the tonnage transported through one of Canada's busiest transcontinental routes.

In so doing it did many an oil tank car out of a job and ate into the loads the giant locomotives lifted over the mountains. The oil industry, not content with humbling the pride of the great mountain engines, began conniving at their death. At first, in its battle with coal, it had arranged to feed the huge puffing steam locomotives with oil. Next, in 1949, about the time that the Trans Mountain line was in the planning stage, the oil industry had conspired with the CNR management to send a diesel locomotive to try its prowess on the mountain division. Then like Norway rats, where one got a foothold others soon swept in, the unromantic but wholly efficient diesels took over. By 1952 the Trans Mountain crews stringing their line seldom saw the magnificent white plume as a proud steam locomotive puffed its way up the hill east of Tête Jaune Cache. The steam locomotives' doom had been sealed.

The old steamer, however, was only one of the many links with the past which fate had notched for snapping. Some could be replaced, like the famous old wooden Jasper Park Lodge, which burned in July, 1952, and was rebuilt in a more palatial manner. With a plane load of imported European masons to rebuild it of stone, it reopened the following spring.

Some of the links, like the well-loved Dr. Thomas O'Hagan, who had first served in Lucerne in 1920 and died in January, 1957, could only be lamented. In due course the Jasper people put up a memorial to this man whose cheerful smile and skillful hand had served them so long. Then, in 1962, Willard S. Jeffery died. He had followed the railway construction from Edmonton and had operated stores in the camps of Wolf Creek, Bickerdike, Prairie Creek, and Hinton, and in 1914 had started a general store in Jasper. Another of the genial, kindly men, whose toil and forethought had helped Jasper's people through some hard places, had gone.

More and more Jasper citizens, like Canadians as a whole, were beginning to think of their history and to take steps to preserve what souvenirs they could. Through the courtesy of the CNR, one of the old mountain engines, locomotive C.N. 6015, was spared the destruction of the cutting torches, and was refurbished and returned to Jasper. This giant, the ultimate in steam locomotive design, was rolled onto tracks near the station from which she had pulled out so often, and there, looking west up the pass which in winter's blizzard or summer's breeze she had bested so often, she stands. And if she, and the graying men who come to see and to pat her, dream of the past, they dream of heroic days.

With all the present-day conveniences, with paved roads and sweetly purring cars, the modern age perhaps tends to forget the rigors their forerunners endured (and enjoyed). Horses and pack saddles indeed are still to be found in Jasper Park, but they are for pleasure jaunts. The bears have lost their independence and loll at their ease within sniffing distance of garbage dumps or pad their way along the white man's pavements, sometimes to the embarrassment of well-meaning park authorities.

About the time locomotive C.N. 6015 came back to her old home, bears gobbling garbage had become such a nuisance that the park wardens decreed that those which continued to do so, should be daubed with paint, chased away and told to stay away. "If," said the head warden, "they come back, we'll fix them." But the bears did not heed, and came back. Thereupon they were trapped, loaded into trucks and hauled thirty miles away to the vicinity of Brulé. "That'll fix 'em," said the staff, "that'll teach 'em a lesson, that's the last we'll see of them fellows!"

But the bears did not understand, and thirty-six hours later tourists in Gordon Bried's Palisades Motel on the old Swift place watched an amusing procession of bears with painted bums. Hungry, footsore, and vexed at the trick played on them, they shuffled along the shoulder of the pavement in a long line, hobbling home to the garbage dumps for their first meal in nearly two days.

All of this Fred Brewster lived to see. When in 1969, after nurturing the area along for sixty years, he died at the age of eighty, no other man had come to typify Jasper as he did. During his earlier jaunts into every pass and valley he had seen the messages blazed on trees by his forerunners as far back as 1837. In his youth, some of the men he had met on the mountain trails could remember back to the days of the Overlanders of 1862 and many of them could recall the years of the CPR surveys. He had packed supplies for the CNR and GTP surveyors, and he had guided many a mountain-climbing party. In every subsequent work planned for Jasper's advancement, he had played a major role.

When he had made his first trip through the Jasper valley it had been with pack horses over crude trails. When on his last trip he was carried to the cemetery in which nearly sixty years earlier he had dug the first grave, splendid highways let thousands of tourists speed along in comfort to enjoy the mountains he had loved. Where sixty years earlier, with great effort, his pack train, making fifteen miles a day, had toted a ton of supplies over the summit, now at express speed train loads of freight from all over Canada swished across it effortlessly. Moreover, many of the millions of tons came from nearby resources he had studied: carloads of paper from the Hinton mill, which belched steam over the Iroquois' Cache Picotte of sad memory; long and daily train loads of coal destined for Japan from Cardinal's river in the Coal Branch, or from the new mine on the Smoky River where Ignace Giasson had made his grande cache. And an hour or so after flashing by the growing city of Jasper, the train loads roared over the summit and passed the flat where long ago, glancing from time to time at the awesome face of Mount Robson, Tête Jaune had notched together the poles of his cache.

Fred Brewster had seen all the real development of the

Yellowhead area. And now, at last, Tête Jaune's pass had come into its own as one of Canada's main transportation routes and Jasper, its handmaiden, had become one of Canada's foremost holiday resorts.

15

AND THE YELLOWHEAD ROUTE

TO JASPER'S growth, of course, the new highway now known as the Yellowhead Interprovincial Highway, or more simply as the Yellowhead Route, has contributed significantly. With its hundreds of miles marked by signs bearing a yellow profile of Tête Jaune against a background of pine trees, it is in effect an alternative Trans-Canada Highway to the official southern route. Leaving the Trans-Canada Highway at Portage la Prairie it traverses the photogenic, rolling parklands of Manitoba, Saskatchewan, and Alberta and sweeps past Roche Miette, the guardian of the Yellowhead Pass, and on to Tête Jaune Cache. There it divides and offers travelers the same choice of routes faced over a century ago by the Overlanders of '62; south 211 miles to Kamloops by Highway No. 5, or west 150 miles to Prince George by continuing on Highway No. 16. But unlike the portion of the Overlanders who went down the North Thompson River and reached Kamloops some forty days later or the other portion who floated down the Fraser in eight days, motorists can reach either city in three or four hours' luxurious touring. At Kamloops they can rejoin the southern Trans-Canada Highway and sweep on to salt water at Vancouver. From Prince George, on the other hand, following in Simon Fraser's steps, they can go west to his Fort Fraser and then by continuing through a history-steeped land can finally descend the last one hundred miles of the scenic Skeena River to tide-water at Prince Rupert.

And almost continuously along all of its hundreds of miles from Portage la Prairie to Kamloops or Prince Rupert the Yellowhead Highway clings far more closely than any other to the fur traders' routes across the prairies and through the mountains. Passing, at times, through the sites of old trading posts and between them following in the steps of the Oregon-bound settlers of 1841 and of the Overlanders of '62, or the gold seekers and the homesteaders, the modern road smacks of the past. Riding in luxurious comfort as the miles of rich scenic parkland or the majestic mountain peaks pass in endless, effortless review beside him, the present-day traveler's experience is a far cry from that of those who used these routes over a century ago.

In general, from Manitoba through Yorkton and Saskatoon

to Edmonton, the Yellowhead Route follows the first cart trail across the prairies. That was the Carlton Trail, starting at Fort Garry, reaching first to Fort Carlton in Saskatchewan, and later continuing to Fort Edmonton — about one thousand miles by the old trail and less than eight hundred by the Yellowhead Route.

While today's Yellowhead Route has cut off some of the bends of the Carlton Trail and from the very nature of a modern highway, seldom follows exactly in the wheel ruts of its older counterpart, it is rarely very far from them. Here and there the two routes diverge considerably. In one stretch, for instance, they separate slightly over a hundred miles west of Yorkton and near Lanigan where the Yellowhead Route crosses the old trail and heads nearly straight west to Saskatoon. The cart trail, working northward through Humboldt, headed for the Métis settlement near Batoche's ferry over the South Saskatchewan River. Thence it crossed the neck of land to Fort Carlton on the North Saskatchewan River. From there it advanced over the rolling hills to pass south of Jackfish Lake, some fifteen miles north of North Battleford. The Yellowhead Route, after leaving Saskatoon, crosses the North Saskatchewan River at Ceepee and then, after paralleling the mighty river, swings down to cross its beautiful valley to reach historic old Battleford.

Once more the old trail, headed toward Edmonton along the river's north bank as far as Fort Pitt followed a different route from the modern highway, for the pavement heads for Lloydminster on the Alberta border some twenty-five miles south and west of the old fort.

At Fort Pitt the Carlton Trail split into two alternate routes to Edmonton, one keeping north of the North Saskatchewan River and the other, the shorter, crossing that stream and heading west. At Two Hills it was twenty miles north of the Yellowhead Route, which has trended in the same direction through Vermilion and on to Vegreville. From there the modern highway, passing through Elk Island Buffalo Park in the heart of the Beaver Hills and then leaping over cloverleafs and swishing under overpasses, heads into the center of Edmonton, whereas the old cart trail swung around the north flank of those hills.

From Edmonton the Yellowhead Route follows the old Jasper Trail as far as Tête Jaune Cache, a trail described quite fully in previous chapters. It is interesting, therefore, to turn back to Portage la Prairie and proceed west along the Carlton Trail in more detail.

Portage la Prairie, the city built on the flats along the winding Assiniboine River, has a long history dating back to 1738 when in its general vicinity the famous explorer La Vérendrye built the first fur trade post on the open prairies. As the years went by, white and Métis traders and hunters worked out a cart trail from the Red River Settlement around Fort Garry to the site of the town and on to Brandon and then south and west from there. Eventually a few settlers began laying claim to parts of the rich farm land surrounding Portage la Prairie. There, in 1868, one settler, Thomas Spence, dreamed up and brought into being the short-lived Republic of Manitoba. As the capital of that abortive republic Portage's reign lasted about a week. Six years later the first steamboat to ascend the Assinboine River that far tied up in the village and from that time on until now, when it is the third largest city in Manitoba, Portage la Prairie has never looked back.

Well before 1840, however, the traders and the Métis were pioneering another cart trail heading north and west from Portage la Prairie to Fort Ellice, the Hudson's Bay post near the junction of the Assiniboine and Qu'Appelle rivers. In doing so they were taking the first step toward the creation of the Carlton Trail and thus of the Yellowhead Highway. For decades before that, of course, Hudson's Bay Company men had traveled a general route by which they rode across the prairie to and from the Saskatoon area but it was merely a route and in no sense a trail or even a path. It was left to Red River carts to turn the route into a trail.

And in the midst of a fur-trade milieu it was left to a group of farming-oriented mixed bloods bound from the Red River Settlement to Oregon in 1841 to take the first cart along the route west of Fort Ellice. According to George Simpson, the Governor of the Hudson's Bay Company who had inspired their departure for Oregon, they consisted of twenty-three families, each with two or three carts together with bands of horses and cattle. They left Fort Garry on June 3 and were more than two months getting to Fort Edmonton.

George Simpson, however, who left Fort Garry early in July, made the trip in twenty-two days and, as he passed the settlers on the way, was the first to take carts all the way to Edmonton. He was on his way around the world and because he wrote a book of his adventures it is possible to follow him fairly accurately as he crossed the prairies and to get some conception of the discomforts and dangers of crossing the plains in 1841.

With a number of carts making up his procession, Simpson left Portage la Prairie on horseback accompanied by Chief Factor John Rowand of Fort Edmonton and some twenty men. Following the trail, which is paralleled by the highway to beyond Minnedosa, he made his second night's camp south of modern Neepawa and "the mosquitoes were so numerous, that they literally mottled the poor horses with black patches of great size, extending at the same time a very unreasonable share of their attention to ourselves. We had some compensations, however, for this annoyance in the excellence of the water, for we had been fortunate enough to fix our halt on a running stream, instead of being doomed to swallow the seething dregs of half-dried lakes . . ."

Next day the group came to a band of Saulteaux Indians who watched them spend about an hour fording the river near Minnedosa. That day they considered stopping for a meal at beautiful Salt Lake (south of Strathclair) but John Rowand insisted that they give it a wide berth. According to Simpson, when Rowand had been eastbound on his way to meet him at Fort Garry he had been attracted by the lake's beauty and had camped for the night "with his kettle bubbling and steaming all comfortably about him, when, lo and behold, the first sip of the welcome beverage revealed the horrible truth, that the lovely lake was no better than it should be, being filled with salt water."

A day or so later, after using a craft tied there by the Hudson's Bay people to cross the Assiniboine, the party reached Fort Ellice (thirty miles south of modern Russell) and went on to ford the nearby Qu'Appelle River, as described by Simpson: "Our horses and carts forded the stream; and we ourselves traversed it in a canoe of alarmingly simple construction, being neither more nor less than a few branches covered with buffalo robes. This make-shift barely served the purpose of taking us over before it got altogether filled with water."

The cart trail ended at Fort Ellice but Simpson's party was able to follow the wheel marks left by the Oregon settlers. Fording several streams in what is now the rich farming area embracing Langenburg, Melville, and Yorkton in Saskatchewan and finally traversing "about twenty-five miles of prairie among several large and beautiful lakes," they formed a notable procession. "The guide was followed by four or five horsemen to beat a track; then came the carts, each with a driver attended by one or two cavaliers; and lastly followed the unmounted animals, whether loaded or light, under the charge of the rest of our people. Our ordinary rate of traveling was four or five miles an hour for ten, twelve or fourteen hours a day, — the carts sometimes requiring a longer time to accomplish the day's march."

Having crossed the little plain they traveled around the edge of the Quill Lakes, and incidentally, crossed the route of the Yellowhead Highway near modern Dafoe. Next morning, traveling toward Humboldt, north of the present highway, they "marched till ten o'clock in a soaking rain. An encampment in such weather is by no means an exhilarating sight. On halting we were wet and chilly, but had no place to shelter ourselves from the shower. After a drawn battle of nearly an hour with the wind and rain in the way of making a fire, we at last succeeded; and then, heaping on whole piles of wood, we contrived to keep ourselves tolerably comfortable till our tents were pitched. The horses were the very picture of misery, as they huddled themselves together."

That afternoon, however, they pressed on and passed a spot which reminded Simpson of a worrisome matter which had occurred in 1825 when he had ridden along the same route from Fort Carlton to Fort Garry. At that point his servant, Tom Taylor, and another man named George Bird had dismounted to stalk an elk and had wandered off. When they did not come back Simpson had halted his party for twenty-four hours, but when they still had not returned he had moved on, having felt that somehow or other the two men would make their way back to Fort Garry. Two weeks later the two famished men, having made their way practically straight east for two hundred miles had turned up at the Hudson's Bay Company's Swan River Post.

Simpson described their adventures: "After a day or two their ammunition was expended and their flints became useless, while their feet were lacerated by the thorns, timber, stones and prickly grass. They had no other clothing than their trousers and shirts, having parted from us in the heat of the day; so that they were now exposed to the chills of the night without even the comfort of a fire, — a privation which placed them, as it were, at the mercy of the wolves. From day to day they lived on whatever the chances of the wilderness afforded them, such as roots, and bark, and eggs, in every stage of progress."

When they had reached the post of which Mr. McDonell had been in charge "they crawled rather than walked to his private room, standing before him with their torn and emaciated limbs, while their haggard cheeks and glaring eyes gave them the appearance of maniacs. After a minute inspection of his visitors, Mr. McDonell with the aid of sundry expletives, ascertained, by degrees, that one of his friends was 'the Governor's Tom' ". He had nursed them back to health and had sent them to Norway House where weeks later they had rejoined Simpson.

From the spot where Tom Taylor had wandered away Simpson continued and crossed the South Saskatchewan River near later Batoche and made his way to Fort Carlton, an important post on the North Saskatchewan River. There, of course, he came into contact with the fur traders' long-established water route up and down the river from Fort Edmonton to Lake Winnipeg. There, too, he learned that the Blackfoot and Cree had recently had a battle in the parklands farther west, and that because both tribes were stirred up, any travelers heading west to Fort Pitt (north of Lloydminster) faced considerable risks.

In spite of the warning he continued west, noting the recent passage of the Oregon-bound settlers' carts and experiencing ". . . a good deal of inconvenience from thirst. In the afternoon, after marching a considerable distance without seeing a drop of water, we reached a small lake; but as the hour was too early for encamping, we passed it, more particularly as its stagnant surface was by no means attractive; but we soon regretted our fastidiousness, for, when the evening began to darken, we had seen neither lake nor brook, though searching for the luxury on both sides of our track." Late that evening they came to Jackfish Lake north of Battleford.

Next morning, a few miles west, Simpson's party caught up with the Oregon-bound settlers and traveled with them for the rest of the day. Before noon in that beautiful parklike country west of North Battleford (across the river from the Yellowhead Route), the party encountered buffalo ". . . grazing or stalking about in bands between twenty and a hundred, to the number of about five thousand in all." All of the hunting men took after them. "The morning's chase resulted in about fifty killed;

but so abundant were provisions at this moment, that, after taking the tongues, we left the carcases to the mercy of the wolves."

At the Turtle River, somewhere across the North Saskatchewan from the Yellowhead Route's village of Bresaylor, Simpson ordered a halt for the rest of the day and to honor ". . . the first occasion perhaps, on which two large bands of civilized men had met as friends on these vast prairies . . ." he poured out a few drinks. As well as that, their late breakfast "was a complete specimen of a hunter's meal, consisting of enormous piles of roasted ribs, with marrow and tripe at discretion — the spoils of the morning's chase."

When parting from the settlers to hurry on to Fort Pitt Simpson's cavalcade was "on the verge of an immense prairie, where no water could be obtained, we filled every pot and kettle for our supper. During the whole day, comprising a march of fifty miles, we saw no other water than that of the Turtle River; nor was there any for more than half that distance beyond our night's encampment." The next day after dark Simpson's party reached Fort Pitt. In spite of the fact that the Blackfoot were belligerently patrolling the area north of today's Lloydminster, Simpson decided to risk taking the route on the southern side of the North Saskatchewan River. Five days later, following the pack trail from modern Fort Saskatchewan, his route eventually merged with the present Yellowhead Highway and shortly after he was looking across the river at Fort Edmonton. From there on he chose to pioneer a new route which took him southwest to Banff, and in due course, the settlers left Edmonton along his trail.

In taking carts from Fort Garry to Fort Edmonton Simpson's party and the Oregon-bound settlers had been the first to travel on wheels the route which later evolved into the Yellowhead Highway. From then on for some decades practically everyone crossing to the mountains or the Pacific coast wound his way along that sometimes wearisome but ever-interesting long trail along the edge of the parklands.

Out of scores of such travelers, three groups in particular stand out. The first is the large party of Overlanders of '62. They not only followed the Carlton Trail to Edmonton but went on to Tête Jaune Cache along what is now the Yellowhead Route and then, splitting into two sections, went down either the North Thomspon or the upper Fraser rivers to Kamloops and Prince George respectively. The other two sets of travelers, both very interesting but vastly different, were Métis hunters on the one hand and the farming-oriented Barr Colonists on the other.

After the Red River Rebellion of 1869 in which Louis Riel led the Métis in the hope of rectifying some of their grievances, many of his people found the pressure of white people flocking into the Red River district too uncomfortable to tolerate. As a result, many a Métis family loaded its belongings into its creaking Red River carts and in little groups headed west along the Carlton Trail. From time to time during their famous buffalo hunts some of them had camped where the trail crossed the South Saskatchewan River. After 1869 they decided to go west and form a settlement near that crossing. By 1872 Xavier Letendre (better known as Batoche) had opened a store there and was operating a ferry, while Gabriel Dumont operated another farther up the river.

By 1885 conditions in their one-time happy Batoche settlement had also become intolerable. Everything had gone wrong. The CPR had been built across the southern prairies to the mountains and consequently their livelihood of freighting along the Carlton Trail had dried to a dribble. The buffalo had vanished. Moreover, once more white settlers were beginning to come too close for comfort. North of them the little town of Prince Albert had sprung up in the midst of its farming community. South of them, in 1882, the Temperance Colonization Company had come in to found the village of Saskatoon and farmers were radiating out from it. East of them, well back along the old trail to Winnipeg, a new village called Yorkton had started from the efforts of the York Farmers Colonization Company. West of Batoche a farming settlement had sprouted around Battleford, which in 1877 had been declared the capital of the Northwest Territories and had become quite a town and then in 1883 had been deserted by the Government for a new capital, Regina, built along the CPR far to the south. By 1885 the Métis were unemployed, hungry, and unhappy at white men's encroachment. The conditions which had set off the Red River Rebellion sixteen years earlier were being duplicated, and Louis Riel, returning from exile in Montana and making his headquarters at Batoche, was leading them again.

On a raw spring day toward the end of March that year at nearby Duck Lake, Riel and his Métis clashed with NWMP and killed twelve of them before the police retired. The North-West Rebellion had started.

That part of the old Carlton Trail north of Humboldt and extending west to the Alberta border saw renewed activity. Other trails had come into being; notably one from Saskatoon through the Eagle Hills to Battleford and another from the CPR at Qu'Appelle to intersect the older one at Humboldt. Before many weeks soldiers from Eastern Canada came marching north from Qu'Appelle to attack Riel's fighting men who were led in battle by the able and brave Gabriel Dumont.

The outcome of the campaign was never in doubt. Nevertheless it took several sharp battles — the army's defeat at Fish Creek, the troops' defeat at Cut Knife Hill, the army's decisive victory at Batoche on May 12, and the final clean-up operation against the Indians at Frenchman Butte some two weeks later.

Throughout the two months of exictement the Carlton Trail and parts of the new trails which were later to become bits of the Yellowhead Route felt the tramp of soldiers, the stealthy stride of Indian couriers, the cautious steps of Métis messengers and the rumble of wagons bearing the wounded back to Saskatoon to hospitalization at the hands of the kindly townsfolk. The Mounties took over Fort Carlton (after they abandoned it the old fort caught fire and was destroyed). The villages of Prince Albert, Yorkton, and Saskatoon felt themselves beleaguered and took defensive measures. As well as killing nine white men and taking two women prisoners at Frog Lake (north of Lloydminster), the Indians pillaged the town of Battleford and captured Fort Pitt.

Far different from the Métis' trek to Batoche some thirty years earlier was that of the Barr Colony cavalcade bound for Lloydminster in 1903. Thirteen years before that the railway heading north through Duck Lake to Prince Albert had reached the growing town of Saskatoon. Traveling that far in three trains some two thousand Barr Colonists, drawn from several strata of mainly English society, arrived in one day. They set out west late in April to face their 170-mile trek through snow and mudholes. Few had any experience in farming and none had any experience with such traveling. Taking the road through the Eagle Hills to Battleford and then, with many a misadventure and many a mishap, heading west to found their new town of Lloydminster, they were a courageous, if confused, lot.

Land had been reserved for them around the point in the Northwest Territories where the survey of the proposed Canadian Northern Railway crossed the 4th Meridian. Right on that meridian they started their village, all unaware that two years later when the provinces of Alberta and Saskatchewan came to be created, that road allowance — their main street — was to be the boundary line between them. Once that happened their town became two villages, one incorporated in Saskatchewan and the other in Alberta. With gumption and persistence, however, radiating out from the town for miles, the Barr Colonists homesteaded and overcame pioneer difficulties. Today their two villages have become one large city which stands as a monument to their courage and labor. Today the Yellowhead Route from Battleford to Vermilion follows most of the trail they took west in 1903.

The Barr Colonists were only a few of the thousands of the settlers who during a span of twenty-five years took up most of the arable land in Manitoba, Saskatchewan, and Alberta. By the time the CPR had been built to Brandon in 1881, hundreds of land seekers preceded it out into the prairies. A large share of them had chosen to follow the old Carlton Trail. By 1878 many of them, including some brought out by one of the colonization companies, had settled around Neepawa and along the river at Minnedosa and Rapid City. By 1881, along the trail which forty years earlier George Simpson had traveled, they had advanced to Fort Ellice. Settlement along that line received further impetus when in 1883 the Westbourne and North Western Railway reached Minnedosa. While the railway advanced — to Langenburg in 1886, to Saltcoats in 1888, and on to Yorkton in 1890 — the agricultural pioneers kept ahead of it. By 1892 the sodbusters' advance guard was building shacks immediately east of the Quill Lakes.

By that time, however, the CPR had long since crossed the prairies and mountains to Vancouver. Moreover, northward-oriented branch railway lines had been completed; through Saskatoon to Prince Albert in 1890 and from Calgary to Edmonton a year later. Thereby the continuous advance of farmers along the Carlton Trail was augmented by settlers heading north along the branch lines and intersecting the old trail, and spreading out along it to fill in the wide spaces left between the hardiest pioneers who had not waited for the whistle of locomotives. Finally, about 1905, from Portage la Prairie to Edmonton an almost continuous agricultural settlement extended along the route of the Yellowhead Highway.

For the next seventy-five years, through hardship, wars,

depressions, and periods of prosperity, the farming folk cultivated their lands, and their well-ordered fields have brought a harmony to the primitive beauty that once extended along the eight-hundred-mile Yellowhead Route across the prairie. Moreover, their efforts laid alongside those of three generations of business-oriented men, who likewise pioneered, created a string of villages, towns, and cities along the route.

It was because of those businessmen, starting back in 1922 with Charlie Grant, that nearly half a century later the Yellowhead Route came into being. After World War II governments began considering a Trans-Canada highway, which was to be a high standard, hard-surfaced road from the Atlantic to the Pacific. The first problem to be settled was what route it would take, a southern one through Regina, Medicine Hat, and Calgary or a northern route by way of Yorkton, Saskatoon, and Edmonton. In 1947, to try to insure that it would pass through their cities, those who favored the northern route banded together and organized the Trans-Canada Highway System Association (Yellowhead Route).

The movement started in Edmonton where Mayor Harry Ainlay headed it up, assisted by E. T. Love as secretary-treasurer. Almost immediately it caught on, with enthusiastic meetings in Yorkton in May, 1947, Minnedosa in June, followed by one in Blue River, B.C. in July, and another in Vermilion in October. The association held its first annual meeting in Saskatoon in November, 1947, with delegates representing the towns and cities from Russell, Manitoba, on the east to McBride and Kamloops on the west. With Edmonton's Mayor Ainlay and Saskatoon's Mayor A. W. Macpherson as president and vice-president, E. T. Love as secretary-treasurer, O. C. Olson, of Jasper, and Charles H. Grant as the rest of the executive commitee, the body got away to a good start. Aided by Reg Easton and F. J. Mitchell, of Edmonton, the organization soon embraced the leading figures of all the towns from Portage la Prairie west. Amongst other pioneer mayors were Mrs. N. E. Arnold of Prince Rupert, C. A. Peaker of Yorkton and A. Mather of Russell.

To dramatize their demand that the Trans-Canada Highway should be built through the Yellowhead Pass, Reg Easton and Edd Neighbour, of Jasper, made a pilot trip over an old railway tote road which for some years had been blocked by slides. Then in August, 1948, the group organized a caravan of cars and trucks which, starting from the east, gathered strength as it went on through Edmonton to Jasper and finally passed through Kamloops. Though their efforts focused attention on the Yellowhead Route, they failed in their main purpose, and during the next few years the official Trans-Canada Highway was built through Calgary and the Rogers Pass.

The official highway did not kill the Trans-Canada Highway System Association (Yellowhead Route), because over the years enthusiastic men from Portage la Prairie to Kamloops and Prince Rupert kept it alive. Over those years, because of the most active part he played, Reg Easton came to be known as Mr. Yellowhead, the "Passionate Pioneer" of the route. During the late sixties Reg and his wife toured the route two or three times a year in their camper truck emblazoned with the message "Travel the Yellowhead Highway — Canada's Evergreen Route." At various times the most prominent men of the prairie cities and their boards of trade all had a hand in carrying the torch for their highway.

Finally, in August, 1970, Premier W. A. C. Bennett of British Columbia presided at its official opening, but by that time it had come to be called the Yellowhead Interprovincial Highway. About that time, too, a new organization closely tied in with the older one, which continues to exist, came into being — the Yellowhead Interprovincial Highway Association. At present, as its executive director, Ted Sample, a former Saskatchewan boy, carries on the promotional work from the Edmonton office used for so many years by Reg Easton. Moreover, in the same building in the law office he has occupied for decades, Charles H. Grant, L.L.D., now over ninety, regales interested visitors with stories of his half-century-long connection with the Yellowhead Route.

Today, owing to the efforts of so many men like Grant, the trip from Winnipeg through Tête Jaune's Pass to the Pacific is a brief, enjoyable experience. As one drives effortlessly along the pavement where once the Red River carts squealed, conditions are so vastly different that even observant old George Simpson would barely recognize the parklands he crossed in 1841 in the record time of twenty-two days. Starting from Winnipeg on a summer's day, planning to "camp" only one night on the way, the traveler passes through some eighty villages, towns, and cities before reaching Edmonton.

Some fifty miles west of Portage la Prairie, Neepawa, a typical sturdy town, the shopping center for a large farming area in that land of plenty, houses its 3,400 people in the security of its tree-shaded streets. Until 1970 when its sixty-year-old salt plant closed down, it was the source of most of western Canada's table salt — drawn from wells which undoubtedly tapped the same strata as those which impregnated the Salt Lake whose waters had spoiled John Rowand's breakfast tea well over a hundred years ago.

A few of Minnedosa's 2,500 citizens, being sixteen miles closer to that salty lake, devote a part of their effort to manufacturing various liquors in its thriving distillery. Many others find congenial employment catering to the adjacent well-off farming area in several ways, including manufacturing agricultural machinery. All of them enjoy the serenity of the historic town which came into existence some forty years after the Saulteaux Indians watched George Simpson cross the town's river.

Sixty or so miles farther along the Yellowhead Route and some thirty miles north of old Fort Ellice, the town of Russell was subdivided by Col. C. A. Boulton. The colonel played a risky part in the Red River Rebellion and some years later, during 1885, raised a force of Boulton's Scouts which marched west along the Carlton Trail to fight in the battles of the North-West Rebellion.

Ninety-five miles north and west of Russell the Yellowhead Route enters the city of Yorkton, which, with its population of over 14,000, is the second largest city along the route between Portage la Prairie and Edmonton. With its many industries and its prominence as an education center, it is a far cry from the little hamlet which during the North-West Rebellion raised a military unit and put itself into a posture of defense.

Westward from Yorkton to Saskatoon two hundred miles away the Yellowhead Route flows along through a variety of prairie and parkland scenery glowing in season with vast fields of yellow rape or golden ripening wheat. Between the two largest towns of Wynyard (population 2,000) and Lanigan (1,600), both near the Quill Lakes, the old Carlton Trail, as noted, crosses the highway. It was in this vicinity in a pouring rain on George Simpson's eleventh day out from Fort Garry that his men had such a difficult time to make a fire to eat by.

By the time the modern tourist reaches this area after traveling a greater distance in an hour than Simpson did in a day, he too may well be looking forward to his night's camp. His campground, of course, could be where the Yellowhead Route crosses the South Saskatchewan River at Saskatoon and will be vastly different from Simpson's; for in the midst of Saskatoon's 130,000 people he can find any accommodation that suits his taste — a dry roof, electricity or natural gas for his cooking, or indeed a multitude of restaurants to supply meals and wines to his taste. How George Simpson, with his love for a bottle of Madeira, would have appreciated the lip-smacking conveniences!

Saskatoon, once the Temperance City, then the Hub City, and now the Potash Capital of the World, has established an amazing record of growth. A prairie oasis, a university city, it is a restful haven of trees and bridges across the river which coils its way seductively through many a beautiful subdivision. And yet an active city, capable of rising to the challenge of the 1971 Canada Winter Games and building a mountain on its prairie environs to provide the necessary ski slopes. Moreover, scores of millions of dollars came cascading into its trading area to dig six massive mines and build mills to harvest the largest and richest potash deposits in the world. Its surging growth has culminated for the present in replacing a maze of midtown-railway tracks by a four-block-square luxurious Plaza.

Refreshed by his night's "camping" in Saskatoon, the traveler heads west and after crossing the nearby North Saskatchewan River makes his way to the Battlefords through some of the beautiful and productive farming country near the route Simpson took when he suffered "a great deal of inconvenience from thirst." Straddling their magnificent valley, The Battlefords serve a large and interesting area of Saskatchewan's parklands. Recalling the days of 1885 when the Indians sacked and pillaged it, old Battleford maintains its fascinating Mounted Police post and museum, for old Battleford on the south side of the river has many a memory.

In 1885, with the North-West Rebellion raging all around it — the battles of Duck Lake, Fish Creek, and Batoche off to the east, the fight at Cut Knife Hill to the west, the troubles at Fort Pitt and the Battle of Frenchman Butte, both to the northwest — the little village saw plenty of activity as policemen, soldiers, Indians, and settlers galloped in or hurried off. From it Col. Otter and his troops marched to their defeat at Cut Knife Hill. To it Inspector Dickens and his Mounties retreated from Fort Pitt. In due course, General Middleton arrived with his troops on board the sternwheeler the *Northcote*, and finally, the great chief Poundmaker came in and surrendered. Battleford's museum has much to tell.

Past its old buildings the Barr Colonists continued on their way along what is essentially the Yellowhead Route to found Lloydminster some eighty-five miles west. Halfway there as they passed the site of the future Paynton they could see off to the south across the Battle River Valley the hills around the Cut Knife Battle site and the nearer blue, misty Maskwa Hill on which over a hundred years ago battling Cree and Blackfoot — perhaps some of the Indians Simpson had met — left several of their dead.

Lloydminster, for long a spirited town serving a fine farming area, had its date with destiny in the thirties when the first of its 2,000 oil wells revealed the riches beneath the Barr Colonists' fields. Since then with its population of over 8,000 straddling the Alberta-Saskatchewan border and its Husky Oil plant refining the wells' wealth, Lloydminster has become the Black Oil Capital of the Prairies.

Before he reaches Edmonton the traveler still has the pleasure of another 150 miles over the rich, rolling parklands. The first forty miles while the pavement skirts the northern edge of the Blackfoot Hills take him to Vermilion, a center of 3,000 people enjoying life on the high bank above the Vermilion River. In another fifty-odd miles he skirts misty blue Sick Man Hill north of Lavoy and arrives at Vegreville (population 3,900), which for so long has served Alberta's huge Ukrainian colony, which dates back to 1892. Half an hour's additional journey takes the tourist through the Beaver Hills and Elk Island Park, where in succulent pastures most of Canada's remaining plains buffalo graze as they did in George Simpson's day. Beyond it, another half an hour away, with its great buildings towering high over the magnificent North Saskatchewan River valley stands the metropolis of Edmonton with its ever-growing population, now reaching 464,000.

Its eastern edge is a complex of oil refineries, pumping stations, and chemical plants — a complex which with the surrounding vast aggregation of oil and gas fields, supports Edmonton's claim to being the Oil Capital of Canada.

It was at Edmonton's old fort, first established nearby in 1795, where George Simpson, having ended the prairie leg of his round-the-world trip, turned off the Yellowhead Route to head for the coast by way of Banff. The modern traveler, however, can continue on the pavement of the Yellowhead Highway until he links up with Tête Jaune's stamping ground and his famous cache in the Yellowhead Pass. On the first part of that 300-mile stretch he will pass through a continuation of prairie-type farms until a hundred miles west of Edmonton he reaches Edson, the flourishing center of the foothills country. In that town of some 4,000 people who have found its lumbering, mining and natural gas-bearing areas their chosen land, he will enter the foothills and get his first view of the mountains.

Beyond Edson a delightful hour's drive will take him to where with the Athabasca River lapping at its feet the pulp mill town of Hinton (population 4,700) gives him a striking view of the eastern wall of the Rocky Mountains where bold Roche Miette stands as the great guardian of the pass. Soon he enters the famed pass itself and by following up its Athabasca River for a few miles comes to Jasper, where 3,000 citizens enjoy the year-round splendors of the vast national park. Driving west another sixty-five miles — up the Miette River, over the actual pass and down the Fraser River past magnificent Mount Robson — he reaches the "Y" of the Yellowhead Route at Tête Jaune Cache. There, he can turn left as the main line of the CNR does and head for Kamloops some 200 miles south, or he can continue west down the mighty Fraser River 150 miles as the Grand Trunk Pacific Railway did to Prince George.

The trip south, along the route followed by the courageous Mrs. Schubert of the Overlanders, takes the modern tourist through the old mica mining area and over a low summit and then starts him descending along the river named after David Thompson until he comes to the busy town of Blue River. Beyond it another 140 miles or so of ever-changing mountain and pastoral scenery along the North Thompson River lead him to Kamloops. There this leg of the Yellowhead Route ends as it merges with the southern Trans-Canada Highway from which it diverged at Portage la Prairie 1,200 miles to the east.

Long before it reached the present metropolitan population of over 52,000 in its immediate environs, Kamloops, the capital of the drier ranching lands of British Columbia's southern interior, had a long history. The first white man on the site arrived during the winter of 1811-12 — the same winter that Selkirk's first settlers spent at Hudson Bay on their way to his colony at Red River, and six months after David Thompson finally reached the mouth of the Columbia only to find J. J.

Astor's Pacific Fur Company building Fort Astoria there. On Thompson's return trip upstream two of Astor's men, David Stuart and Alexander Ross, kept him company as far as Pasco, Washington, where he left the Columbia River. Astor's two men, however, continued up that majestic stream to the mouth of the Okanogan (in Canada, "Okanagan") and built Fort Okanogan there. Late in 1811 David Stuart left Ross and pushed on upstream with pack horses until he arrived at the junction of the North and South Thompson rivers, Kamloops' situation, where he stayed trading with the Shuswap until February, 1812.

Some six months later Stuart and Ross built their Fort Kamloops. All the while, of course, David Thompson's colleagues were keeping track of their movements and within months Joseph La Rocque (who was to be at Jasper a few years later) built a North West Company post beside that of the Pacific Fur Company. During the War of 1812 the Pacific Fur Company sold out to La Rocque's firm and for several years in its hands and in those of its successors after 1821, the Hudson's Bay Company, Fort Kamloops led an uneventful existence.

When in 1858 the gold rush to the Fraser River was in full swing and the famous Cariboo mines were on the verge of discovery, Kamloops began to see its share of wandering prospectors. Perhaps the most exciting of them all were the Overlanders, who reached there on October 13, 1862, bringing the hardy Mrs. Schubert, who, pregnant and looking after three young children, had crossed the prairies and the Yellowhead Pass. When next morning her daughter Rose became the first white girl to be born in the interior of British Columbia, the pair were the talk of both the fort and the Indian camps.

The next equally momentous event in Kamloops' life occurred nearly a quarter of a century later when on July 11, 1885, the first CPR train from the coast reached the town. When Donald Smith drove the last spike in the transcontinental at Craigellachie on November 5, Kamloops found itself a divisional point on the railway. Ideally located to become the headquarters of a developing area, the town grew rapidly and in April, 1893, it was incorporated as a city.

In November, 1914, the first Canadian Northern Railway train passed through, and as the meeting place of two transcontinentals, the city grew some more. Following a course somewhat similar to the Yellowhead Route, the CNR had set off from Portage la Prairie to swing north and west over the parklands.

Passing north of the Quill Lakes and just north of Saskatoon, it headed to where on the north side of the Saskatchewan River it created North Battleford, and then following in the steps of the Barr Colonists, it reached Lloydminster. By way of Vermilion and Vegreville it went on to Edmonton. Thence it followed the old pack trail to Tête Jaune Cache and finally descended the North Thompson River to Kamloops.

From Edmonton west for three hundred miles the CNR had Canada's third transcontinental, the Grand Trunk Pacific, to keep it company — often for mile after mile within a hundred yards of it. From Tête Jaune's Cache, however, the GTP kept on west along the same route that the most westerly leg of the modern Yellowhead Route follows, down the Fraser to Prince George, and continued west to build the port of Prince Rupert some six hundred miles from the cache.

For those six hundred miles the GTP made its way through a terrain vastly different from that over which it had cantered in crossing the plains. It was a land of continuous mountains of limited use for agriculture but dotted here and there with old Hudson's Bay Company fur trading posts set in an almost endless region of cedar, pine, spruce, and fir, drained by salmon-spawning rivers. The Indian folk, also, differed from those of the prairie, utilizing the runs of salmon as their main food supply, and near the west coast, living in villages built of great logs hewn from the huge coastal forests.

For forty miles below Tête Jaune Cache to the town of McBride, the cedar pole shipping center, the Yellowhead Route and the old GTP (now the Canadian National Railway) run on opposite sides of the Fraser River. From that town for some ninety more miles a nearly continuous forest of swaying cedars hems in the highway almost to Prince George, the expanding city where a population of over 30,000 lives well off pulp, lumber and other forest products.

Seeing its first white man's building in 1807 when Simon Fraser built his Fort George, it remained for a long time a fur trade post occupied only once in a while. Indeed, the site's most important claim to fame was that it was the jumping-off place from which he set out to explore the lands farther west and later on embarked on his discovery voyage down the Fraser River. For decades thereafter, aside from occasional visits from Tête Jaune and other fur-seeking men, Fort George languished in relative obscurity. Even the gold rush days when miners ascended the Fraser and tramped far and wide exploring the mountain valleys for hundreds of miles did little to awaken it. It saw its first steamboat in 1871, but that was for one trip only when the *Enterprise* landed with a load of supplies bound for the Omineca gold fields. Another thirty-eight years elapsed before, in 1909, the *Nechako* ascended the Fraser and started a short but action-packed era of steamboat days centering about Fort George.

By that time, of course, everyone knew that the GTP had been surveyed so as to pass through Fort George. Immediately the embryo center at the junction of the Nechako and the Fraser rivers began to boom, as businessmen, promoters, and some farm-minded folk flocked in. Thousands of lots and hundreds of streets in two or three separate townsites were staked out extending back for miles from the rivers' banks. At last, by means of the railway hundreds of square miles of forests surrounding the town in every direction were capable of being exploited. Prosperity seemed just around the corner; the GTP was on its way down the Fraser from Tête Jaune Cache and the much-talked-of Pacific Great Eastern Railway was about to hurry up the Fraser from Vancouver.

While on every count Fort George deserved prosperity, that blissful condition was to turn out to be decades away. The GTP did indeed reach there and everybody rejoiced when on January 27, 1914, the track layer pushed its way over the new Fraser Bridge and the town was renamed Prince George. The rejoicing did not last long; the GTP went on west to drive its last spike at Fort Fraser in April, 1914, and hundreds of men were laid off; World War I started and the PGE, suffering a difficult gestation, got as far as Clinton in 1916 and five years later straggled into Quesnel and stopped. Prince George settled into a long slumber, and decades passed before the fairy prince of post-World War II prosperity came to arouse it.

Prosperity woke up the PGE, and some forty years late, its first trains came rolling in to Prince George. That railway was extended to the north and in the fall of 1958 reached Dawson Creek and at long last Prince George found itself the crossing point of two railways. But by that time the White Spruce City was so busy with other matters — larger sawmills, pulp mills scattered about its bailiwick, and smaller industries tumbling over themselves to find space to build on — that only oldtimers remembered the long doldrum years. Everybody else was busy building up the new city, whose population continued to soar year by year until it exceeded 30,000, with more people coming in on every train as well as by the Yellowhead Route.

All of that, however, lay a century and a half in the future when Simon Fraser, looking up the Nechako River during the summer of 1806, decided to ascend it and, along with James Stuart, established Fort St. James on Stuart Lake. A little later that summer Simon Fraser went farther up the Nechako and built Fort Fraser on Fraser Lake. The advance along the future route of the Yellowhead Highway had started.

Over the decades fur traders, miners, missionaries, and ranchers penetrated the territory, many to remain. When the Yellowhead Route was finally paved, three busy towns, Vanderhoof (population 2,000), Burns Lake (1,600), and Smithers (4,000) became headquarters for an extensive district two hundred miles long embracing a large ranching area in what has been called the "Lakes District of British Columbia." At the base of Hudson Bay Mountain (8,700 feet), Smithers has become a major center for mining and mixed-farming activity.

Near Burns Lake the Yellowhead Route crosses the divide between the waters draining east by the Nechako and thus reaching the sea by the Fraser River, and those starting westward as the Bulkley River and ultimately sweeping down the broad Skeena to enter the Pacific Ocean near Prince Rupert. The Bulkley was named after Col. Charles S. Bulkley, who about 1866 was in charge of building the Western Union Telegraph Line through that area. It was projected to connect the old world with the new — to join the telegraph systems of Russia with those of America by a land line from the mouth of the Fraser River near modern Vancouver to the tip of Alaska, where it was to link up with a cable across the Bering Sea. The venture failed but not before a line had been built from Quesnel to the headwaters of the Bulkley River and thence down it to Hazelton on the Skeena. As it approached Hazelton the telegraph line, like the GTP and the Yellowhead Route, passed from the lands claimed by the Carrier, the interior Indians, to those owned by the Tsimshain family of coastal natives. Both groups had an interesting civilization and both lived mainly on salmon.

One of their preferred fishing spots was on the Bulkley River halfway between Smithers and Hazelton. There, at the falls named after Father A. G. Morice, the famous Oblate missionary, the modern Carrier still spear and dry salmon as their ancestors did long ago.

If at the falls the men building the telegraph line watched with interest as the natives landed salmon, they stared in amazement a few miles farther down the river where it narrows to another canyon shortly before entering the Skeena, for at a favorite campground called Hagwilget the Indians had strung up one of their unbelievable suspension bridges. To span the canyon's considerable width they had lashed poles together with cedar withes and braced the swaying structure with spars to provide a quick if nerve-racking crossing a hundred feet above the stream. The telegraph crew decided to strengthen it and added many strands of wire to that structure, which was still in service half a century later when the GTP construction crews came along.

But other marvels lay in store for white men entering that region — Indian houses and halls built of great square logs, two feet through, and nearby, tall totem poles — in some villages a veritable forest of them. Though the Hagwilget bridge has been allowed to fall away, the artistic totem poles remain to amaze the modern Yellowhead Route tourist. This is an interesting land, this upper Skeena area, where, usually at the mouths of rivers, Indian villages remain. This is the land of the Tsimshian who still live along the Skeena, the K-shian, the mighty "River of the Clouds." Listen to the lilt of the names of some of their villages — Kisgegas and Kispiox, Kitselas, Kitwanga, Kitwancool and Kitsumgalum.

If, however, their fascinating villages, their impressive totem poles, and their great canoes carved from cedar astound the modern tourist and tell of an astonishing development, the history of white men on the Skeena River is no less interesting. Over a hundred years ago they, too, brought their craft up the "River of the Clouds," craft not lovingly wrought nor caressingly carved but rough things of timbers and boards and fire-breathing machinery that fought their way up the river's raging canyons. First in 1864 they ascended the river for ninety miles and a few years later blew their whistles at Hazelton village, 180 miles upstream at the head of navigation.

Many a tale there is to tell of hardy, sternwheeler skippers fighting each other, racing each other, and ramming each other as they battled all the whims of the river, which fluctuated sixty feet between high and low water, could rise seventeen feet in a day, and could tear a steamer's planking in a dozen rapid-torn canyons or boulder-strewn rapids. Some of the captains who later on were to navigate the upper Fraser gained experience on that stream with the long easy stretches and the many rough spots. Amongst them were several men like Captain J. H. Bonser who later on ran the first sternwheeler, the *Fort Fraser,* up to Tête Jaune Cache. He was the skipper who christened the eleven major rapids and canyons up the Skeena as far as Hazelton with such names as Whirly Gig, The Hornet's Nest, and The Devil's Elbow.

Though the old sternwheelers have long since left the Skeena's tricky waters, more people than ever ascend or descend along the mighty river either by the CNR or the Yellowhead Route. As that route nears Terrace a branch highway thirty-seven miles long swings down to another of the Indian names, Kitimat, now a town housing some 12,000 people whose livelihood is obtained from the tremendous Alcan aluminum smelter.

Terrace itself, once known as Kitsumgalum, was first staked out in 1905. When about 1910 the GTP railway began blasting its way out of the Skeena's rocky cliffs the town came into being. Today with its population nearing the 15,000 mark, Terrace, relying on the tremendous forests, some mining enterprises, and the magnetic tourist attraction of the great river and its tributaries which abound in trout and salmon, has become a rapidly growing center. Not its least claim to fame is the 92½-pound world's record spring salmon caught four miles above the town.

Magnificent as is the Skeena River scenery viewed from the Yellowhead Route between Hazelton and Terrace, nevertheless for sheer magic, few areas in the world can compare with that one-hundred-mile portion of the stream from there down to Prince Rupert. Along that stretch the highway swings gently around the undulating shoreline as the broad river, reflecting the blue of the magnificent coast mountains, moves calmly along past the point where it becomes tidal and then continues its long sweep to the sea. Well-chosen indeed was the name "K-shian" — "the River of the Clouds." As mile after mile the climate comes more and more under the influence of the sea, the vegetation becomes lusher and greener, the huge trees thicker and taller. Where here and there some of their stranded hulks have been washed up on the shore, their roots soar upwards higher than a big house.

Finally, in its very last stretch the highway leaves the broad tidal river and after a wild scramble over a short mountain route drops down to the port town of Prince Rupert. Now a town with a population of over 15,000, its first settlers arrived in May, 1906, when the GTP officials had found its great inlet to be a remarkably safe harbor. Within a year or so streets had been laid out hither and yon over its rocky knobs, and in March, 1910, it was incorporated as a city. For years the GTP had been building its grade up the Skeena and Bulkley rivers to meet the construction men working west from Prince George, and finally on April 8, 1914, the first transcontinental train steamed into its station where Pacific waves lapped at its rocky roadbed.

In time, two pulp mills were established within its boundary as was a terminal elevator for storing prairie grain destined for consumers across the wide Pacific. Fishing and fish canning and processing plants bulk large in Prince Rupert's economy, and its claim to being the Halibut Capital of the World is no idle boast. At present the Dominion Government is considering expanding its harbor facilities and turning it into Canada's tenth National Harbours Board port. Prospects for Prince Rupert are promising.

In such an interesting city, 1,600 miles west of Portage la Prairie, the Yellowhead Route terminates. From Winnipeg in the land of the manito and maple, through Saskatchewan's poplar bluffs, over Alberta's pine-clad foothills, beside towering Mount Robson and into British Columbia's cedar and fir forests, it has made its way to tidewater. Every mile of its whole length has some story to tell of Indians, traders, explorers, or early settlers. Every mile of its predecessors, the Carlton and Jasper trails, had seen the plodding progress of pioneers of all sorts — Oregon settlers, Overlanders, Métis and Barr Colonists — including David Thompson, who had first mapped the Athabasca Pass, and Pierre Hatsinaton, Tête Jaune, long since forgotten as a man but living forever as the almost legendary pathfinder of the Yellowhead Pass.

INDEX

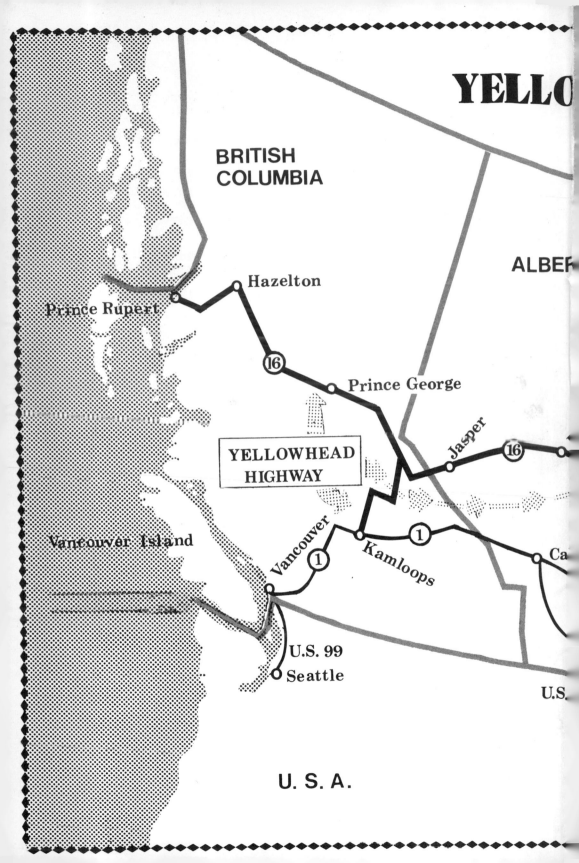